Jane Austen

MANSFIELD PARK

Jane Austen

MANSFIELD PARK

[Edited with Introduction, Author's Background, Histotical Context, Summary, Study Questins and Critical Essays]

Misha Kandhari
M.A., M. Phil. English,
Delhi University

ANMOL PUBLICATIONS PVT. LTD.
NEW DELHI - 110 002 (INDIA)

ANMOL PUBLICATIONS PVT. LTD.

H.O.: 4374/4B, Ansari Road, Darya Ganj,
New Delhi-110 002 (India)
Ph.: 23278000, 23261597

B.O.: No. 1015, Ist Main Road, BSK IIIrd Stage
IIIrd Phase, IIIrd Block
Bangalore - 560 085 (India)
Visit us at: www.anmolpublications.com

Mansfield Park

First Published, 2009

PRINTED IN INDIA

Printed at Mehra Offset Press, Delhi.

Contents

Preface

The present book is a critical appreciation of Mansfeild Park the most celebrated and unforgettable novel of Jane Austen, who is acknowledged as the innovator of novels of manners. Although not recognized in her times, her popularity has increased with the passing of years and today her novels, like Pride and Prejudice, Sense and Sensibility, and Emma, to name but a few, are not only widely read but have also been included in the syllabi of various universities across the world. Jane Austen's work is known for its calmness, delicacy, exquisite touch, subtle irony and miniature grace. Mansfield Park was written between 1811 and 1813, although it did not appear in print until 1814. It is an even more socially-aware novel than Austen's others, focusing as it does on the slave trade and the roots of the British upper-crust's wealth in corruption and exploitation. It is probably the least romantic and most pragmatic of Austen's novels, as its abrupt and rather matter-of-fact ending shows

Chapter 1

Introduction

MANSFIELD PARK: JANE AUSTEN THE CONTRARIAN

Mansfield Park is probably the most controversial and least favored of all six Austen novels. Drawing the issue of slavery into the limelight, post-colonialist critic Edward Said had certainly stirred up some ripples in alleging Austen's acceptance of British imperialism with her mention of Sir Thomas Bertram's Antigua plantation. Susan Fraiman has aptly presented her rebuttal to Said's argument, noting in particular Austen's brilliant irony and metaphor upon deeper reading. So here, I would just like to concentrate on Austen's characterization, which I believe is more in line with her central purpose in *Mansfield Park.* That brings me to the other major controversy.

What makes a heroine?Published after *Pride and Prejudice, Mansfield Park* presents a very different heroine from that of Austen's previous success. Fanny Price is often measured against Elizabeth Bennet, consequently being looked upon as inferior. On the outset, Fanny is indeed everything Lizzy is not. First of all, she is physically fragile, easily succumbs to exhaustion and fainting spells, very unlike Lizzy who can take on extensive walks in the outdoors, happily treading through miles of muddy paths. No rosy cheeks from such exercise for Fanny. She may have grown into a fair lady at eighteen, but she does not have Lizzy's athletic prowess, or her pair of fine eyes, the trademark of her exuberance.

Further, Fanny Price is painfully shy, an introvert. Readers may find her insipid, lacking glamour, but they may be more impatient with her passive, yielding personality. Why does Jane Austen present to us such a heroine, especially after the very lively and charismatic Lizzy Bennet? Well, I, for one, am glad to see Austen has demonstrated her wisdom by depicting an anti-stereotyped heroine. With Fanny Price, Austen has shattered the image of the typical heroine: a captivating beauty, quick witted and forthright, even audacious at times, endowed with energy and charisma. Why is reticence, or introvert nature being frowned upon? When did we start thinking of long-suffering and perseverance as negative traits? Why is humility not getting its rightful esteem? And, why are the quiet, observant and thinking female not as attractive as those who are more expressive, or who possess only outward beauty?

What Fanny lacks in physical vigor, she more than compensates with her inner strength. And it is in the nobility of character that Austen has chosen to depict her heroine. Underneath Fanny's fragile appearance is a quiet and principled perseverance. Seeing the impropriety of staging a play which entails the remodelling of Sir Thomas' very private library in his absence, Fanny stands firm in not participating, despite the pressures and insults from her older cousins, the persuasion from the Crawfords, the scornful criticisms from Mrs. Norris, and even the eventual yielding of Edmund himself.

In her ingenious manner with biting irony, Austen pits Fanny Price against her formidable foe, Mary Crawford. At first sight, "Mary Crawford was remarkably pretty." Not long after that, Austen adds:

"She had none of Fanny's delicacy of taste, of mind, of feeling; she saw nature, inanimate nature, with little observation; her attention was all for men and women, her talents for the light and lively."

When it comes to moral uprightness, Mary Crawford is no match. Thanks to the way she defends her brother Henry who has snatched Maria away from her husband, even Edmund can now see clearly. Henry Crawford is a carnal schemer, and Mary Crawford is equally manipulative and egotistic. Unfortunately, it takes a scandal and trepidations for others to learn what Fanny has seen clearly from the very beginning.

In a way, Fanny Price is more lucid than Elizabeth Bennet in not succumbing to the lure of vanity with Henry Crawford's superfluous praise and wooing. If only Elizabeth had conquered that soft spot regarding Wickham earlier on....but of course, there wouldn't be any story then. And if it is admirably bold for Lizzy to resist Lady Catherine de Bourgh, someone who is of no relation to her, Fanny is all the more courageous in her refusing to marry Henry Crawford by standing up against the very guardian to whom she owes her upbringing and her present living, the patriarch Sir Thomas Bertram. It takes extraordinary fortitude to go against everyone in Mansfield Park, and follow her own heart, while the privilege to explain herself is infeasible.

Compared to other Austen heroines, Fanny Price is equally, if not more, worthy. Fanny has the passion of Marianne, while possessing the rationale of Elinor. That is why her secret love for Edmund can endure unfavorable conditions. Her lucid sense of judgement restrains her to reveal it to Edmund, who, with his emotional frailty, would be exasperated knowing his own beloved cousin is a rival rather than a friend of Mary Crawford. Her perseverance can easily match and surpass that of Anne Elliot. And, she may be uneducated and naive like Catherine Morland to start with, and is equally moldable and respectful when taught, she has way surpassed her mentor in insights and maturity as the story progresses.

By presenting a heroine who may not be a typical favorite, Austen seems to be writing contrary to conventional norms. (But is it just modern audience who have differed in their expectations, resulting in recent film adaptations altering the very spirit and essence of Austen's characters to appeal to them?) Has Austen created a character so different from her other heroines? Comparing *Mansfield Park* with all her other novels, I do not feel she is particularly off her usual standpoint.

As with her other heroines, Austen is more concerned with character, virtues, and morals, the inner qualities of the person rather than the outer appearance. *Mansfield Park* is the best manifestation of her stance. Ultimately, what shine through for our Austenian heroine are:

"The sweetness of her temper, the purity of her mind, and the excellence of her principles."

At the end, the steadfast and long-suffering Fanny Price triumphs. And for critics who assert that Austen had silently condoned slavery, the ending of *Mansfield Park* should silent them all, for it is the socially and economically disenfranchised and marginalized that is exalted and vindicated. In my view, Edmund does not deserve her. However, it is Fanny's heart and long unrequited love that Austen attempts to satisfy. And I totally concur with that, for *our heroine* deserves it. And no, Fanny does not become mistress of Mansfield Park, which is also ideal: It is not affluence and materialism that win after all, but spiritual values and nobility of character that overcome, and they are their own rewards. The Parsonage is a most fitting place for both Edmund and Fanny to begin their life together.

Chapter 2

Short Biography of Jane Austen

Jane Austen was the author of several enduringly popular English novels, including: Pride and Prejudice, Emma and Mansfield Park.

Early Life

Jane Austen was born in Steventon, Hampshire on 16th December 1775. She was the 7th daughter of an 8 child family. Her father, George Austen, was a vicar and lived on a reasonable income of £600 a year. However, although they were middle class, they were not rich; her father would have been unable to give much to help her daughters get married. Jane was brought up with her 5 brothers and her elder sister Cassandra. (Another brother, Edward, was adopted by a rich, childless couple and went to live with them). Jane was close to her siblings, especially Cassandra, to whom she was devoted. The two sisters shared a long correspondence throughout her life; much of what we know about Jane comes from these letters, although, unfortunately Cassandra burnt a number of these on Jane's death.

Jane was educated at Oxford and later a boarding school in Reading. In the early 1800s two of Jane's brother's joined the navy, leaving to fight in the Napoleonic wars; they would go on to become admirals. The naval connections can be seen in novels like Mansfield Park. After the death of her father in 1805, Jane, with her mother and sister returned to Hampshire. In 1809, her brother, Edward who had been brought up by the Knights, invited the family to the estate he had inherited at Chawton. It was in the country house of Chawton, that Jane was able to produce some of her greatest novels.

Novels of Jane Austen

Her novels are a reflection of her outlook on life. She spent most of her life insulated from certain sections of society. Her close friends were mainly her family, and those of similar social standing. It is not surprising then that her novels focused on 2 or 3 families of the middle or upper classes. Most novels were also based on the idyll of rural country houses that Jane was so fond of.

Her novels also focus on the issue of gaining a suitable marriage. Marriage was a big issue facing women and men of her time; often financial considerations were paramount in deciding marriages. As an author, Jane used to satirize these financial motivations, for example, in Pride and Prejudice the mother is ridiculed for her ambitions to marry her daughters for maximum financial remuneration. Jane, herself remained single throughout her life. Apart from brief flirtations, Jane remained single, and appeared to have little interest in getting married (unlike the characters of her novels.

The strength of Jane's novels was her ability to gain penetrating insights into the character and nature of human relationships, from even a fairly limited range of environments and characters. In particular, she helped to redefine the role and aspirations of middle class women like herself. Through providing a witty satire of social conventions, she helped to liberate contemporary ideas of what women could strive for.

During her lifetime the novels were reasonably popular. One of her strongest supporters was Walter Scott. He said of her novels:

"That young lady has a talent for describing the involvements of feelings and characters of ordinary life which is to me the most wonderful I ever met with."

King George IV actually requested that one novel could be dedicated to him. Emma is therefore dedicated to the King, even though Jane did not maintain any liking towards the

King.

Not all were favorable to Jane. The literary critic and wit Mark Twain said:

"Jane Austen? Why, I go so far as to say that any library is a good library that does not contain a volume by Jane Austen. Even if it contains no other book."

Death of Jane Austen

Jane died in 1816, aged only 41. She died of Addison's disease, a disorder of the adrenal glands. She was buried at Winchester Cathedral.

There are two museums dedicated to Jane Austen.

- The Jane Austen Centre in Bath and
- The Jane Austen's House Museum, located in Chawton cottage, in Hampshire, where she lived from 1809 –1917

In 2005, Pride and Prejudice was voted best British novel of all time in a BBC poll.

Jane was also voted as one of the

- Top 100 greatest Britons
- And features in a list: 50 women who changed the world

Chronology Age

1775	(16 Dec) Jane Austen born at Steventon in Hants, seventh child of the Rev. George Austen (1731-1805) and Cassandra Leigh (1739-1827)
1784/5	J. A. and her sister, Cassandra, leave the Abbey School, Reading 9
1795	*Elinor and Marianne* written. *Lady Susan* written 20
1796	(Oct) *First Impressions* begun (finished Aug 1797) 21
1797	(Nov) *Sense and Sensibility* begun. *First Impressions* unsuccessfully offered to Cadell 22
1798/9	*Northanger Abbey* (Susan) written. Sold to Crosby and Go. in 1803
1801	Austens settle in Bath 26
1805	Rev. George Austen dies. *The Watsons* and *Lady*

	Susan (R. W. Chapman's dating) written about this time 30
1806	Austens leave Bath for Clifton with 'happy feelings of escape', and visit Adlestrop and Stoneleigh 31
1807	(Mar) Austens settle in at Castle Square, Southampton 32
1809	Austens move to Chawton, Hampshire (owned by Jane's brother Edward) 34
1811	*Mansfield Park* begun (Feb). Sense and Sensibility published 36 (Nov.) 36
1812	(Nov) *Pride and Prejudice* sold to Egerton 37
1813	(Jan) *Pride and Prejudice* published (Nov.) second editions of this and *Sense and Sensibility* 38
1814	(21 Jan) *Emma* begun (finished 29 Mar 1815) (May) *Mansfield Park* published by Egerton 39
1815	*Persuasion* begun (finished August 1816) (Dec) *Emma* published by John Murray. 40
1816	*Mansfield Park,* second edition. 41
1817	(Jan-Mar) *Sanditon* begun (28 July) Jane Austen dies at Winchester; buried in Winchester Cathedral (Dec) *Northanger Abbey; and Persuasion* published by Murray.

Chapter 3

Historical Context

INTRODUCTION TO THE TIMES

During Austen's career, Romanticism reached its zenith of acceptance and influence, but she rejected the tenets of that movement. The romantics extolled the power of feeling, whereas Austen upheld the supremacy of the rational faculty. Romanticism advocated the abandonment of restraint; Austen was a staunch exponent of the neo-classical belief in order and discipline. The romantics saw in nature a transcendental power to stimulate men to better the existing order of things, which they saw as essentially tragic in its existing state. Austen supported traditional values and the established norms, and viewed the human condition in the comic spirit. The romantics exuberantly celebrated natural beauty, but Austen's dramatic technique decreed sparse description of setting. The beauties of nature are seldom detailed in her work.

Just as Austen's works display little evidence of the Romantic Movement, they also reveal no awareness of the international upheavals and consequent turmoil in England that took place during her lifetime. Keep in mind, however, that such forces were remote from the restricted world that she depicts. Tumultuous affairs, such as the Napoleonic wars, in her day did not significantly affect the daily lives of middle-class provincial families. The ranks of the military were recruited from the lower orders of the populace, leaving gentlemen to purchase a commission, the way Wickham does in the novel, and thereby become officers.

Additionally, the advancement of technology had not yet

disrupted the stately eighteenth-century patterns of rural life. The effects of the industrial revolution, with its economic and social repercussions, were still most sharply felt by the underprivileged laboring classes. Unrest was widespread, but the great reforms that would launch a new era of English political life did not come until later. Consequently, newer technology that existed in England at the time of *Pride and Prejudice*'s publication does not appear in the work.

Jane Austen's England

Jane Austin's major novels, including *Pride and Prejudice,* were all composed within a short period of about twenty years. Those twenty years (1795-1815) also mark a period in history when England was at the height of its power. England stood as the bulwark against French revolutionary extremism and against Napoleonic imperialism. The dates Austen was writing almost exactly coincide with the great English military victories over Napoleon and the French: the Battle of the Nile, in which Admiral Nelson crippled the French Mediterranean fleet, and the battle of Waterloo, in which Lord Wellington and his German allies defeated Napoleon decisively and sent him into exile. However, so secure in their righteousness were the English middle and upper classes — the "landed gentry" featured in Austen's works — that these historical events impact *Pride and Prejudice* very little.

The French Revolution and Napoleonic Wars

The period from 1789 to 1799 marks the time of the French Revolution, while the period from 1799 to 1815 marks the ascendancy of Napoleon — periods of almost constant social change and upheaval. In England, the same periods were times of conservative reaction, in which society changed very little. The British government, led by Prime Minister William Pitt, maintained a strict control over any ideas or opinions that seemed to support the revolution in France. Pitt's government suspended the right of *habeas corpus,* giving them the power to imprison people for an indefinite time without trial. It also passed laws against public criticism of government policies, and suppressed working-class trade unions. At the same time, the Industrial Revolution permanently changed the British economy. It provided the money Pitt's government needed to oppose Napoleon. At the same time, it also created a large wealthy class and an even larger middle class. These are the people that Jane Austen depicts in *Pride and Prejudice,* the "landed gentry" who have eamed their property, not by inheriting it from their aristocratic ancestors, but by purchasing it with their new wealth. They have few of the manners and graces of the aristocracy and, like the Collins's in *Pride and Prejudice,* are primarily conceded with their own futures in their own little worlds.

Unlike other Romantic-era writers, such as William Wordsworth and Samuel Taylor Coleridge, Austen's works are very little impacted by the French Revolution and revolutionary rhetoric. Members of Austen's own family served in the war against Bonaparte and the French; two of her brothers became admirals in the Royal Navy. The only hint of war and military behavior in *Pride and Prejudice,* however, lies in the continued presence of the British soldiers in Meryton, near the Bennet estate at Longbourn. The soldiers include George Wickham, who later elopes with Lydia Bennet, disgracing the family. In the world of *Pride and Prejudice,* the soldiers are present only to give the younger Bennet daughters men in uniforms to chase after. Their world is limited to their own home, those of their friends and neighbors, a few major resort towns, and, far off, the city of London. There is no hint of the revolutionary affairs going on just across the English Channel in France.

English Regency Society

On the other hand, contemporary English society is a preoccupation of *Pride and Prejudice.* At the time the novel was published, King George III had been struck down by the periodic madness (now suspected to be caused by the metabolic disease porphyria) that plagued his final years. The powers he was no longer capable of using were placed in the hands of his son the Prince Regent, later George IV. The Prince

Regent was widely known as a man of dissolute morals, and his example was followed by many of society's leading figures. Young men regularly went to universities not to learn, but to see and be seen, to drink, gamble, race horses, and spend money. Perhaps the greatest example of this type in *Pride and Prejudice* is the unprincipled George Wickham, who seduces sixteen-year-old Lydia Bennet. Lydia for her part also participates willingly in Regency culture; her thoughts are not for her family's disgrace, but about the handsomeness of her husband and the jealousy of her sisters.

Most "respectable" middle- and upper-class figures, such as Elizabeth Bennet and Fitzwilliam Darcy, strongly disapproved of the immorality of Regency culture. But they did participate in the fashions of the time, influenced by French styles (even though France was at war with England). During the period of the Directory and the Consulate in France (from 1794-1804), styles were influenced by the costumes of the Roman Republic. The elaborate hairstyles and dresses that had characterized the French aristocracy before the Revolution were discarded for simpler costumes. Women, including Elizabeth Bennet, would have worn a simple dress that resembled a modern nightgown. Loose and flowing, it was secured by a ribbon tied just below the breasts. Darcy for his part would have worn a civilian costume of tight breeches, a ruffled shirt with a carefully folded neck cloth, and a high-collared jacket. Even though these costumes were in part a reaction to the excesses of early eighteenth-century dress, they became themselves quite elaborate as the century progressed, sparked by the Prince Regent himself and his friend, the impeccable dresser Beau Brummel. Brummel's mystique, known as "dandyism," expressed in clothing the same idleness and effortless command of a situation that characterizes many of Austen's heroes and heroines.

Chronology of Mansfield Park

1808-1809
Thurs. 22 Dec.
The ball at Mansfield Park.

Fri. 23 Dec.
Edmund goes to Lessingby, "to receive ordination in the course of the Christmas week".
Henry and William go to town.
Fri. Sat. Sun., 30 Dec.-1 Jan.
Edmund does not return, though his week was up.
Mon. 2 Jan.
Mary makes her way to the Park. Henry returns.
Tues. 3 Jan.
He sits with Lady Bertram and Fanny.
Wed. 4 Jan.
He tells Fanny of William's promotion, and makes his offer.
Thurs. 5 Jan.
Fanny's interview with Sir Thomas.
Fri. 6 Jan.
Henry's interview with Sir Thomas.
Mon. 9 Jan. or Tues. 10 Jan.
Edmund returns, after an absence of more than a fortnight.
Tues. 10 Jan. or Wed. 11 Jan.
Henry dines at the Park.
Thurs. 12 Jan.
Edmund dines at the Parsonage.
Fri. 13 Jan.
Edmund and Fanny discuss her affairs, and his.
Sat. 14 Jan.
Fanny expects Mary's visit.
Sun. 15 Jan.
Mary says good-bye to Fanny.

Mon. 16 Jan.The Crawfords leave Mansfield. (Edmund had stayed away more than a fortnight from 23 Dec., and if he had stayed five or six days longer would have returned on that very Monday.)

Sat. 28 Jan.
William arrives on ten days' leave.
Mon. 6 Feb.

Three weeks after the Crawfords' departure Fanny and William leave Mansfield Park and sleep at Newbury.

Tues. 7 Feb.

They reach Portsmouth in daylight.

Sat. 11 Feb.

The Thrush sails "within four days".

Thurs. 16 Feb.

Mary writes to Fanny that Henry went to Norfolk ten days ago, perhaps "for the sake of being travelling at the same time that you were".

Sat. 25 Feb.

Edmund goes to London.

Tues. *28* Feb.

Mrs. Rushworth opens one of the best houses in Wimpole Street.

Sat. 4 March.

Fanny had been nearly four weeks from Mansfield. Henry walks into the room.

Sun. 5 March.

They walk on the ramparts, in April weather though it was really March. Accused of having been in Portsmouth a month, Fanny says: "Not quite a month. — It is only four weeks tomorrow since I left Mansfield." "You are a most accurate and honest reckoner. I should call that a month." "I did not arrive here till Tuesday evening."

Mon. 6 March.

Henry leaves for London.

Wed. 8 March.

Mary's letter (written no doubt on Tuesday) reaches Portsmouth. Henry, she says cannot be allowed to go to Norfolk again "before the middle of next week, that is, he cannot any how be spared till after the 14th, for we have a party that evening".

Tues. *14 March.*

Mrs. Frazer's party.

Sat. 18 March.

Edmund returns to Mansfield.

Sat. 25 or Sun. 26 March.

Fanny receives Edmund's letter. On this day "seven weeks

of the two months were very nearly gone" — they would be up on Mon. 27 March. *At latest* therefore it is Sun. 26 March. The *Saturday*, therefore, on which Edmund returned to Mansfield is 18, not 25, March. He was in London three weeks, which would make his arrival there Sat. 25 Feb. He was not in London when Mary wrote on 16 Feb.; and about 4 March Fanny was supposing him to have been there a week. He had not seen Henry since 14 March.

Mon. 27 March.

The Grants leave for Bath. A few days later Fanny receives Lady Bertram's letter announcing Tom's illness. Some days after this — for her aunt writes "again and again" — comes the news of his being at Mansfield. About a week later comes the letter from Edmund revealing the truth. "Such was the state of Mansfield, and so it continued, with scarcely any change till Easter", which was "particularly late this year". Easter came, and Fanny had no prospect of leaving Portsmouth. "The end of April was coming on; it would soon be almost three months instead of two that she had been absent".

[Easter was on April 2nd in 1809 and March 26th in 1815, neither especially late. In 1810, Easter was on April 22nd.]

Fri. 21 April.

Mary's letter inquiring about Tom's chances of recovery. Mrs. Rushworth is at Twickenham for Easter.

Fri. 28 April.

About a week later, Mary's letter about the "scandalous, ill-natured rumour".

Sat. 29 April

[This day] brought no second letter. Fanny "had, indeed, been three months there".

Sun. 30 April, Mon. 1 May.

"Nothing happened the next day, or the next".

Tues. 2 May.

The third day brings Edmund's letter. "I shall be at Portsmouth the morning after you receive this." (Sir Thomas and he had been in London two days, when he wrote on 1 May).

Wed. 3 May.

Edmund arrives, and they leave Portsmouth, sleeping at Oxford.

Thurs. 4 May.

They reach Mansfield Park. "It was three months, full three months, since her quitting it."

Sun. 7 May.

Edmund opens his heart.

Chapter 4

Character List

Tom Bertram: The profligate older son and the sole heir to Mansfield Park. Tom causes his father and brother hardship for his excessive debts. Eventually, his lifestyle causes his collapse, as he acquires an illness from which he nearly fails to recover.

Edmund Bertram: The second son of Lord and Lady Bertram. Because he is not heir to the estate, he must pick an occupation, and chooses to become a clergyman-much to the chagrin of Mary Crawford, with whom he falls in love. Fanny Price loves him quietly and patiently.

Julia Bertram: The second daughter of Sir Thomas and Lady Bertram. Julia and her sister fall in love with Henry Crawford, but Henry favors her married sister, Maria. Eventually, Julia runs away with Yates.

Lady Bertram: An extremely indolent woman who spends the day on her couch petting her lap dog. Lady Bertram is kind to Fanny, and manages to make a happy marriage with Sir Thomas Bertram.

Maria Bertram: Sir Thomas and Lady Bertrams' narcissistic older daughter. Maria marries Mr. Rushworth for money and social standing despite her attraction to Henry Crawford, with whom she ultimately runs away.

Sir Thomas Bertram: A baronet, the patriarch of Mansfield Park, and Fanny Price's uncle through marriage. Strict and stern, Sir Bertram's financial investments take him to his Antigua plantation, and he returns to find that his children have met the wrong sort of people, the Crawfords.

Mrs. Norris: Lady Bertrams's miserly busybody sister and the scourge of every inhabitant of Mansfield Park. Mrs. Norris is married to the parson, Mr. Norris, until he dies and is replaced by Dr. Grant in the parsonage. She thinks only of herself, and treats Fanny like a servant.

Mary Crawford: Mrs. Grant's younger sister, who hails from London. Although on the surface Mary appears beautiful and charming, underneath she is manipulative, proud, and narcissistic. She feigns friendship with Fanny to get Edmund's attention.

Henry Crawford: Mrs. Grant's wealthy younger brother, who also hails from London. Henry's charm makes up for his plain looks, and he entices women to fall in love with him. He plays Maria Bertram off against her sister Julia, and seems to fall in love with Fanny until he runs away with the married Maria.

Fanny Price: The protagonist, and the poor ward and niece of Sir Thomas and Lady Bertram. Fanny comes to Mansfield Park as a child of nine. Although she is initially kept in her place as a poor relation, over time her good sense and modesty cause her to become be an accepted member of the family. Fanny secretly loves her cousin Edmund, who is himself attracted to Mary Crawford. At the end of the novel, Fanny marries Edmund and moves with him to the Mansfield Park parsonage.

Susan Price: Fanny's younger sister. Because Susan is smart and well-mannered, she comes to replace her sister at Mansfield Park after Fanny marries.

William Price: Fanny's younger brother, who has retained a commission in the Navy. Henry arranges with his admiral uncle to get William promoted to lieutenant in an effort to entice Fanny into marrying him. Fanny and William illustrate how siblings should act, and stand in contrast to the more "high-class" Bertrams.

Mr. Rushworth: The bumbling owner of Sotherton, Mansfield Park's neighboring estate. Blinded by Maria Bertram's beauty, he fails to see that she has married him strictly for his fortune.

Mr. Yates: A visitor to Mansfield Park who puts together the troubling play, *Lover's Vows*. Mr. Yates eventually elopes with Julia Bertram.

Chapter 5

Selected Chapters

Mansfield Park by Jane Austen

Chapter I

About thirty years ago Miss Maria Ward, of Huntingdon, with only seven thousand pounds, had the good luck to captivate Sir Thomas Bertram, of Mansfield Park, in the county of Northampton, and to be thereby raised to the rank of a baronet's lady, with all the comforts and consequences of an handsome house and large income. All Huntingdon exclaimed on the greatness of the match, and her uncle, the lawyer, himself, allowed her to be at least three thousand pounds short of any equitable claim to it.

She had two sisters to be benefited by her elevation; and such of their acquaintance as thought Miss Ward and Miss Frances quite as handsome as Miss Maria, did not scruple to predict their marrying with almost equal advantage. But there certainly are not so many men of large fortune in the world as there are pretty women to deserve them. Miss Ward, at the end of half a dozen years, found herself obliged to be attached to the Rev. Mr. Norris, a friend of her brother-in-law, with scarcely any private fortune, and Miss Frances fared yet worse. Miss Ward's match, indeed, when it came to the point, was not contemptible: Sir Thomas being happily able to give his friend an income in the living of Mansfield; and Mr. and Mrs. Norris began their career of conjugal felicity with very little less than a thousand a year. But Miss Frances married, in the common phrase, to disoblige her family, and by fixing on a lieutenant of marines, without education, fortune, or connexions, did it very thoroughly. She could hardly have made a more untoward choice. Sir Thomas Bertram had interest, which, from principle as well as pride—from a general wish of doing right, and a desire of seeing all that were connected with him in situations of respectability, he would have been glad to exert for the advantage of Lady Bertram's sister; but her husband's profession was such as no interest could reach; and before he had time to devise any other method of assisting them, an absolute breach between the sisters had taken place. It was the natural result of the conduct of each party, and such as a very imprudent marriage almost always produces. To save herself from useless remonstrance, Mrs. Price never wrote to her family on the subject till actually married. Lady Bertram, who was a woman of very tranquil feelings, and a temper remarkably easy and indolent, would have contented herself with merely giving up her sister, and thinking no more of the matter; but Mrs. Norris had a spirit of activity, which could not be satisfied till she had written a long and angry letter to Fanny, to point out the folly of her conduct, and threaten her with all its possible ill consequences. Mrs. Price, in her turn, was injured and angry; and an answer, which comprehended each sister in its bitterness, and bestowed such very disrespectful reflections on the pride of Sir Thomas as Mrs. Norris could not possibly keep to herself, put an end to all intercourse between them for a considerable period.

Their homes were so distant, and the circles in which they moved so distinct, as almost to preclude the means of ever hearing of each other's existence during the eleven following years, or, at least, to make it very wonderful to Sir Thomas that Mrs. Norris should ever have it in her power to tell them, as she now and then did, in an angry voice, that Fanny had got another child. By the end of eleven years, however, Mrs. Price could no longer afford to cherish pride or resentment, or to lose one connexion that might possibly assist her. A large and still increasing family, an husband disabled for active service, but not the less equal to company and good liquor, and a very small income to supply their wants, made her eager to regain the friends she had so carelessly sacrificed; and she addressed Lady Bertram in a letter which spoke so much contrition and despondence, such a superfluity of children, and such a want of almost everything else, as could not but dispose them all to a reconciliation. She was preparing for her ninth lying-in; and after bewailing the circumstance, and imploring their countenance as sponsors to the expected child, she could not conceal how important she felt they might be to the future maintenance of the eight already in being. Her eldest was a boy of ten years old, a fine spirited fellow, who longed to be out in the world; but what could she do? Was there any chance of his being hereafter useful to Sir Thomas in the concerns of his West Indian property? No situation would be beneath him; or what did Sir Thomas think of Woolwich? or how could a boy be sent out to the East?

The letter was not unproductive. It re-established peace and kindness. Sir Thomas sent friendly advice and professions, Lady Bertram dispatched money and baby-linen, and Mrs. Norris wrote the letters. Such were its immediate effects, and within a twelvemonth a more important advantage to Mrs. Price resulted from it. Mrs.

Norris was often observing to the others that she could not get her poor sister and her family out of her head, and that, much as they had all done for her, she seemed to be wanting to do more; and at length she could not but own it to be her wish that poor Mrs. Price should be relieved from the charge and expense of one child entirely out of her great number. "What if they were among them to undertake the care of her eldest daughter, a girl now nine years old, of an age to require more attention than her poor mother could possibly give? The trouble and expense of it to them would be nothing, compared with the benevolence of the action." Lady Bertram agreed with her instantly. "I think we cannot do better," said she; "let us send for the child."

Sir Thomas could not give so instantaneous and unqualified a consent. He debated and hesitated;—it was a serious charge;— a girl so brought up must be adequately provided for, or there would be cruelty instead of kindness in taking her from her family. He thought of his own four children, of his two sons, of cousins in love, etc.;—but no sooner had he deliberately begun to state his objections, than Mrs. Norris interrupted him with a reply to them all, whether stated or not.

"My dear Sir Thomas, I perfectly comprehend you, and do justice to the generosity and delicacy of your notions, which indeed are quite of a piece with your general conduct; and I entirely agree with you in the main as to the propriety of doing everything one could by way of providing for a child one had in a manner taken into one's own hands; and I am sure I should be the last person in the world to withhold my mite upon such an occasion. Having no children of my own, who should I look to in any little matter I may ever have to bestow, but the children of my sisters?— and I am sure Mr. Norris is too just— but you know I am a woman of few words and professions. Do not let us be frightened from a good deed by a trifle. Give a girl an education, and introduce her properly into the world, and ten to one but she has the means of settling well, without farther expense to anybody.

A niece of ours, Sir Thomas, I may say, or at least of yours, would not grow up in this neighbourhood without many advantages. I don't say she would be so handsome as her cousins. I dare say she would not; but she would be introduced into the society of this country under such very favourable circumstances as, in all human probability, would get her a creditable establishment. You are thinking of your sons— but do not you know that, of all things upon earth, thatis the least likely to happen, brought up as they would be, always together like brothers and sisters?

It is morally impossible. I never knew an instance of it. It is, in fact, the only sure way of providing against the connexion. Suppose her a pretty girl, and seen by Tom or Edmund for the first time seven years hence, and I dare say there would be mischief. The very idea of her having been suffered to grow up at a distance from us all in poverty and neglect, would be enough to make either of the dear, sweet-tempered boys in love with her. But breed her up with them from this time, and suppose her even to have the beauty of an angel, and she will never be more to either than a sister." "There is a great deal of truth in what you say," replied Sir Thomas, "and far be it from me to throw any fanciful impediment in the way of a plan which would be so consistent with the relative situations of each. I only meant to observe that it ought not to be lightly engaged in, and that to make it really serviceable to Mrs. Price, and creditable to ourselves, we must secure to the child, or consider ourselves engaged to secure to her hereafter, as circumstances may arise, the provision of a gentlewoman, if no such establishment should offer as you are so sanguine in expecting."

"I thoroughly understand you," cried Mrs. Norris, "you are everything that is generous and considerate, and I am sure we shall never disagree on this point. Whatever I can do, as you well know, I am always ready enough to do for the good of those I love; and, though I could never feel for this little girl the hundredth part of the regard I bear your own dear children, nor consider her, in any respect, so much my own, I should hate myself if I were capable of neglecting her. Is not she a sister's child? and could I bear to see her want while I had a bit of bread to give her? My dear Sir Thomas, with all my faults I have a warm heart; and, poor as I am, would rather deny myself the necessaries of life than do an ungenerous thing. So, if you are not against it, I will write to my poor sister tomorrow, and make the proposal; and, as soon as matters are settled, Iwill engage to get the child to Mansfield; youshall have no trouble about it.

My own trouble, you know, I never regard. I will send Nanny to London on purpose, and she may have a bed at her cousin the saddler's, and the child be appointed to meet her there. They may easily get her from Portsmouth to town by the coach, under the care of any creditable person that may chance to be going. I dare say there is always some reputable tradesman's wife or other going up."

Except to the attack on Nanny's cousin, Sir Thomas no longer made any objection, and a more respectable, though less economical rendezvous being accordingly substituted, everything was considered as settled, and the pleasures of so benevolent a scheme were already enjoyed. The division of gratifying sensations ought not, in strict justice, to have been equal; for Sir Thomas was fully resolved to be the real and consistent patron of the selected child, and Mrs. Norris had not the least intention of being at any expense whatever in her maintenance. As far as walking, talking, and contriving reached, she was thoroughly benevolent, and nobody knew better how to dictate liberality to others; but her love of money was equal to her love of directing, and she knew quite as well how to save her own as to spend that of her friends.

Having married on a narrower income than she had been used to look forward to, she had, from the first, fancied a very strict line of economy necessary; and what was begun as a matter of prudence, soon grew into a matter of choice, as an object of that needful solicitude which there were no children to supply. Had there been a family to provide for, Mrs. Norris might never have saved her money; but having no care of that kind, there was nothing to impede her frugality, or lessen the comfort of making a yearly addition to an income which they had never lived up to. Under this infatuating principle, counteracted by no real affection for her sister, it was impossible for her to aim at more than the credit of projecting and arranging so expensive a charity; though perhaps she might so little know herself as to walk home to the Parsonage, after this conversation, in the happy belief of being the most liberal-minded sister and aunt in the world.

When the subject was brought forward again, her views were more fully explained; and, in reply to Lady Bertram's calm inquiry of "Where shall the child come to first, sister, to you or to us?" Sir Thomas heard with some surprise that it would be totally out of Mrs. Norris's power to take any share in the personal charge of her. He had been considering her as a particularly welcome addition at the Parsonage, as a desirable companion to an aunt who had no children of her own; but he found himself wholly mistaken. Mrs. Norris was sorry to say that the little girl's staying with them, at least as things then were, was quite out of the question. Poor Mr.

Norris's indifferent state of health made it an impossibility: he could no more bear the noise of a child than he could fly; if, indeed, he should ever get well of his gouty complaints, it would be a different matter: she should then be glad to take her turn, and think nothing of the inconvenience; but just now, poor Mr. Norris took up every moment of her time, and the very mention of such a thing she was sure would distract him. "Then she had better come to us," said Lady Bertram, with the utmost composure. After a short pause Sir Thomas added with dignity, "Yes, let her home be in this house. We will endeavour to do our duty by her, and she will, at least, have the advantage of companions of her own age, and of a regular instructress."

"Very true," cried Mrs. Norris, "which are both very important considerations; and it will be just the same to Miss Lee whether she has three girls to teach, or only two—there can be no difference. I only wish I could be more useful; but you see I do all in my power. I am not one of those that spare their own trouble; and Nanny shall fetch her, however it may put me to inconvenience to have my chief counsellor away for three days. I suppose, sister, you will put the child in the little white attic, near the old nurseries. It will be much the best place for her, so near Miss Lee, and not far from the girls, and close by the housemaids, who could either of them help to dress her, you know, and take care of her clothes, for I suppose you would not think it fair to expect Ellis to wait on her as well as the others. Indeed, I do not see that you could possibly place her anywhere else."

Lady Bertram made no Opposition.

"I hope she will prove a well-disposed girl," continued Mrs. Norris, "and be sensible of her uncommon good fortune in having such friends."

"Should her disposition be really bad," said Sir Thomas, "we must not, for our own children's sake, continue her in the family; but there is no reason to expect so great an evil. We shall probably see much to wish altered in her, and must prepare ourselves for gross ignorance, some meanness of opinions, and very distressing vulgarity of manner; but these are not incurable faults; nor, I trust, can they be dangerous for her associates. Had my daughters been youngerthan herself, I should have considered the introduction of such a companion as a matter of very serious moment; but, as it is, I hope there can be nothing to fear for them, and everything to hope for her, from the association."

"That is exactly what I think," cried Mrs. Norris, "and what I was saying to my husband this morning. It will be an education for the child, said I, only being with her cousins; if Miss Lee taught her nothing, she would learn to be good and clever from them."

"I hope she will not tease my poor pug," said Lady Bertram; "I have but just got Julia to leave it alone."

"There will be some difficulty in our way, Mrs. Norris," observed Sir Thomas, "as to the distinction proper to be made between the girls as they grow up: how to preserve in the minds of my daughtersthe consciousness of what they are, without making them think too lowly of their cousin; and how, without depressing her spirits too far, to make her remember that she is not a Miss Bertram. I should wish to see them very good friends, and would, on no account, authorise in my girls the smallest degree of arrogance towards their relation; but still they cannot be equals. Their rank, fortune, rights, and expectations will always be different. It is a point of great delicacy, and you must assist us in our endeavours to choose exactly the right line of conduct."

Mrs. Norris was quite at his service; and though she perfectly agreed with him as to its being a most difficult thing, encouraged him to hope that between them it would be easily managed.

It will be readily believed that Mrs. Norris did not write to her sister in vain. Mrs. Price seemed rather surprised that a girl should be fixed on, when she had so many fine boys, but accepted the offer most thankfully, assuring them of her daughter's being a very well-disposed, good-humoured girl, and trusting they would never have cause to throw her off. She spoke of her farther as somewhat delicate and puny, but was sanguine in the hope of her being materially better for change of air. Poor woman! she probably thought change of air might agree with many of her children.

Chapter II

The little girl performed her long journey in safety; and at Northampton was met by Mrs. Norris, who thus regaled in the credit of being foremost to welcome her, and in the importance of leading her in to the others, and recommending her to their kindness.

Fanny Price was at this time just ten years old, and though there might not be much in her first appearance to captivate, there was, at least, nothing to disgust her relations. She was small of her age, with no glow of complexion, nor any other striking beauty; exceedingly timid and shy, and shrinking from notice; but her air, though awkward, was not vulgar, her voice was sweet, and when she spoke her countenance was pretty. Sir Thomas and Lady Bertram received her very kindly; and Sir Thomas, seeing how much she needed encouragement, tried to be all that was conciliating: but he had to work against a most untoward gravity of deportment; and Lady Bertram, without taking half so much trouble, or speaking one word where he spoke ten, by the mere aid of a good-humoured smile, became immediately the less awful character of the two.

The young people were all at home, and sustained their share in the introduction very well, with much good humour, and no embarrassment, at least on the part of the sons, who, at seventeen and sixteen, and tall of their age, had all the grandeur of men in the eyes of their little cousin. The two girls were more at a loss from being younger and in greater awe of their father, who addressed them on the occasion with rather an injudicious particularity. But they were too much used to company and praise to have anything like natural shyness; and their confidence increasing from their cousin's total want of it, they were soon able to take a full survey of her face and her frock in easy indifference.

They were a remarkably fine family, the sons very well-looking, the daughters decidedly handsome, and all of them well-grown and forward of their age, which produced as striking a difference between the cousins in person, as education had given to their address; and no one would have supposed the girls so nearly of an age as they really were. There were in fact but two years between the youngest and Fanny. Julia Bertram was only twelve, and Maria but a year older. The little visitor meanwhile was as unhappy as possible. Afraid of everybody, ashamed of herself, and longing for the home she had left, she knew not how to look up, and could scarcely speak to be heard, or without crying.

Mrs. Norris had been talking to her the whole way from Northampton of her wonderful good fortune, and the extraordinary degree of gratitude and good behaviour which it ought to produce, and her consciousness of misery was therefore increased by the idea of its being a wicked thing for her not to be happy. The fatigue, too, of so long a journey, became soon no trifling evil. In vain were the well-meant condescensions of Sir Thomas, and all the officious prognostications of Mrs. Norris that she would be a good girl; in vain did Lady Bertram smile and make her sit on the sofa with herself and pug, and vain was even the sight of a gooseberry tart towards giving her comfort; she could scarcely swallow two mouthfuls before tears interrupted her, and sleep seeming to be her likeliest friend, she was taken to finish her sorrows in bed.

"This is not a very promising beginning," said Mrs. Norris, when Fanny had left the room. "After all that I said to her as we came along, I thought she would have behaved better; I told her how much might depend upon her acquitting herself well at first. I wish there may not be a little sulkiness of temper—her poor mother had a good deal; but we must make allowances for such a child—and I do not know that her being sorry to leave her home is really against her, for, with all its faults, it washer home, and she cannot as yet understand how much she has changed for the better; but then there is moderation in all things."

It required a longer time, however, than Mrs. Norris was inclined to allow, to reconcile Fanny to the novelty of

Mansfield Park, and the separation from everybody she had been used to. Her feelings were very acute, and too little understood to be properly attended to. Nobody meant to be unkind, but nobody put themselves out of their way to secure her comfort.

The holiday allowed to the Miss Bertrams the next day, on purpose to afford leisure for getting acquainted with, and entertaining their young cousin, produced little union. They could not but hold her cheap on finding that she had but two sashes, and had never learned French; and when they perceived her to be little struck with the duet they were so good as to play, they could do no more than make her a generous present of some of their least valued toys, and leave her to herself, while they adjourned to whatever might be the favourite holiday sport of the moment, making artificial flowers or wasting gold paper.

Fanny, whether near or from her cousins, whether in the schoolroom, the drawing-room, or the shrubbery, was equally forlorn, finding something to fear in every person and place. She was disheartened by Lady Bertram's silence, awed by Sir Thomas's grave looks, and quite overcome by Mrs. Norris's admonitions. Her elder cousins mortified her by reflections on her size, and abashed her by noticing her shyness: Miss Lee wondered at her ignorance, and the maid-servants sneered at her clothes; and when to these sorrows was added the idea of the brothers and sisters among whom she had always been important as playfellow, instructress, and nurse, the despondence that sunk her little heart was severe.

The grandeur of the house astonished, but could not console her. The rooms were too large for her to move in with ease: whatever she touched she expected to injure, and she crept about in constant terror of something or other; often retreating towards her own chamber to cry; and the little girl who was spoken of in the drawing-room when she left it at night as seeming so desirably sensible of her peculiar good fortune, ended every day's sorrows by sobbing herself to sleep. A week had passed in this way, and no suspicion of it conveyed by her quiet passive manner, when she was found one morning by her cousin Edmund, the youngest of the sons, sitting crying on the attic stairs.

"My dear little cousin," said he, with all the gentleness of an excellent nature, "what can be the matter?" And sitting down by her, he was at great pains to overcome her shame in being so surprised, and persuade her to speak openly. Was she ill? or was anybody angry with her? or had she quarrelled with Maria and Julia? or was she puzzled about anything in her lesson that he could explain? Did she, in short, want anything he could possibly get her, or do for her?

For a long while no answer could be obtained beyond a "no, no—not at all—no, thank you"; but he still persevered; and no sooner had he begun to revert to her own home, than her increased sobs explained to him where the grievance lay. He tried to console her. "You are sorry to leave Mama, my dear little Fanny," said he, "which shows you to be a very good girl; but you must remember that you are with relations and friends, who all love you, and wish to make you happy. Let us walk out in the park, and you shall tell me all about your brothers and sisters."

On pursuing the subject, he found that, dear as all these brothers and sisters generally were, there was one among them who ran more in her thoughts than the rest. It was William whom she talked of most, and wanted most to see. William, the eldest, a year older than herself, her constant companion and friend; her advocate with her mother (of whom he was the darling) in every distress. "William did not like she should come away; he had told her he should miss her very much indeed." "But William will write to you, I dare say." "Yes, he had promised he would, but he had told herto write first." "And when shall you do it?" She hung her head and answered hesitatingly, "she did not know; she had not any paper."

"If that be all your difficulty, I will furnish you with paper and every other material, and you may write your letter whenever you choose. Would it make you happy to write to William?"

"Yes, very."

"Then let it be done now. Come with me into the

breakfast-room, we shall find everything there, and be sure of having the room to ourselves."

"But, cousin, will it go to the post?"

"Yes, depend upon me it shall: it shall go with the other letters; and, as your uncle will frank it, it will cost William nothing."

"My uncle!" repeated Fanny, with a frightened look.

"Yes, when you have written the letter, I will take it to my father to frank."

Fanny thought it a bold measure, but offered no further resistance; and they went together into the breakfast-room, where Edmund prepared her paper, and ruled her lines with all the goodwill that her brother could himself have felt, and probably with somewhat more exactness. He continued with her the whole time of her writing, to assist her with his penknife or his orthography, as either were wanted; and added to these attentions, which she felt very much, a kindness to her brother which delighted her beyond all the rest. He wrote with his own hand his love to his cousin William, and sent him half a guinea under the seal.

Fanny's feelings on the occasion were such as she believed herself incapable of expressing; but her countenance and a few artless words fully conveyed all their gratitude and delight, and her cousin began to find her an interesting object. He talked to her more, and, from all that she said, was convinced of her having an affectionate heart, and a strong desire of doing right; and he could perceive her to be farther entitled to attention by great sensibility of her situation, and great timidity. He had never knowingly given her pain, but he now felt that she required more positive kindness; and with that view endeavoured, in the first place, to lessen her fears of them all, and gave her especially a great deal of good advice as to playing with Maria and Julia, and being as merry as possible.

From this day Fanny grew more comfortable. She felt that she had a friend, and the kindness of her cousin Edmund gave her better spirits with everybody else. The place became less strange, and the people less formidable; and if there were some amongst them whom she could not cease to fear, she began at least to know their ways, and to catch the best manner of conforming to them. The little rusticities and awkwardnesses which had at first made grievous inroads on the tranquillity of all, and not least of herself, necessarily wore away, and she was no longer materially afraid to appear before her uncle, nor did her aunt Norris's voice make her start very much. To her cousins she became occasionally an acceptable companion. Though unworthy, from inferiority of age and strength, to be their constant associate, their pleasures and schemes were sometimes of a nature to make a third very useful, especially when that third was of an obliging, yielding temper; and they could not but own, when their aunt inquired into her faults, or their brother Edmund urged her claims to their kindness, that "Fanny was good-natured enough."

Edmund was uniformly kind himself; and she had nothing worse to endure on the part of Tom than that sort of merriment which a young man of seventeen will always think fair with a child of ten. He was just entering into life, full of spirits, and with all the liberal dispositions of an eldest son, who feels born only for expense and enjoyment. His kindness to his little cousin was consistent with his situation and rights: he made her some very pretty presents, and laughed at her.

As her appearance and spirits improved, Sir Thomas and Mrs. Norris thought with greater satisfaction of their benevolent plan; and it was pretty soon decided between them that, though far from clever, she showed a tractable disposition, and seemed likely to give them little trouble A mean opinion of her abilities was not confined to them. Fanny could read, work, and write, but she had been taught nothing more; and as her cousins found her ignorant of many things with which they had been long familiar, they thought her prodigiously stupid, and for the first two or three weeks were continually bringing some fresh report of it into the drawing-room. "Dear mama, only think, my cousin cannot put the map of Europe together— or my cousin cannot tell the principal rivers in Russia— or, she never heard of Asia Minor—or she does not know the difference between water-colours and crayons!— How strange!—Did you ever hear anything so stupid?"

"My dear," their considerate aunt would reply, "it is very bad, but you must not expect everybody to be as forward and quick at learning as yourself."

"But, aunt, she is really so very ignorant!—Do you know, we asked her last night which way she would go to get to Ireland; and she said, she should cross to the Isle of Wight. She thinks of nothing but the Isle of Wight, and she calls it theIsland, as if there were no other island in the world. I am sure I should have been ashamed of myself, if I had not known better long before I was so old as she is. I cannot remember the time when I did not know a great deal that she has not the least notion of yet. How long ago it is, aunt, since we used to repeat the chronological order of the kings of England, with the dates of their accession, and most of the principal events of their reigns!"

"Yes," added the other; "and of the Roman emperors as low as Severus; besides a great deal of the heathen mythology, and all the metals, semi-metals, planets, and distinguished philosophers." "Very true indeed, my dears, but you are blessed with wonderful memories, and your poor cousin has probably none at all. There is a vast deal of difference in memories, as well as in everything else, and therefore you must make allowance for your cousin, and pity her deficiency. And remember that, if you are ever so forward and clever yourselves, you should always be modest; for, much as you know already, there is a great deal more for you to learn."

"Yes, I know there is, till I am seventeen. But I must tell you another thing of Fanny, so odd and so stupid. Do you know, she says she does not want to learn either music or drawing." "To be sure, my dear, that is very stupid indeed, and shows a great want of genius and emulation. But, all things considered, I do not know whether it is not as well that it should be so, for, though you know (owing to me) your papa and mama are so good as to bring her up with you, it is not at all necessary that she should be as accomplished as you are;—on the contrary, it is much more desirable that there should be a difference."

Such were the counsels by which Mrs. Norris assisted to

form her nieces' minds; and it is not very wonderful that, with all their promising talents and early information, they should be entirely deficient in the less common acquirements of self-knowledge, generosity and humility. In everything but disposition they were admirably taught. Sir Thomas did not know what was wanting, because, though a truly anxious father, he was not outwardly affectionate, and the reserve of his manner repressed all the flow of their spirits before him.

To the education of her daughters Lady Bertram paid not the smallest attention. She had not time for such cares. She was a woman who spent her days in sitting, nicely dressed, on a sofa, doing some long piece of needlework, of little use and no beauty, thinking more of her pug than her children, but very indulgent to the latter when it did not put herself to inconvenience, guided in everything important by Sir Thomas, and in smaller concerns by her sister. Had she possessed greater leisure for the service of her girls, she would probably have supposed it unnecessary, for they were under the care of a governess, with proper masters, and could want nothing more. As for Fanny's being stupid at learning, "she could only say it was very unlucky, but some people werestupid, and Fanny must take more pains: she did not know what else was to be done; and, except her being so dull, she must add she saw no harm in the poor little thing, and always found her very handy and quick in carrying messages, and fetching, what she wanted."

Fanny, with all her faults of ignorance and timidity, was fixed at Mansfield Park, and learning to transfer in its favour much of her attachment to her former home, grew up there not unhappily among her cousins. There was no positive ill-nature in Maria or Julia; and though Fanny was often mortified by their treatment of her, she thought too lowly of her own claims to feel injured by it.

From about the time of her entering the family, Lady Bertram, in consequence of a little ill-health, and a great deal of indolence, gave up the house in town, which she had been used to occupy every spring, and remained wholly in the country, leaving Sir Thomas to attend his duty in Parliament, with whatever increase or diminution of comfort might arise from her absence. In the country, therefore, the Miss Bertrams continued to exercise their memories, practise their duets, and grow tall and womanly: and their father saw them becoming in person, manner, and accomplishments, everything that could satisfy his anxiety. His eldest son was careless and extravagant, and had already given him much uneasiness; but his other children promised him nothing but good. His daughters, he felt, while they retained the name of Bertram, must be giving it new grace, and in quitting it, he trusted, would extend its respectable alliances; and the character of Edmund, his strong good sense and uprightness of mind, bid most fairly for utility, honour, and happiness to himself and all his connexions. He was to be a clergyman.

Amid the cares and the complacency which his own children suggested, Sir Thomas did not forget to do what he could for the children of Mrs. Price: he assisted her liberally in the education and disposal of her sons as they became old enough for a determinate pursuit; and Fanny, though almost totally separated from her family, was sensible of the truest satisfaction in hearing of any kindness towards them, or of anything at all promising in their situation or conduct. Once, and once only, in the course of many years, had she the happiness of being with William. Of the rest she saw nothing: nobody seemed to think of her ever going amongst them again, even for a visit, nobody at home seemed to want her; but William determining, soon after her removal, to be a sailor, was invited to spend a week with his sister in Northamptonshire before he went to sea.

Their eager affection in meeting, their exquisite delight in being together, their hours of happy mirth, and moments of serious conference, may be imagined; as well as the sanguine views and spirits of the boy even to the last, and the misery of the girl when he left her. Luckily the visit happened in the Christmas holidays, when she could directly look for comfort to her cousin Edmund; and he told her such charming things of what William was to do, and be hereafter, in consequence of his profession, as made her gradually admit that the separation might have some use. Edmund's friendship never failed her: his leaving Eton for Oxford made no change in his kind dispositions, and only afforded more frequent opportunities of proving them. Without any display of doing more than the rest, or any fear of doing too much, he was always true to her interests, and considerate of her feelings, trying to make her good qualities understood, and to conquer the diffidence which prevented their being more apparent; giving her advice, consolation, and encouragement.

Kept back as she was by everybody else, his single support could not bring her forward; but his attentions were otherwise of the highest importance in assisting the improvement of her mind, and extending its pleasures. He knew her to be clever, to have a quick apprehension as well as good sense, and a fondness for reading, which, properly directed, must be an education in itself. Miss Lee taught her French, and heard her read the daily portion of history; but he recommended the books which charmed her leisure hours, he encouraged her taste, and corrected her judgment: he made reading useful by talking to her of what she read, and heightened its attraction by judicious praise. In return for such services she loved him better than anybody in the world except William: her heart was divided between the two.

Chapter III

The first event of any importance in the family was the death of Mr. Norris, which happened when Fanny was about fifteen, and necessarily introduced alterations and novelties. Mrs. Norris, on quitting the Parsonage, removed first to the Park, and afterwards to a small house of Sir Thomas's in the village, and consoled herself for the loss of her husband by considering that she could do very well without him; and for her reduction of income by the evident necessity of stricter economy.

The living was hereafter for Edmund; and, had his uncle died a few years sooner, it would have been duly given to some friend to hold till he were old enough for orders. But Tom's extravagance had, previous to that event, been so great as to render a different disposal of the next presentation necessary, and the younger brother must help to pay for the pleasures of the elder. There was another family living actually held for Edmund; but though this circumstance had made the arrangement somewhat easier to Sir Thomas's conscience, he could not but feel it to be an act of injustice, and he earnestly tried to impress his eldest son with the same conviction, in the hope of its producing a better effect than anything he had yet been able to say or do.

"I blush for you, Tom," said he, in his most dignified manner; "I blush for the expedient which I am driven on, and I trust I may pity your feelings as a brother on the occasion. You have robbed Edmund for ten, twenty, thirty years, perhaps for life, of more than half the income which ought to be his. It may hereafter be in my power, or in yours (I hope it will), to procure him better preferment; but it must not be forgotten that no benefit of that sort would have been beyond his natural claims on us, and that nothing can, in fact, be an equivalent for the certain advantage which he is now obliged to forego through the urgency of your debts."

Tom listened with some shame and some sorrow; but escaping as quickly as possible, could soon with cheerful selfishness reflect, firstly, that he had not been half so much in debt as some of his friends; secondly, that his father had made a most tiresome piece of work of it; and, thirdly, that the future incumbent, whoever he might be, would, in all probability, die very soon.

On Mr. Norris's death the presentation became the right of a Dr. Grant, who came consequently to reside at Mansfield; and on proving to be a hearty man of forty-five, seemed likely to disappoint Mr. Bertram's calculations. But "no, he was a short-necked, apoplectic sort of fellow, and, plied well with good things, would soon pop off."

He had a wife about fifteen years his junior, but no children; and they entered the neighbourhood with the usual fair report of being very respectable, agreeable people.

The time was now come when Sir Thomas expected his sister-in-law to claim her share in their niece, the change in

Mrs. Norris's situation, and the improvement in Fanny's age, seeming not merely to do away any former objection to their living together, but even to give it the most decided eligibility; and as his own circumstances were rendered less fair than heretofore, by some recent losses on his West India estate, in addition to his eldest son's extravagance, it became not undesirable to himself to be relieved from the expense of her support, and the obligation of her future provision. In the fullness of his belief that such a thing must be, he mentioned its probability to his wife; and the first time of the subject's occurring to her again happening to be when Fanny was present, she calmly observed to her, "So, Fanny, you are going to leave us, and live with my sister. How shall you like it?"

Fanny was too much surprised to do more than repeat her aunt's words, "Going to leave you?"

"Yes, my dear; why should you be astonished? You have been five years with us, and my sister always meant to take you when Mr. Norris died. But you must come up and tack on my patterns all the same."

The news was as disagreeable to Fanny as it had been unexpected. She had never received kindness from her aunt Norris, and could not love her.

"I shall be very sorry to go away," said she, with a faltering voice.

"Yes, I dare say you will; that'snatural enough. I suppose you have had as little to vex you since you came into this house as any creature in the world."

"I hope I am not ungrateful, aunt," said Fanny modestly.

"No, my dear; I hope not. I have always found you a very good girl."

"And am I never to live here again?"

"Never, my dear; but you are sure of a comfortable home. It can make very little difference to you, whether you are in one house or the other."

Fanny left the room with a very sorrowful heart; she could not feel the difference to be so small, she could not think of living with her aunt with anything like satisfaction. As soon as she met with Edmund she told him her distress.

"Cousin," said she, "something is going to happen which I do not like at all; and though you have often persuaded me into being reconciled to things that I disliked at first, you will not be able to do it now. I am going to live entirely with my aunt Norris."

"Indeed!"

"Yes; my aunt Bertram has just told me so. It is quite settled. I am to leave Mansfield Park, and go to the White House, I suppose, as soon as she is removed there."

"Well, Fanny, and if the plan were not unpleasant to you, I should call it an excellent one."

"Oh, cousin!"

"It has everything else in its favour. My aunt is acting like a sensible woman in wishing for you. She is choosing a friend and companion exactly where she ought, and I am glad her love of money does not interfere. You will be what you ought to be to her. I hope it does not distress you very much, Fanny?"

"Indeed it does: I cannot like it. I love this house and everything in it: I shall love nothing there. You know how uncomfortable I feel with her."

"I can say nothing for her manner to you as a child; but it was the same with us all, or nearly so. She never knew how to be pleasant to children. But you are now of an age to be treated better; I think she is behaving better already; and when you are her only companion, you mustbe important to her."

"I can never be important to any one."

"What is to prevent you?"

"Everything. My situation, my foolishness and awkwardness." "As to your foolishness and awkwardness, my dear Fanny, believe me, you never have a shadow of either, but in using the words so improperly. There is no reason in the world why you should not be important where you are known. You have good sense, and a sweet temper, and I am sure you have a grateful heart, that could never receive kindness without wishing to return it. I do not know any better qualifications for a friend and companion."

"You are too kind," said Fanny, colouring at such praise; "how shall I ever thank you as I ought, for thinking so well of me. Oh! cousin, if I am to go away, I shall remember your goodness to the last moment of my life." "Why, indeed, Fanny, I should hope to be remembered at such a distance as the White House. You speak as if you were going two hundred miles off instead of only across the park; but you will belong to us almost as much as ever. The two families will be meeting every day in the year. The only difference will be that, living with your aunt, you will necessarily be brought forward as you ought to be. Herethere are too many whom you can hide behind; but with heryou will be forced to speak for yourself."

"Oh! I do not say so."

"I must say it, and say it with pleasure. Mrs. Norris is much better fitted than my mother for having the charge of you now. She is of a temper to do a great deal for anybody she really interests herself about, and she will force you to do justice to your natural powers."

Fanny sighed, and said, "I cannot see things as you do; but I ought to believe you to be right rather than myself, and I am very much obliged to you for trying to reconcile me to what must be. If I could suppose my aunt really to care for me, it would be delightful to feel myself of consequence to anybody. Here, I know, I am of none, and yet I love the place so well." "The place, Fanny, is what you will not quit, though you quit the house. You will have as free a command of the park and gardens as ever. Even yourconstant little heart need not take fright at such a nominal change. You will have the same walks to frequent, the same library to choose from, the same people to look at, the same horse to ride."

"Very true. Yes, dear old grey pony! Ah! cousin, when I remember how much I used to dread riding, what terrors it gave me to hear it talked of as likely to do me good (oh! how I have trembled at my uncle's opening his lips if horses were talked of), and then think of the kind pains you took to reason and persuade me out of my fears, and convince me that I should like it after a little while, and feel how right you proved to be, I am inclined to hope you may always prophesy as well."

"And I am quite convinced that your being with Mrs. Norris will be as good for your mind as riding has been for your health, and as much for your ultimate happiness too." So ended their discourse, which, for any very appropriate service it could render Fanny, might as well have been spared, for Mrs. Norris had not the smallest intention of taking her. It had never occurred to her, on the present occasion, but as a thing to be carefully avoided. To prevent its being expected, she had fixed on the smallest habitation which could rank as genteel among the buildings of Mansfield parish, the White House being only just large enough to receive herself and her servants, and allow a spare room for a friend, of which she made a very particular point. The spare rooms at the Parsonage had never been wanted, but the absolute necessity of a spare room for a friend was now never forgotten. Not all her precautions, however, could save her from being suspected of something better; or, perhaps, her very display of the importance of a spare room might have misled Sir Thomas to suppose it really intended for Fanny. Lady Bertram soon brought the matter to a certainty by carelessly observing to Mrs. Norris—

"I think, sister, we need not keep Miss Lee any longer, when Fanny goes to live with you."

Mrs. Norris almost started. "Live with me, dear Lady Bertram! what do you mean?"

"Is she not to live with you? I thought you had settled it with Sir Thomas."

"Me! never. I never spoke a syllable about it to Sir Thomas, nor he to me. Fanny live with me! the last thing in the world for me to think of, or for anybody to wish that really knows us both. Good heaven! what could I do with Fanny? Me! a poor, helpless, forlorn widow, unfit for anything, my spirits quite broke down; what could I do with a girl at her time of life? A girl of fifteen! the very age of all others to need most attention and care, and put the cheerfullest spirits to the test! Sure Sir Thomas could not seriously expect such a thing! Sir Thomas is too much my friend. Nobody that wishes me well, I am sure, would propose it. How came Sir Thomas to speak to you about it?" "Indeed, I do not know. I suppose he thought it best." "But what did he say? He could not say he wishedme to take Fanny.

I am sure in his heart he could not wish me to do it." "No; he only said he thought it very likely; and I thought so too. We both thought it would be a comfort to you. But if you do not like it, there is no more to be said. She is no encumbrance here."

"Dear sister, if you consider my unhappy state, how can she be any comfort to me? Here am I, a poor desolate widow, deprived of the best of husbands, my health gone in attending and nursing him, my spirits still worse, all my peace in this world destroyed, with hardly enough to support me in the rank of a gentlewoman, and enable me to live so as not to disgrace the memory of the dear departed— what possible comfort could I have in taking such a charge upon me as Fanny? If I could wish it for my own sake, I would not do so unjust a thing by the poor girl. She is in good hands, and sure of doing well. I must struggle through my sorrows and difficulties as I can." "Then you will not mind living by yourself quite alone?"

"Lady Bertram, I do not complain. I know I cannot live as I have done, but I must retrench where I can, and learn to be a better manager. I havebeena liberal housekeeper enough, but I shall not be ashamed to practise economy now. My situation is as much altered as my income. A great many things were due from poor Mr. Norris, as clergyman of the parish, that cannot be expected from me. It is unknown how much was consumed in our kitchen by odd comers and goers. At the White House, matters must be better looked after. I mustlive within my income, or I shall be miserable; and I own it would give me great satisfaction to be able to do rather more, to lay by a little at the end of the year." "I dare say you will. You always do, don't you?"

"My object, Lady Bertram, is to be of use to those that come after me. It is for your children's good that I wish to be richer. I have nobody else to care for, but I should be very glad to think I could leave a little trifle among them worth their having." "You are very good, but do not trouble yourself about them. They are sure of being well provided for. Sir Thomas will take care of that."

"Why, you know, Sir Thomas's means will be rather

straitened if the Antigua estate is to make such poor returns." "Oh! thatwill soon be settled. Sir Thomas has been writing about it, I know." "Well, Lady Bertram," said Mrs. Norris, moving to go, "I can only say that my sole desire is to be of use to your family: and so, if Sir Thomas should ever speak again about my taking Fanny, you will be able to say that my health and spirits put it quite out of the question; besides that, I really should not have a bed to give her, for I must keep a spare room for a friend."

Lady Bertram repeated enough of this conversation to her husband to convince him how much he had mistaken his sister-in-law's views; and she was from that moment perfectly safe from all expectation, or the slightest allusion to it from him. He could not but wonder at her refusing to do anything for a niece whom she had been so forward to adopt; but, as she took early care to make him, as well as Lady Bertram, understand that whatever she possessed was designed for their family, he soon grew reconciled to a distinction which, at the same time that it was advantageous and complimentary to them, would enable him better to provide for Fanny himself.

Fanny soon learnt how unnecessary had been her fears of a removal; and her spontaneous, untaught felicity on the discovery, conveyed some consolation to Edmund for his disappointment in what he had expected to be so essentially serviceable to her. Mrs. Norris took possession of the White House, the Grants arrived at the Parsonage, and these events over, everything at Mansfield went on for some time as usual.

The Grants showing a disposition to be friendly and sociable, gave great satisfaction in the main among their new acquaintance. They had their faults, and Mrs. Norris soon found them out. The Doctor was very fond of eating, and would have a good dinner every day; and Mrs. Grant, instead of contriving to gratify him at little expense, gave her cook as high wages as they did at Mansfield Park, and was scarcely ever seen in her offices. Mrs. Norris could not speak with any temper of such grievances, nor of the quantity of butter and eggs that were regularly consumed in the house. "Nobody loved plenty and hospitality more than herself; nobody more hated pitiful doings; the Parsonage, she believed, had never been wanting in comforts of any sort, had never borne a bad character in hertime, but this was a way of going on that she could not understand. A fine lady in a country parsonage was quite out of place. Herstore-room, she thought, might have been good enough for Mrs. Grant to go into. Inquire where she would, she could not find out that Mrs. Grant had ever had more than five thousand pounds."

Lady Bertram listened without much interest to this sort of invective. She could not enter into the wrongs of an economist, but she felt all the injuries of beauty in Mrs. Grant's being so well settled in life without being handsome, and expressed her astonishment on that point almost as often, though not so diffusely, as Mrs. Norris discussed the other.

These opinions had been hardly canvassed a year before another event arose of such importance in the family, as might fairly claim some place in the thoughts and conversation of the ladies. Sir Thomas found it expedient to go to Antigua himself, for the better arrangement of his affairs, and he took his eldest son with him, in the hope of detaching him from some bad connexions at home. They left England with the probability of being nearly a twelvemonth absent.

The necessity of the measure in a pecuniary light, and the hope of its utility to his son, reconciled Sir Thomas to the effort of quitting the rest of his family, and of leaving his daughters to the direction of others at their present most interesting time of life. He could not think Lady Bertram quite equal to supply his place with them, or rather, to perform what should have been her own; but, in Mrs. Norris's watchful attention, and in Edmund's judgment, he had sufficient confidence to make him go without fears for their conduct. Lady Bertram did not at all like to have her husband leave her; but she was not disturbed by any alarm for his safety, or solicitude for his comfort, being one of those persons who think nothing can be dangerous, or difficult, or fatiguing to anybody but themselves.

The Miss Bertrams were much to be pitied on the occasion: not for their sorrow, but for their want of it. Their father was no object of love to them; he had never seemed the friend of their pleasures, and his absence was unhappily most welcome. They were relieved by it from all restraint; and without aiming at one gratification that would probably have been forbidden by Sir Thomas, they felt themselves immediately at their own disposal, and to have every indulgence within their reach. Fanny's relief, and her consciousness of it, were quite equal to her cousins'; but a more tender nature suggested that her feelings were ungrateful, and she really grieved because she could not grieve. "Sir Thomas, who had done so much for her and her brothers, and who was gone perhaps never to return! that she should see him go without a tear! it was a shameful insensibility." He had said to her, moreover, on the very last morning, that he hoped she might see William again in the course of the ensuing winter, and had charged her to write and invite him to Mansfield as soon as the squadron to which he belonged should be known to be in England.

"This was so thoughtful and kind!" and would he only have smiled upon her, and called her "my dear Fanny," while he said it, every former frown or cold address might have been forgotten. But he had ended his speech in a way to sink her in sad mortification, by adding, "If William does come to Mansfield, I hope you may be able to convince him that the many years which have passed since you parted have not been spent on your side entirely without improvement; though, I fear, he must find his sister at sixteen in some respects too much like his sister at ten." She cried bitterly over this reflection when her uncle was gone; and her cousins, on seeing her with red eyes, set her down as a hypocrite.

Chapter IV

Tom Bertram had of late spent so little of his time at home that he could be only nominally missed; and Lady Bertram was soon astonished to find how very well they did even without his father, how well Edmund could supply his place in carving, talking to the steward, writing to the attorney, settling with the servants, and equally saving her from all possible fatigue or exertion in every particular but that of directing her letters. The earliest intelligence of the travellers' safe arrival at Antigua, after a favourable voyage, was received; though not before Mrs. Norris had been indulging in very dreadful fears, and trying to make Edmund participate them whenever she could get him alone; and as she depended on being the first person made acquainted with any fatal catastrophe, she had already arranged the manner of breaking it to all the others, when Sir Thomas's assurances of their both being alive and well made it necessary to lay by her agitation and affectionate preparatory speeches for a while.

The winter came and passed without their being called for; the accounts continued perfectly good; and Mrs. Norris, in promoting gaieties for her nieces, assisting their toilets, displaying their accomplishments, and looking about for their future husbands, had so much to do as, in addition to all her own household cares, some interference in those of her sister, and Mrs. Grant's wasteful doings to overlook, left her very little occasion to be occupied in fears for the absent.

The Miss Bertrams were now fully established among the belles of the neighbourhood; and as they joined to beauty and brilliant acquirements a manner naturally easy, and carefully formed to general civility and obligingness, they possessed its favour as well as its admiration. Their vanity was in such good order that they seemed to be quite free from it, and gave themselves no airs; while the praises attending such behaviour, secured and brought round by their aunt, served to strengthen them in believing they had no faults.

Lady Bertram did not go into public with her daughters. She was too indolent even to accept a mother's gratification in witnessing their success and enjoyment at the expense of any personal trouble, and the charge was made over to her sister, who desired nothing better than a post of such honourable representation, and very thoroughly relished the means it afforded her of mixing in society without having horses to hire. Fanny had no share in the festivities of the season; but she enjoyed being avowedly useful as her aunt's companion when they called away the rest of the family; and, as Miss Lee had left Mansfield, she naturally became everything to Lady Bertram during the night of a ball or a party. She talked to her, listened to her, read to her; and the tranquillity of such evenings, her perfect security in such a tete-a-tetefrom any sound of unkindness, was unspeakably welcome to a mind which had seldom known a pause in its alarms or embarrassments.

As to her cousins' gaieties, she loved to hear an account of them, especially of the balls, and whom Edmund had danced with; but thought too lowly of her own situation to imagine she should ever be admitted to the same, and listened, therefore, without an idea of any nearer concern in them. Upon the whole, it was a comfortable winter to her; for though it brought no William to England, the never-failing hope of his arrival was worth much.

The ensuing spring deprived her of her valued friend, the old grey pony; and for some time she was in danger of feeling the loss in her health as well as in her affections; for in spite of the acknowledged importance of her riding on horse-back, no measures were taken for mounting her again, "because," as it was observed by her aunts, "she might ride one of her cousin's horses at any time when they did not want them," and as the Miss Bertrams regularly wanted their horses every fine day, and had no idea of carrying their obliging manners to the sacrifice of any real pleasure, that time, of course, never came.

They took their cheerful rides in the fine mornings of April and May; and Fanny either sat at home the whole day with one aunt, or walked beyond her strength at the instigation of the other: Lady Bertram holding exercise to be as unnecessary for everybody as it was unpleasant to herself; and Mrs. Norris, who was walking all day, thinking everybody ought to walk as much. Edmund was absent at this time, or the evil would have been earlier remedied. When he returned, to understand how Fanny was situated, and perceived its ill effects, there seemed with him but one thing to be done; and that "Fanny must have a horse" was the resolute declaration with which he opposed whatever could be urged by the supineness of his mother, or the economy of his aunt, to make it appear unimportant. Mrs. Norris could not help thinking that some steady old thing might be found among the numbers belonging to the Park that would do vastly well; or that one might be borrowed of the steward; or that perhaps Dr. Grant might now and then lend them the pony he sent to the post.

She could not but consider it as absolutely unnecessary, and even improper, that Fanny should have a regular lady's horse of her own, in the style of her cousins. She was sure Sir Thomas had never intended it: and she must say that, to be making such a purchase in his absence, and adding to the great expenses of his stable, at a time when a large part of his income was unsettled, seemed to her very unjustifiable. "Fanny must have a horse," was Edmund's only reply. Mrs. Norris could not see it in the same light. Lady Bertram did: she entirely agreed with her son as to the necessity of it, and as to its being considered necessary by his father; she only pleaded against there being any hurry; she only wanted him to wait till Sir Thomas's return, and then Sir Thomas might settle it all himself. He would be at home in September, and where would be the harm of only waiting till September?

Though Edmund was much more displeased with his aunt than with his mother, as evincing least regard for her niece, he could not help paying more attention to what she said; and at length determined on a method of proceeding which would obviate the risk of his father's thinking he had done too much, and at the same time procure for Fanny the immediate means of exercise, which he could not bear she should be without. He had three horses of his own, but not one that would carry a woman. Two of them were hunters; the third, a useful road-horse: this third he resolved to exchange for one that his cousin might ride; he knew where such a one was to be met with; and having once made up his mind, the whole business was soon completed. The new mare proved a treasure; with a very little trouble she became exactly calculated for the purpose, and Fanny was then put in almost full possession of her. She had not supposed before that anything could ever suit her like the old grey pony; but her delight in Edmund's mare was far beyond any former pleasure of the sort; and the addition it was ever receiving in the consideration of that kindness from which her pleasure sprung, was beyond all her words to express. She regarded her cousin as an example of everything good and great, as possessing worth which no one but herself could ever appreciate, and as entitled to such gratitude from her as no feelings could be strong enough to pay. Her sentiments towards him were compounded of all that was respectful, grateful, confiding, and tender.

As the horse continued in name, as well as fact, the property of Edmund, Mrs. Norris could tolerate its being for Fanny's use; and had Lady Bertram ever thought about her own objection again, he might have been excused in her eyes for not waiting till Sir Thomas's return in September, for when September came Sir Thomas was still abroad, and without any near prospect of finishing his business. Unfavourable circumstances had suddenly arisen at a moment when he was beginning to turn all his thoughts towards England; and the very great uncertainty in which everything was then involved determined him on sending home his son, and waiting the final arrangement by himself Tom arrived safely, bringing an excellent account of his father's health; but to very little purpose, as far as Mrs. Norris was concerned.

Sir Thomas's sending away his son seemed to her so like a parent's care, under the influence of a foreboding of evil to himself, that she could not help feeling dreadful presentiments; and as the long evenings of autumn came on, was so terribly haunted by these ideas, in the sad solitariness of her cottage, as to be obliged to take daily refuge in the dining-room of the Park. The return of winter engagements, however, was not without its effect; and in the course of their progress, her mind became so pleasantly occupied in superintending the fortunes of her eldest niece, as tolerably to quiet her nerves. "If poor Sir Thomas were fated never to return, it would be peculiarly consoling to see their dear Maria well married," she very often thought; always when they were in the company of men of fortune, and particularly on the introduction of a young man who had recently succeeded to one of the largest estates and finest places in the country.

Mr. Rushworth was from the first struck with the beauty

of Miss Bertram, and, being inclined to marry, soon fancied himself in love. He was a heavy young man, with not more than common sense; but as there was nothing disagreeable in his figure or address, the young lady was well pleased with her conquest. Being now in her twenty-first year, Maria Bertram was beginning to think matrimony a duty; and as a marriage with Mr. Rushworth would give her the enjoyment of a larger income than her father's, as well as ensure her the house in town, which was now a prime object, it became, by the same rule of moral obligation, her evident duty to marry Mr. Rushworth if she could.

Mrs. Norris was most zealous in promoting the match, by every suggestion and contrivance likely to enhance its desirableness to either party; and, among other means, by seeking an intimacy with the gentleman's mother, who at present lived with him, and to whom she even forced Lady Bertram to go through ten miles of indifferent road to pay a morning visit. It was not long before a good understanding took place between this lady and herself. Mrs. Rushworth acknowledged herself very desirous that her son should marry, and declared that of all the young ladies she had ever seen, Miss Bertram seemed, by her amiable qualities and accomplishments, the best adapted to make him happy. Mrs. Norris accepted the compliment, and admired the nice discernment of character which could so well distinguish merit. Maria was indeed the pride and delight of them all— perfectly faultless— an angel; and, of course, so surrounded by admirers, must be difficult in her choice: but yet, as far as Mrs. Norris could allow herself to decide on so short an acquaintance, Mr. Rushworth appeared precisely the young man to deserve and attach her.

After dancing with each other at a proper number of balls, the young people justified these opinions, and an engagement, with a due reference to the absent Sir Thomas, was entered into, much to the satisfaction of their respective families, and of the general lookers-on of the neighbourhood, who had, for many weeks past, felt the expediency of Mr. Rushworth's marrying Miss Bertram.

It was some months before Sir Thomas's consent could be received; but, in the meanwhile, as no one felt a doubt of his most cordial pleasure in the connexion, the intercourse of the two families was carried on without restraint, and no other attempt made at secrecy than Mrs. Norris's talking of it everywhere as a matter not to be talked of at present.

Edmund was the only one of the family who could see a fault in the business; but no representation of his aunt's could induce him to find Mr. Rushworth a desirable companion. He could allow his sister to be the best judge of her own happiness, but he was not pleased that her happiness should centre in a large income; nor could he refrain from often saying to himself, in Mr. Rushworth's company— "If this man had not twelve thousand a year, he would be a very stupid fellow."

Sir Thomas, however, was truly happy in the prospect of an alliance so unquestionably advantageous, and of which he heard nothing but the perfectly good and agreeable. It was a connexion exactly of the right sort— in the same county, and the same interest—and his most hearty concurrence was conveyed as soon as possible. He only conditioned that the marriage should not take place before his return, which he was again looking eagerly forward to. He wrote in April, and had strong hopes of settling everything to his entire satisfaction, and leaving Antigua before the end of the summer.

Such was the state of affairs in the month of July; and Fanny had just reached her eighteenth year, when the society of the village received an addition in the brother and sister of Mrs. Grant, a Mr. and Miss Crawford, the children of her mother by a second marriage. They were young people of fortune. The son had a good estate in Norfolk, the daughter twenty thousand pounds. As children, their sister had been always very fond of them; but, as her own marriage had been soon followed by the death of their common parent, which left them to the care of a brother of their father, of whom Mrs. Grant knew nothing, she had scarcely seen them since. In their uncle's house they had found a kind home.

Admiral and Mrs. Crawford, though agreeing in nothing else, were united in affection for these children, or, at least, were no farther adverse in their feelings than that each had their favourite, to whom they showed the greatest fondness of the two. The Admiral delighted in the boy, Mrs. Crawford doted on the girl; and it was the lady's death which now obliged her protegee, after some months' further trial at her uncle's house, to find another home.

Admiral Crawford was a man of vicious conduct, who chose, instead of retaining his niece, to bring his mistress under his own roof; and to this Mrs. Grant was indebted for her sister's proposal of coming to her, a measure quite as welcome on one side as it could be expedient on the other; for Mrs. Grant, having by this time run through the usual resources of ladies residing in the country without a family of children—having more than filled her favourite sitting-room with pretty furniture, and made a choice collection of plants and poultry—was very much in want of some variety at home. The arrival, therefore, of a sister whom she had always loved, and now hoped to retain with her as long as she remained single, was highly agreeable; and her chief anxiety was lest Mansfield should not satisfy the habits of a young woman who had been mostly used to London.

Miss Crawford was not entirely free from similar apprehensions, though they arose principally from doubts of her sister's style of living and tone of society; and it was not till after she had tried in vain to persuade her brother to settle with her at his own country house, that she could resolve to hazard herself among her other relations. To anything like a permanence of abode, or limitation of society, Henry Crawford had, unluckily, a great dislike: he could not accommodate his sister in an article of such importance; but he escorted her, with the utmost kindness, into Northamptonshire, and as readily engaged to fetch her away again, at half an hour's notice, whenever she were weary of the place. The meeting was very satisfactory on each side. Miss Crawford found a sister without preciseness or rusticity, a sister's husband who looked the gentleman, and a house commodious and well fitted up; and Mrs. Grant received in those whom she hoped to love better than ever a young man and woman of very prepossessing appearance. Mary Crawford was remarkably pretty; Henry, though not handsome, had air and countenance; the manners of both were lively and pleasant, and Mrs. Grant immediately gave them credit for everything else. She was delighted with each, but Mary was her dearest object; and having never been able to glory in beauty of her own, she thoroughly enjoyed the power of being proud of her sister's. She had not waited her arrival to look out for a suitable match for her: she had fixed on Tom Bertram; the eldest son of a baronet was not too good for a girl of twenty thousand pounds, with all the elegance and accomplishments which Mrs. Grant foresaw in her; and being a warm-hearted, unreserved woman, Mary had not been three hours in the house before she told her what she had planned.

Miss Crawford was glad to find a family of such consequence so very near them, and not at all displeased either at her sister's early care, or the choice it had fallen on. Matrimony was her object, provided she could marry well: and having seen Mr. Bertram in town, she knew that objection could no more be made to his person than to his situation in life. While she treated it as a joke, therefore, she did not forget to think of it seriously. The scheme was soon repeated to Henry. "And now," added Mrs. Grant, "I have thought of something to make it complete. I should dearly love to settle you both in this country; and therefore, Henry, you shall marry the youngest Miss Bertram, a nice, handsome, good-humoured, accomplished girl, who will make you very happy." Henry bowed and thanked her.

"My dear sister," said Mary, "if you can persuade him into anything of the sort, it will be a fresh matter of delight to me to find myself allied to anybody so clever, and I shall only regret that you have not half a dozen daughters to dispose of. If you can persuade Henry to marry, you must have the address of a Frenchwoman. All that English abilities can do has been tried already. I have three very particular friends who have been all dying for him in their turn; and the pains which they, their mothers (very clever women), as well as my dear aunt and myself, have taken to reason, coax, or trick him into marrying, is inconceivable! He is the most horrible flirt that can be imagined. If your Miss Bertrams do not like to have their hearts broke, let them avoid Henry." "My dear brother, I will not believe this of you."

"No, I am sure you are too good. You will be kinder than Mary. You will allow for the doubts of youth and inexperience. I am of a cautious temper, and unwilling to risk my happiness in a hurry. Nobody can think more highly of the matrimonial state than myself I consider the blessing of a wife as most justly described in those discreet lines of the poet—'Heaven's lastbest gift.'"

"There, Mrs. Grant, you see how he dwells on one word, and only look at his smile. I assure you he is very detestable; the Admiral's lessons have quite spoiled him."

"I pay very little regard," said Mrs. Grant, "to what any young person says on the subject of marriage. If they profess a disinclination for it, I only set it down that they have not yet seen the right person."

Dr. Grant laughingly congratulated Miss Crawford on feeling no disinclination to the state herself.

"Oh yes! I am not at all ashamed of it. I would have everybody marry if they can do it properly: I do not like to have people throw themselves away; but everybody should marry as soon as they can do it to advantage."

Chapter V

The young people were pleased with each other from the first. On each side there was much to attract, and their acquaintance soon promised as early an intimacy as good manners would warrant. Miss Crawford's beauty did her no disservice with the Miss Bertrams. They were too handsome themselves to dislike any woman for being so too, and were almost as much charmed as their brothers with her lively dark eye, clear brown complexion, and general prettiness. Had she been tall, full formed, and fair, it might have been more of a trial: but as it was, there could be no comparison; and she was most allowably a sweet, pretty girl, while they were the finest young women in the country.

Her brother was not handsome: no, when they first saw him he was absolutely plain, black and plain; but still he was the gentleman, with a pleasing address. The second meeting proved him not so very plain: he was plain, to be sure, but then he had so much countenance, and his teeth were so good, and he was so well made, that one soon forgot he was plain; and after a third interview, after dining in company with him at the Parsonage, he was no longer allowed to be called so by anybody. He was, in fact, the most agreeable young man the sisters had ever known, and they were equally delighted with him. Miss Bertram's engagement made him in equity the property of Julia, of which Julia was fully aware; and before he had been at Mansfield a week, she was quite ready to be fallen in love with.

Maria's notions on the subject were more confused and indistinct. She did not want to see or understand. "There could be no harm in her liking an agreeable man— everybody knew her situation—Mr. Crawford must take care of himself." Mr. Crawford did not mean to be in any danger! the Miss Bertrams were worth pleasing, and were ready to be pleased; and he began with no object but of making them like him. He did not want them to die of love; but with sense and temper which ought to have made him judge and feel better, he allowed himself great latitude on such points.

"I like your Miss Bertrams exceedingly, sister," said he, as he returned from attending them to their carriage after the said dinner visit; "they are very elegant, agreeable girls."

"So they are indeed, and I am delighted to hear you say it. But you like Julia best." "Oh yes! I like Julia best."

"But do you really? for Miss Bertram is in general thought the handsomest." "So I should suppose. She has the advantage in every feature, and I prefer her countenance; but I like Julia best; Miss Bertram is certainly the handsomest, and I have found her the most agreeable, but I shall always like Julia best, because you order me."

"I shall not talk to you, Henry, but I know you willlike her best at last." "Do not I tell you that I like her best atfirst?"

"And besides, Miss Bertram is engaged. Remember that,

my dear brother. Her choice is made." "Yes, and I like her the better for it. An engaged woman is always more agreeable than a disengaged. She is satisfied with herself. Her cares are over, and she feels that she may exert all her powers of pleasing without suspicion. All is safe with a lady engaged: no harm can be done."

"Why, as to that, Mr. Rushworth is a very good sort of young man, and it is a great match for her."

"But Miss Bertram does not care three straws for him; thatis your opinion of your intimate friend. Ido not subscribe to it. I am sure Miss Bertram is very much attached to Mr. Rushworth. I could see it in her eyes, when he was mentioned. I think too well of Miss Bertram to suppose she would ever give her hand without her heart." "Mary, how shall we manage him?" "We must leave him to himself, I believe. Talking does no good. He will be taken in at last."

"But I would not have him takenin; I would not have him duped; I would have it all fair and honourable."

"Oh dear! let him stand his chance and be taken in. It will do just as well. Everybody is taken in at some period or other."

"Not always in marriage, dear Mary."

"In marriage especially. With all due respect to such of the present company as chance to be married, my dear Mrs. Grant, there is not one in a hundred of either sex who is not taken in when they marry. Look where I will, I see that it isso; and I feel that it mustbe so, when I consider that it is, of all transactions, the one in which people expect most from others, and are least honest themselves."

"Ah! You have been in a bad school for matrimony, in Hill Street."

"My poor aunt had certainly little cause to love the state; but, however, speaking from my own observation, it is a manoeuvring business. I know so many who have married in the full expectation and confidence of some one particular advantage in the connexion, or accomplishment, or good quality in the person, who have found themselves entirely deceived, and been obliged to put up with exactly the reverse. What is this but a take in?"

"My dear child, there must be a little imagination here. I beg your pardon, but I cannot quite believe you. Depend upon it, you see but half. You see the evil, but you do not see the consolation. There will be little rubs and disappointments everywhere, and we are all apt to expect too much; but then, if one scheme of happiness fails, human nature turns to another; if the first calculation is wrong, we make a second better: we find comfort somewhere—and those evil-minded observers, dearest Mary, who make much of a little, are more taken in and deceived than the parties themselves."

"Well done, sister! I honour your espritducorps. When I am a wife, I mean to be just as staunch myself; and I wish my friends in general would be so too. It would save me many a heartache."

"You are as bad as your brother, Mary; but we will cure you both. Mansfield shall cure you both, and without any taking in. Stay with us, and we will cure you."

The Crawfords, without wanting to be cured, were very willing to stay. Mary was satisfied with the Parsonage as a present home, and Henry equally ready to lengthen his visit. He had come, intending to spend only a few days with them; but Mansfield promised well, and there was nothing to call him elsewhere. It delighted Mrs. Grant to keep them both with her, and Dr. Grant was exceedingly well contented to have it so: a talking pretty young woman like Miss Crawford is always pleasant society to an indolent, stay-at-home man; and Mr. Crawford's being his guest was an excuse for drinking claret every day.

The Miss Bertrams' admiration of Mr. Crawford was more rapturous than anything which Miss Crawford's habits made her likely to feel. She acknowledged, however, that the Mr. Bertrams were very fine young men, that two such young men were not often seen together even in London, and that their manners, particularly those of the eldest, were very good. Hehad been much in London, and had more liveliness and gallantry than Edmund, and must, therefore, be preferred; and, indeed, his being the eldest was another strong claim. She had felt an early presentiment that she shouldlike the eldest best.

She knew it was her way. Tom Bertram must have been thought pleasant, indeed, at any rate; he was the sort of young man to be generally liked, his agreeableness was of the kind to be oftener found agreeable than some endowments of a higher stamp, for he had easy manners, excellent spirits, a large acquaintance, and a great deal to say; and the reversion of Mansfield Park, and a baronetcy, did no harm to all this. Miss Crawford soon felt that he and his situation might do.

She looked about her with due consideration, and found almost everything in his favour: a park, a real park, five miles round, a spacious modern-built house, so well placed and well screened as to deserve to be in any collection of engravings of gentlemen's seats in the kingdom, and wanting only to be completely new furnished—pleasant sisters, a quiet mother, and an agreeable man himself—with the advantage of being tied up from much gaming at present by a promise to his father, and of being Sir Thomas hereafter. It might do very well; she believed she should accept him; and she began accordingly to interest herself a little about the horse which he had to run at the B races. These races were to call him away not long after their acquaintance began; and as it appeared that the family did not, from his usual goings on, expect him back again for many weeks, it would bring his passion to an early proof. Much was said on his side to induce her to attend the races, and schemes were made for a large party to them, with all the eagerness of inclination, but it would only do to be talked of.

And Fanny, what was shedoing and thinking all this while? and what was heropinion of the newcomers? Few young ladies of eighteen could be less called on to speak their opinion than Fanny. In a quiet way, very little attended to, she paid her tribute of admiration to Miss Crawford's beauty; but as she still continued to think Mr. Crawford very plain, in spite of her two cousins having repeatedly proved the contrary, she never mentioned him. The notice, which she excited herself, was to this effect. "I begin now to understand you all, except Miss Price," said Miss Crawford, as she was walking with the Mr. Bertrams. "Pray, is she out, or is she not? I am puzzled. She dined at the Parsonage, with the rest of you, which seemed like being out; and yet she says so little, that I can hardly suppose she is."

Edmund, to whom this was chiefly addressed, replied, "I believe I know what you mean, but I will not undertake to answer the question. My cousin is grown up. She has the age and sense of a woman, but the outs and not outs are beyond me." "And yet, in general, nothing can be more easily ascertained. The distinction is so broad. Manners as well as appearance are, generally speaking, so totally different. Till now, I could not have supposed it possible to be mistaken as to a girl's being out or not.

A girl not out has always the same sort of dress: a close bonnet, for instance; looks very demure, and never says a word. You may smile, but it is so, I assure you; and except that it is sometimes carried a little too far, it is all very proper. Girls should be quiet and modest. The most objectionable part is, that the alteration of manners on being introduced into company is frequently too sudden. They sometimes pass in such very little time from reserve to quite the opposite—to confidence! Thatis the faulty part of the present system. One does not like to see a girl of eighteen or nineteen so immediately up to every thing—and perhaps when one has seen her hardly able to speak the year before. Mr. Bertram, I dare say youhave sometimes met with such changes."

"I believe I have, but this is hardly fair; I see what you are at. You are quizzing me and Miss Anderson."

"No, indeed. Miss Anderson! I do not know who or what you mean. I am quite in the dark. But I willquiz you with a great deal of pleasure, if you will tell me what about."

"Ah! you carry it off very well, but I cannot be quite so far imposed on. You must have had Miss Anderson in your eye, in describing an altered young lady. You paint too accurately for mistake. It was exactly so. The Andersons of Baker Street. We were speaking of them the other day, you know. Edmund, you have heard me mention Charles Anderson. The circumstance was precisely as this lady has represented it. 'When Anderson first introduced me to his family, about two years ago, his sister was not out, and I could not get her to speak to me. I sat there an hour one morning waiting for Anderson, with only her and a little girl or two in the room, the governess being sick or run away, and the mother in and out every moment with letters of business, and I could hardly get a word or a look from the young lady—nothing like a civil answer—she screwed up her mouth, and turned from me with such an air! I did not see her again for a twelvemonth. She was then out. I met her at Mrs. Holford's, and did not recollect her. She came up to me, claimed me as an acquaintance, stared me out of countenance; and talked and laughed till I did not know which way to look. I felt that I must be the jest of the room at the time, and Miss Crawford, it is plain, has heard the story."

"And a very pretty story it is, and with more truth in it, I dare say, than does credit to Miss Anderson. It is too common a fault. Mothers certainly have not yet got quite the right way of managing their daughters. I do not know where the error lies. I do not pretend to set people right, but I do see that they are often wrong."

"Those who are showing the world what female manners shouldbe," said Mr. Bertram gallantly, "are doing a great deal to set them right."

"The error is plain enough," said the less courteous Edmund; "such girls are ill brought up. They are given wrong notions from the beginning. They are always acting upon motives of vanity, and there is no more real modesty in their behaviour beforethey appear in public than afterwards."

"I do not know," replied Miss Crawford hesitatingly. "Yes, I cannot agree with you there. It is certainly the modestest part of the business. It is much worse to have girls not out give themselves the same airs and take the same liberties as if they were, which I have seen done. That is worse than anything—quite disgusting!"

"Yes, thatis very inconvenient indeed," said Mr. Bertram. "It leads one astray; one does not know what to do. The close bonnet and demure air you describe so well (and nothing was ever juster), tell one what is expected; but I got into a dreadful scrape last year from the want of them. I went down to Ramsgate for a week with a friend last September, just after my return from the West Indies. My friend Sneyd—you have heard me speak of Sneyd, Edmund— his father, and mother, and sisters, were there, all new to me. When we reached Albion Place they were out; we went after them, and found them on the pier: Mrs. and the two Miss Sneyds, with others of their acquaintance. I made my bow in form; and as Mrs. Sneyd was surrounded by men, attached myself to one of her daughters, walked by her side all the way home, and made myself as agreeable as I could; the young lady perfectly easy in her manners, and as ready to talk as to listen.

I had not a suspicion that I could be doing anything wrong. They looked just the same: both well-dressed, with veils and parasols like other girls; but I afterwards found that I had been giving all my attention to the youngest, who was not out, and had most excessively offended the eldest. Miss Augusta ought not to have been noticed for the next six months; and Miss Sneyd, I believe, has never forgiven me."

"That was bad indeed. Poor Miss Sneyd. Though I have no younger sister, I feel for her. To be neglected before one's time must be very vexatious; but it was entirely the mother's fault. Miss Augusta should have been with her governess. Such half-and-half doings never prosper. But now I must be satisfied about Miss Price. Does she go to balls? Does she dine out every where, as well as at my sister's?" "No," replied Edmund; "I do not think she has ever been to a ball. My mother seldom goes into company herself, and dines nowhere but with Mrs. Grant, and Fanny stays at home with her."

"Oh! then the point is clear. Miss Price is not out."

Chapter VI

Mr. Bertram set off for— — — —, and Miss Crawford was prepared to find a great chasm in their society, and to miss him decidedly in the meetings which were now becoming almost daily between the families; and on their all dining together at the Park soon after his going, she retook her chosen place near the bottom of the table, fully expecting to feel a most melancholy difference in the change of masters. It would be a very flat business, she was sure. In comparison with his brother, Edmund would have nothing to say. The soup would be sent round in a most spiritless manner, wine drank without any smiles or agreeable trifling, and the venison cut up without supplying one pleasant anecdote of any former haunch, or a single entertaining story, about "my friend such a one." She must try to find amusement in what was passing at the upper end of the table, and in observing Mr. Rushworth, who was now making his appearance at Mansfield for the first time since the Crawfords' arrival. He had been visiting a friend in the neighbouring county, and that friend having recently had his grounds laid out by an improver, Mr. Rushworth was returned with his head full of the subject, and very eager to be improving his own place in the same way; and though not saying much to the purpose, could talk of nothing else. The subject had been already handled in the drawing-room; it was revived in the dining-parlour. Miss Bertram's attention and opinion was evidently his chief aim; and though her deportment showed rather conscious superiority than any solicitude to oblige him, the mention of Sotherton Court, and the ideas attached to it, gave her a feeling of complacency, which prevented her from being very ungracious.

"I wish you could see Compton," said he; "it is the most complete thing! I never saw a place so altered in my life. I told Smith I did not know where I was. The approach now, is one of the finest things in the country: you see the house in the most surprising manner. I declare, when I got back to Sotherton yesterday, it looked like a prison— quite a dismal old prison."

"Oh, for shame!" cried Mrs. Norris. "A prison indeed? Sotherton Court is the noblest old place in the world."

"It wants improvement, ma'am, beyond anything. I never saw a place that wanted so much improvement in my life; and it is so forlorn that I do not know what can be done with it."

"No wonder that Mr. Rushworth should think so at present," said Mrs. Grant to Mrs. Norris, with a smile; "but depend upon it, Sotherton will have everyimprovement in time which his heart can desire." "I must try to do something with it," said Mr. Rushworth, "but I do not know what. I hope I shall have some good friend to help me."

"Your best friend upon such an occasion," said Miss Bertram calmly, "would be Mr. Repton, I imagine."

"That is what I was thinking of. As he has done so well by Smith, I think I had better have him at once. His terms are five guineas a day."

"Well, and if they were ten," cried Mrs. Norris, "I am sure youneed not regard it. The expense need not be any impediment. If I were you, I should not think of the expense. I would have everything done in the best style, and made as nice as possible. Such a place as Sotherton Court deserves everything that taste and money can do. You have space to work upon there, and grounds that will well reward you. For my own part, if I had anything within the fiftieth part of the size of Sotherton, I should be always planting and improving, for naturally I am excessively fond of it. It would be too ridiculous for me to attempt anything where I am now, with my little half acre. It would be quite a burlesque. But if I had more room, I should take a prodigious delight in improving and planting. We did a vast deal in that way at the Parsonage: we made it quite a different place from what it was when we first had it. You young ones do not remember much about it, perhaps; but if dear Sir Thomas were here, he could tell you what improvements we made: and a great deal more would have been done, but for poor Mr. Norris's sad state of health. He could hardly ever get out, poor man, to enjoy anything, and thatdisheartened me from doing several things that Sir Thomas and I used to talk of. If it had not been for that, we should have carried on the garden wall, and made the plantation to shut out the churchyard, just as Dr. Grant has done. We were always doing something as it was. It was only the spring twelvemonth before Mr. Norris's death that we put in the apricot against the stable wall, which is now grown such a noble tree, and getting to such perfection, sir," addressing herself then to Dr. Grant.

"The tree thrives well, beyond a doubt, madam," replied

Dr. Grant. "The soil is good; and I never pass it without regretting that the fruit should be so little worth the trouble of gathering."

"Sir, it is a Moor Park, we bought it as a Moor Park, and it cost us—that is, it was a present from Sir Thomas, but I saw the bill—and I know it cost seven shillings, and was charged as a Moor Park."

"You were imposed on, ma'am," replied Dr. Grant: "these potatoes have as much the flavour of a Moor Park apricot as the fruit from that tree. It is an insipid fruit at the best; but a good apricot is eatable, which none from my garden are."

"The truth is, ma'am," said Mrs. Grant, pretending to whisper across the table to Mrs. Norris, "that Dr. Grant hardly knows what the natural taste of our apricot is: he is scarcely ever indulged with one, for it is so valuable a fruit; with a little assistance, and ours is such a remarkably large, fair sort, that what with early tarts and preserves, my cook contrives to get them all."

Mrs. Norris, who had begun to redden, was appeased; and, for a little while, other subjects took place of the improvements of Sotherton. Dr. Grant and Mrs. Norris were seldom good friends; their acquaintance had begun in dilapidations, and their habits were totally dissimilar.

After a short interruption Mr. Rushworth began again. "Smith's place is the admiration of all the country; and it was a mere nothing before Repton took it in hand. I think I shall have Repton."

"Mr. Rushworth," said Lady Bertram, "if I were you, I would have a very pretty shrubbery. One likes to get out into a shrubbery in fine weather."

Mr. Rushworth was eager to assure her ladyship of his acquiescence, and tried to make out something complimentary; but, between his submission to hertaste, and his having always intended the same himself, with the superadded objects of professing attention to the comfort of ladies in general, and of insinuating that there was one only whom he was anxious to please, he grew puzzled, and Edmund was glad to put an end to his speech by a proposal of wine. Mr. Rushworth, however, though not usually a great talker, had still more to say on the subject next his heart. "Smith has not much above a hundred acres altogether in his grounds, which is little enough, and makes it more surprising that the place can have been so improved. Now, at Sotherton we have a good seven hundred, without reckoning the water meadows; so that I think, if so much could be done at Compton, we need not despair. There have been two or three fine old trees cut down, that grew too near the house, and it opens the prospect amazingly, which makes me think that Repton, or anybody of that sort, would certainly have the avenue at Sotherton down: the avenue that leads from the west front to the top of the hill, you know," turning to Miss Bertram particularly as he spoke. But Miss Bertram thought it most becoming to reply—

"The avenue! Oh! I do not recollect it. I really know very little of Sotherton."

Fanny, who was sitting on the other side of Edmund, exactly opposite Miss Crawford, and who had been attentively listening, now looked at him, and said in a low voice—

"Cut down an avenue! What a pity! Does it not make you think of Cowper? 'Ye fallen avenues, once more I mourn your fate unmerited.'"

He smiled as he answered, "I am afraid the avenue stands a bad chance, Fanny.""I should like to see Sotherton before it is cut down, to see the place as it is now, in its old state; but I do not suppose I shall."

"Have you never been there? No, you never can; and, unluckily, it is out of distance for a ride. I wish we could contrive it."

"Oh! it does not signify. Whenever I do see it, you will tell me how it has been altered."

"I collect," said Miss Crawford, "that Sotherton is an old place, and a place of some grandeur. In any particular style of building?"

"The house was built in Elizabeth's time, and is a large, regular, brick building; heavy, but respectable looking, and has many good rooms. It is ill placed. It stands in one of the lowest spots of the park; in that respect, unfavourable for improvement. But the woods are fine, and there is a stream, which, I dare say, might be made a good deal of. Mr. Rushworth is quite right, I think, in meaning to give it a modern dress, and I have no doubt that it will be all done extremely well."

Miss Crawford listened with submission, and said to herself, "He is a well-bred man; he makes the best of it."

"I do not wish to influence Mr. Rushworth," he continued; "but, had I a place to new fashion, I should not put myself into the hands of an improver. I would rather have an inferior degree of beauty, of my own choice, and acquired progressively. I would rather abide by my own blunders than by his."

"Youwould know what you were about, of course; but that would not suit me. I have no eye or ingenuity for such matters, but as they are before me; and had I a place of my own in the country, I should be most thankful to any Mr. Repton who would undertake it, and give me as much beauty as he could for my money; and I should never look at it till it was complete." "It would be delightful to meto see the progress of it all," said Fanny.

"Ay, you have been brought up to it. It was no part of my education; and the only dose I ever had, being administered by not the first favourite in the world, has made me consider improvements inhandas the greatest of nuisances. Three years ago the Admiral, my honoured uncle, bought a cottage at Twickenham for us all to spend our summers in; and my aunt and I went down to it quite in raptures; but it being excessively pretty, it was soon found necessary to be improved, and for three months we were all dirt and confusion, without a gravel walk to step on, or a bench fit for use.

I would have everything as complete as possible in the country, shrubberies and flower-gardens, and rustic seats innumerable: but it must all be done without my care. Henry is different; he loves to be doing." Edmund was sorry to hear Miss Crawford, whom he was much disposed to admire, speak so freely of her uncle. It did not suit his sense of propriety, and he was silenced, till induced by further smiles and liveliness to put the matter by for the present. "Mr. Bertram," said she, "I have tidings of my harp at last. I am assured that it is safe at Northampton; and there it has probably been these ten days, in spite of the solemn assurances we have so often received to the contrary." Edmund expressed his pleasure and surprise. "The truth is, that our inquiries were too direct; we sent a servant, we went ourselves: this will not do seventy miles from London; but this morning we heard of it in the right way. It was seen by some farmer, and he told the miller, and the miller told the butcher, and the butcher's son-in-law left word at the shop."

"I am very glad that you have heard of it, by whatever means, and hope there will be no further delay."

"I am to have it to-morrow; but how do you think it is to be conveyed? Not by a wagon or cart: oh no! nothing of that kind could be hired in the village. I might as well have asked for porters and a handbarrow."

"You would find it difficult, I dare say, just now, in the middle of a very late hay harvest, to hire a horse and cart?"

"I was astonished to find what a piece of work was made of it! To want a horse and cart in the country seemed impossible, so I told my maid to speak for one directly; and as I cannot look out of my dressing-closet without seeing one farmyard, nor walk in the shrubbery without passing another, I thought it would be only ask and have, and was rather grieved that I could not give the advantage to all. Guess my surprise, when I found that I had been asking the most unreasonable, most impossible thing in the world; had offended all the farmers, all the labourers, all the hay in the parish! As for Dr. Grant's bailiff, I believe I had better keep out of hisway; and my brother-in-law himself, who is all kindness in general, looked rather black upon me when he found what I had been at."

"You could not be expected to have thought on the subject before; but when you dothink of it, you must see the importance of getting in the grass. The hire of a cart at any time might not be so easy as you suppose: our farmers are not in the habit of letting them out; but, in harvest, it must be quite out of their power to spare a horse." "I shall understand all your ways in time; but, coming down with the true London maxim, that everything is to be got with money, I was a little embarrassed at first by the sturdy independence of your country customs. However, I am to have my harp fetched to-morrow. Henry, who is good-nature itself, has offered to fetch it in his barouche. Will it not be honourably conveyed?"

Edmund spoke of the harp as his favourite instrument, and hoped to be soon allowed to hear her. Fanny had never heard the harp at all, and wished for it very much.

"I shall be most happy to play to you both," said Miss Crawford; "at least as long as you can like to listen: probably much longer, for I dearly love music myself, and where the natural taste is equal the player must always be best off, for she is gratified in more ways than one. Now, Mr. Bertram, if you write to your brother, I entreat you to tell him that my harp is come: he heard so much of my misery about it. And you may say, if you please, that I shall prepare my most plaintive airs against his return, in compassion to his feelings, as I know his horse will lose."

"If I write, I will say whatever you wish me; but I do not, at present, foresee any occasion for writing."

"No, I dare say, nor if he were to be gone a twelvemonth, would you ever write to him, nor he to you, if it could be helped. The occasion would never be foreseen. What strange creatures brothers are! You would not write to each other but upon the most urgent necessity in the world; and when obliged to take up the pen to say that such a horse is ill, or such a relation dead, it is done in the fewest possible words. You have but one style among you. I know it perfectly. Henry, who is in every other respect exactly what a brother should be, who loves me, consults me, confides in me, and will talk to me by the hour together, has never yet turned the page in a letter; and very often it is nothing more than—'Dear Mary, I am just arrived. Bath seems full, and everything as usual. Yours sincerely.' That is the true manly style; that is a complete brother's letter." "When they are at a distance from all their family," said Fanny, colouring for William's sake, "they can write long letters." "Miss Price has a brother at sea," said Edmund, "whose excellence as a correspondent makes her think you too severe upon us."

"At sea, has she? In the king's service, of course?"

Fanny would rather have had Edmund tell the story, but his determined silence obliged her to relate her brother's situation: her voice was animated in speaking of his profession, and the foreign stations he had been on; but she could not mention the number of years that he had been absent without tears in her eyes. Miss Crawford civilly wished him an early promotion.

"Do you know anything of my cousin's captain?" said Edmund; "Captain Marshall? You have a large acquaintance in the navy, I conclude?"

"Among admirals, large enough; but," with an air of grandeur, "we know very little of the inferior ranks. Post-captains may be very good sort of men, but they do not belong to us. Of various admirals I could tell you a great deal: of them and their flags, and the gradation of their pay, and their bickerings and jealousies. But, in general, I can assure you that they are all passed over, and all very ill used. Certainly, my home at my uncle's brought me acquainted with a circle of admirals. Of Rearsand VicesI saw enough. Now do not be suspecting me of a pun, I entreat."

Edmund again felt grave, and only replied, "It is a noble profession."

"Yes, the profession is well enough under two circumstances: if it make the fortune, and there be discretion in spending it; but, in short, it is not a favourite profession of mine. It has never worn an amiable form to me."

Edmund reverted to the harp, and was again very happy in the prospect of hearing her play.

The subject of improving grounds, meanwhile, was still under consideration among the others; and Mrs. Grant could not help addressing her brother, though it was calling his attention from Miss Julia Bertram.

"My dear Henry, have younothing to say? You have been an improver yourself, and from what I hear of Everingham, it may vie with any place in England. Its natural beauties, I am sure, are great. Everingham, as it usedto be, was perfect in my estimation: such a happy fall of ground, and such timber! What would I not give to see it again?"

"Nothing could be so gratifying to me as to hear your opinion of it," was his answer; "but I fear there would be some disappointment: you would not find it equal to your present ideas. In extent, it is a mere nothing; you would be surprised at its insignificance; and, as for improvement, there was very little for me to do— too little: I should like to have been busy much longer.""You are fond of the sort of thing?" said Julia.

"Excessively; but what with the natural advantages of the ground, which pointed out, even to a very young eye, what little remained to be done, and my own consequent resolutions, I had not been of age three months before Everingham was all that it is now. My plan was laid at Westminster, a little altered, perhaps, at Cambridge, and at one-and-twenty executed. I am inclined to envy Mr. Rushworth for having so much happiness yet before him. I have been a devourer of my own."

"Those who see quickly, will resolve quickly, and act quickly," said Julia. "Youcan never want employment. Instead of envying Mr. Rushworth, you should assist him with your opinion."

Mrs. Grant, hearing the latter part of this speech, enforced it warmly, persuaded that no judgment could be equal to her brother's; and as Miss Bertram caught at the idea likewise, and gave it her full support, declaring that, in her opinion, it was infinitely better to consult with friends and disinterested advisers, than immediately to throw the business into the hands of a professional man, Mr. Rushworth was very ready to request the favour of Mr. Crawford's assistance; and Mr. Crawford, after properly depreciating his own abilities, was quite at his service in any way that could be useful. Mr. Rushworth then began to propose Mr. Crawford's doing him the honour of coming over to Sotherton, and taking a bed there; when Mrs. Norris, as if reading in her two nieces' minds their little approbation of a plan which was to take Mr. Crawford away, interposed with an amendment.

"There can be no doubt of Mr. Crawford's willingness; but why should not more of us go? Why should not we make a little party? Here are many that would be interested in your improvements, my dear Mr. Rushworth, and that would like to hear Mr. Crawford's opinion on the spot, and that might be of some small use to you with theiropinions; and, for my own part, I have been long wishing to wait upon your good mother again; nothing but having no horses of my own could have made me so remiss; but now I could go and sit a few hours with Mrs. Rushworth, while the rest of you walked about and settled things, and then we could all return to a late dinner here, or dine at Sotherton, just as might be most agreeable to your mother, and have a pleasant drive home by moonlight. I dare say Mr. Crawford would take my two nieces and me in his barouche, and Edmund can go on horseback, you know, sister, and Fanny will stay at home with you."

Lady Bertram made no objection; and every one concerned in the going was forward in expressing their ready concurrence, excepting Edmund, who heard it all and said nothing.

Chapter VII

"Well, Fanny, and how do you like Miss Crawford now?" said Edmund the next day, after thinking some time on the subject himself. "How did you like her yesterday?"

"Very well—very much. I like to hear her talk. She entertains me; and she is so extremely pretty, that I have great pleasure in looking at her."

"It is her countenance that is so attractive. She has a wonderful play of feature! But was there nothing in her conversation that struck you, Fanny, as not quite right?"

"Oh yes! she ought not to have spoken of her uncle as she did. I was quite astonished. An uncle with whom she has been living so many years, and who, whatever his faults may be, is so very fond of her brother, treating him, they say, quite like a son. I could not have believed it!" "I thought you would be struck. It was very wrong; very indecorous."

"And very ungrateful, I think." "Ungrateful is a strong

word. I do not know that her uncle has any claim to her gratitude; his wife certainly had; and it is the warmth of her respect for her aunt's memory which misleads her here. She is awkwardly circumstanced. With such warm feelings and lively spirits it must be difficult to do justice to her affection for Mrs. Crawford, without throwing a shade on the Admiral. I do not pretend to know which was most to blame in their disagreements, though the Admiral's present conduct might incline one to the side of his wife; but it is natural and amiable that Miss Crawford should acquit her aunt entirely. I do not censure her opinions; but there certainly isimpropriety in making them public."

"Do not you think," said Fanny, after a little consideration, "that this impropriety is a reflection itself upon Mrs. Crawford, as her niece has been entirely brought up by her? She cannot have given her right notions of what was due to the Admiral."

"That is a fair remark. Yes, we must suppose the faults of the niece to have been those of the aunt; and it makes one more sensible of the disadvantages she has been under. But I think her present home must do her good. Mrs. Grant's manners are just what they ought to be. She speaks of her brother with a very pleasing affection."

"Yes, except as to his writing her such short letters. She made me almost laugh; but I cannot rate so very highly the love or good-nature of a brother who will not give himself the trouble of writing anything worth reading to his sisters, when they are separated. I am sure William would never have used meso, under any circumstances. And what right had she to suppose that youwould not write long letters when you were absent?"

"The right of a lively mind, Fanny, seizing whatever may contribute to its own amusement or that of others; perfectly allowable, when untinctured by ill-humour or roughness; and there is not a shadow of either in the countenance or manner of Miss Crawford: nothing sharp, or loud, or coarse. She is perfectly feminine, except in the instances we have been speaking of. There she cannot be justified. I am glad you saw it all as I did."

Having formed her mind and gained her affections, he had a good chance of her thinking like him; though at this period, and on this subject, there began now to be some danger of dissimilarity, for he was in a line of admiration of Miss Crawford, which might lead him where Fanny could not follow. Miss Crawford's attractions did not lessen. The harp arrived, and rather added to her beauty, wit, and good-humour; for she played with the greatest obligingness, with an expression and taste which were peculiarly becoming, and there was something clever to be said at the close of every air. Edmund was at the Parsonage every day, to be indulged with his favourite instrument: one morning secured an invitation for the next; for the lady could not be unwilling to have a listener, and every thing was soon in a fair train.

A young woman, pretty, lively, with a harp as elegant as herself, and both placed near a window, cut down to the ground, and opening on a little lawn, surrounded by shrubs in the rich foliage of summer, was enough to catch any man's heart. The season, the scene, the air, were all favourable to tenderness and sentiment. Mrs. Grant and her tambour frame were not without their use: it was all in harmony; and as everything will turn to account when love is once set going, even the sandwich tray, and Dr. Grant doing the honours of it, were worth looking at. Without studying the business, however, or knowing what he was about, Edmund was beginning, at the end of a week of such intercourse, to be a good deal in love; and to the credit of the lady it may be added that, without his being a man of the world or an elder brother, without any of the arts of flattery or the gaieties of small talk, he began to be agreeable to her. She felt it to be so, though she had not foreseen, and could hardly understand it; for he was not pleasant by any common rule: he talked no nonsense; he paid no compliments; his opinions were unbending, his attentions tranquil and simple. There was a charm, perhaps, in his sincerity, his steadiness, his integrity, which Miss Crawford might be equal to feel, though not equal to discuss with herself. She did not think very much about it, however: he pleased her for the present; she liked to have him near her;

it was enough. Fanny could not wonder that Edmund was at the Parsonage every morning; she would gladly have been there too, might she have gone in uninvited and unnoticed, to hear the harp; neither could she wonder that, when the evening stroll was over, and the two families parted again, he should think it right to attend Mrs. Grant and her sister to their home, while Mr.

Crawford was devoted to the ladies of the Park; but she thought it a very bad exchange; and if Edmund were not there to mix the wine and water for her, would rather go without it than not. She was a little surprised that he could spend so many hours with Miss Crawford, and not see more of the sort of fault which he had already observed, and of which shewas almost always reminded by a something of the same nature whenever she was in her company; but so it was. Edmund was fond of speaking to her of Miss Crawford, but he seemed to think it enough that the Admiral had since been spared; and she scrupled to point out her own remarks to him, lest it should appear like ill-nature.

The first actual pain which Miss Crawford occasioned her was the consequence of an inclination to learn to ride, which the former caught, soon after her being settled at Mansfield, from the example of the young ladies at the Park, and which, when Edmund's acquaintance with her increased, led to his encouraging the wish, and the offer of his own quiet mare for the purpose of her first attempts, as the best fitted for a beginner that either stable could furnish. No pain, no injury, however, was designed by him to his cousin in this offer: shewas not to lose a day's exercise by it. The mare was only to be taken down to the Parsonage half an hour before her ride were to begin; and Fanny, on its being first proposed, so far from feeling slighted, was almost over-powered with gratitude that he should be asking her leave for it. Miss Crawford made her first essay with great credit to herself, and no inconvenience to Fanny. Edmund, who had taken down the mare and presided at the whole, returned with it in excellent time, before either Fanny or the steady old coachman, who always attended her when she rode without her cousins, were ready to set forward. The second day's trial was not so guiltless. Miss Crawford's enjoyment of riding was such that she did not know how to leave off. Active and fearless, and though rather small, strongly made, she seemed formed for a horsewoman; and to the pure genuine pleasure of the exercise, something was probably added in Edmund's attendance and instructions, and something more in the conviction of very much surpassing her sex in general by her early progress, to make her unwilling to dismount. Fanny was ready and waiting, and Mrs. Norris was beginning to scold her for not being gone, and still no horse was announced, no Edmund appeared. To avoid her aunt, and look for him, she went out.

The houses, though scarcely half a mile apart, were not within sight of each other; but, by walking fifty yards from the hall door, she could look down the park, and command a view of the Parsonage and all its demesnes, gently rising beyond the village road; and in Dr. Grant's meadow she immediately saw the group—Edmund and Miss Crawford both on horse-back, riding side by side, Dr. and Mrs. Grant, and Mr. Crawford, with two or three grooms, standing about and looking on. A happy party it appeared to her, all interested in one object: cheerful beyond a doubt, for the sound of merriment ascended even to her.

It was a sound which did not make hercheerful; she wondered that Edmund should forget her, and felt a pang. She could not turn her eyes from the meadow; she could not help watching all that passed. At first Miss Crawford and her companion made the circuit of the field, which was not small, at a foot's pace; then, at herapparent suggestion, they rose into a canter; and to Fanny's timid nature it was most astonishing to see how well she sat. After a few minutes they stopped entirely. Edmund was close to her; he was speaking to her; he was evidently directing her management of the bridle; he had hold of her hand; she saw it, or the imagination supplied what the eye could not reach. She must not wonder at all this; what could be more natural than that Edmund should be making himself useful, and proving his good-nature by any one? She could not but think, indeed, that Mr. Crawford might as well have saved him the trouble; that it would have been particularly proper and becoming in a brother to have done it himself; but Mr. Crawford, with all his boasted good-nature, and all his coachmanship, probably knew nothing of the matter, and had no active kindness in comparison of Edmund. She began to think it rather hard upon the mare to have such double duty; if she were forgotten, the poor mare should be remembered.

Her feelings for one and the other were soon a little tranquillised by seeing the party in the meadow disperse, and Miss Crawford still on horseback, but attended by Edmund on foot, pass through a gate into the lane, and so into the park, and make towards the spot where she stood. She began then to be afraid of appearing rude and impatient; and walked to meet them with a great anxiety to avoid the suspicion.

"My dear Miss Price," said Miss Crawford, as soon as she was at all within hearing, "I am come to make my own apologies for keeping you waiting; but I have nothing in the world to say for myself—I knew it was very late, and that I was behaving extremely ill; and therefore, if you please, you must forgive me. Selfishness must always be forgiven, you know, because there is no hope of a cure."

Fanny's answer was extremely civil, and Edmund added his conviction that she could be in no hurry. "For there is more than time enough for my cousin to ride twice as far as she ever goes," said he, "and you have been promoting her comfort by preventing her from setting off half an hour sooner: clouds are now coming up, and she will not suffer from the heat as she would have done then. I wish youmay not be fatigued by so much exercise. I wish you had saved yourself this walk home."

"No part of it fatigues me but getting off this horse, I assure you," said she, as she sprang down with his help; "I am very strong. Nothing ever fatigues me but doing what I do not like. Miss Price, I give way to you with a very bad grace; but I sincerely hope you will have a pleasant ride, and that I may have nothing but good to hear of this dear, delightful, beautiful animal."

The old coachman, who had been waiting about with his own horse, now joining them, Fanny was lifted on hers, and they set off across another part of the park; her feelings of discomfort not lightened by seeing, as she looked back, that the others were walking down the hill together to the village; nor did her attendant do her much good by his comments on Miss Crawford's great cleverness as a horse-woman, which he had been watching with an interest almost equal to her own.

"It is a pleasure to see a lady with such a good heart for riding!" said he. "I never see one sit a horse better. She did not seem to have a thought of fear. Very different from you, miss, when you first began, six years ago come next Easter. Lord bless you! how you did tremble when Sir Thomas first had you put on!"

In the drawing-room Miss Crawford was also celebrated. Her merit in being gifted by Nature with strength and courage was fully appreciated by the Miss Bertrams; her delight in riding was like their own; her early excellence in it was like their own, and they had great pleasure in praising it.

"I was sure she would ride well," said Julia; "she has the make for it. Her figure is as neat as her brother's."

"Yes," added Maria, "and her spirits are as good, and she has the same energy of character. I cannot but think that good horsemanship has a great deal to do with the mind."

When they parted at night Edmund asked Fanny whether she meant to ride the next day.

"No, I do not know—not if you want the mare," was her answer. "I do not want her at all for myself," said he; "but whenever you are next inclined to stay at home, I think Miss Crawford would be glad to have her a longer time— for a whole morning, in short. She has a great desire to get as far as Mansfield Common: Mrs. Grant has been telling her of its fine views, and I have no doubt of her being perfectly equal to it. But any morning will do for this. She would be extremely sorry to interfere with you. It would be very wrong if she did. Sherides only for pleasure; youfor health."

"I shall not ride to-morrow, certainly," said Fanny; "I have been out very often lately, and would rather stay at home.

You know I am strong enough now to walk very well." Edmund looked pleased, which must be Fanny's comfort, and the ride to Mansfield Common took place the next morning: the party included all the young people but herself, and was much enjoyed at the time, and doubly enjoyed again in the evening discussion.

A successful scheme of this sort generally brings on another; and the having been to Mansfield Common disposed them all for going somewhere else the day after. There were many other views to be shewn; and though the weather was hot, there were shady lanes wherever they wanted to go.

A young party is always provided with a shady lane. Four fine mornings successively were spent in this manner, in shewing the Crawfords the country, and doing the honours of its finest spots. Everything answered; it was all gaiety and good-humour, the heat only supplying inconvenience enough to be talked of with pleasure— till the fourth day, when the happiness of one of the party was exceedingly clouded. Miss Bertram was the one.

Edmund and Julia were invited to dine at the Parsonage, and shewas excluded. It was meant and done by Mrs. Grant, with perfect good-humour, on Mr. Rushworth's account, who was partly expected at the Park that day; but it was felt as a very grievous injury, and her good manners were severely taxed to conceal her vexation and anger till she reached home. As Mr. Rushworth did notcome, the injury was increased, and she had not even the relief of shewing her power over him; she could only be sullen to her mother, aunt, and cousin, and throw as great a gloom as possible over their dinner and dessert.

Between ten and eleven Edmund and Julia walked into the drawing-room, fresh with the evening air, glowing and cheerful, the very reverse of what they found in the three ladies sitting there, for Maria would scarcely raise her eyes from her book, and Lady Bertram was half-asleep; and even Mrs. Norris, discomposed by her niece's ill-humour, and having asked one or two questions about the dinner, which were not immediately attended to, seemed almost determined to say no more. For a few minutes the brother and sister were too eager in their praise of the night and their remarks on the stars, to think beyond themselves; but when the first pause came, Edmund, looking around, said, "But where is Fanny? Is she gone to bed?"

"No, not that I know of," replied Mrs. Norris; "she was here a moment ago."

Her own gentle voice speaking from the other end of the room, which was a very long one, told them that she was on the sofa. Mrs. Norris began scolding.

"That is a very foolish trick, Fanny, to be idling away all the evening upon a sofa. Why cannot you come and sit here, and employ yourself as wedo? If you have no work of your own, I can supply you from the poor basket. There is all the new calico, that was bought last week, not touched yet. I am sure I almost broke my back by cutting it out. You should learn to think of other people; and, take my word for it, it is a shocking trick for a young person to be always lolling upon a sofa."

Before half this was said, Fanny was returned to her seat at the table, and had taken up her work again; and Julia, who was in high good-humour, from the pleasures of the day, did her the justice of exclaiming, "I must say, ma'am, that Fanny is as little upon the sofa as anybody in the house."

"Fanny," said Edmund, after looking at her attentively, "I am sure you have the headache." She could not deny it, but said it was not very bad.

"I can hardly believe you," he replied; "I know your looks too well. How long have you had it?"

"Since a little before dinner. It is nothing but the heat."

"Did you go out in the heat?""Go out! to be sure she did," said Mrs. Norris: "would you have her stay within such a fine day as this? Were not we allout? Even your mother was out to-day for above an hour."

"Yes, indeed, Edmund," added her ladyship, who had been thoroughly awakened by Mrs. Norris's sharp reprimand to Fanny; "I was out above an hour. I sat three-quarters of an hour in the flower-garden, while Fanny cut the roses; and very pleasant it was, I assure you, but very hot. It was shady enough in the alcove, but I declare I quite dreaded the coming home again."

"Fanny has been cutting roses, has she?"

"Yes, and I am afraid they will be the last this year. Poor thing! Shefound it hot enough; but they were so full-blown that one could not wait." "There was no help for it, certainly," rejoined Mrs. Norris, in a rather softened voice; "but I question whether her headache might not be caught then, sister. There is nothing so likely to give it as standing and stooping in a hot sun; but I dare say it will be well to-morrow. Suppose you let her have your aromatic vinegar; I always forget to have mine filled." "She has got it," said Lady Bertram; "she has had it ever since she came back from your house the second time."

"What!" cried Edmund; "has she been walking as well as cutting roses; walking across the hot park to your house, and doing it twice, ma'am? No wonder her head aches."

Mrs. Norris was talking to Julia, and did not hear.

"I was afraid it would be too much for her," said Lady Bertram; "but when the roses were gathered, your aunt wished to have them, and then you know they must be taken home."

"But were there roses enough to oblige her to go twice?"

"No; but they were to be put into the spare room to dry; and, unluckily, Fanny forgot to lock the door of the room and bring away the key, so she was obliged to go again."

Edmund got up and walked about the room, saying, "And could nobody be employed on such an errand but Fanny? Upon my word, ma'am, it has been a very ill-managed business." "I am sure I do not know how it was to have been done better," cried Mrs. Norris, unable to be longer deaf; "unless I had gone myself, indeed; but I cannot be in two places at once; and I was talking to Mr. Green at that very time about your mother's dairymaid, by herdesire, and had promised John Groom to write to Mrs. Jefferies about his son, and the poor fellow was waiting for me half an hour. I think nobody can justly accuse me of sparing myself upon any occasion, but really I cannot do everything at once. And as for Fanny's just stepping down to my house for me— it is not much above a quarter of a mile—I cannot think I was unreasonable to ask it. How often do I pace it three times a day, early and late, ay, and in all weathers too, and say nothing about it?"

"I wish Fanny had half your strength, ma'am."

"If Fanny would be more regular in her exercise, she would not be knocked up so soon. She has not been out on horseback now this long while, and I am persuaded that, when she does not ride, she ought to walk. If she had been riding before, I should not have asked it of her. But I thought it would rather do her good after being stooping among the roses; for there is nothing so refreshing as a walk after a fatigue of that kind; and though the sun was strong, it was not so very hot. Between ourselves, Edmund," nodding significantly at his mother, "it was cutting the roses, and dawdling about in the flower-garden, that did the mischief."

"I am afraid it was, indeed," said the more candid Lady Bertram, who had overheard her; "I am very much afraid she caught the headache there, for the heat was enough to kill anybody. It was as much as I could bear myself. Sitting and calling to Pug, and trying to keep him from the flower-beds, was almost too much for me."

Edmund said no more to either lady; but going quietly to another table, on which the supper-tray yet remained, brought a glass of Madeira to Fanny, and obliged her to drink the greater part. She wished to be able to decline it; but the tears, which a variety of feelings created, made it easier to swallow than to speak.

Vexed as Edmund was with his mother and aunt, he was still more angry with himself. His own forgetfulness of her was worse than anything which they had done. Nothing of this would have happened had she been properly considered; but she had been left four days together without any choice of companions or exercise, and without any excuse for avoiding whatever her unreasonable aunts might require. He was ashamed to think that for four days together she had not had the power of riding, and very seriously resolved, however unwilling he must be to check a pleasure of Miss Crawford's, that it should never happen again.

Fanny went to bed with her heart as full as on the first evening of her arrival at the Park. The state of her spirits had probably had its share in her indisposition; for she had been feeling neglected, and been struggling against discontent and envy for some days past. As she leant on the sofa, to which she had retreated that she might not be seen, the pain of her mind had been much beyond that in her head; and the sudden change which Edmund's kindness had then occasioned, made her hardly know how to support herself.

Chapter VIII

Fanny's rides recommenced the very next day; and as it was a pleasant fresh-feeling morning, less hot than the weather had lately been, Edmund trusted that her losses, both of health and pleasure, would be soon made good. While she was gone Mr. Rushworth arrived, escorting his mother, who came to be civil and to shew her civility especially, in urging the execution of the plan for visiting Sotherton, which had been started a fortnight before, and which, in consequence of her subsequent absence from home, had since lain dormant. Mrs. Norris and her nieces were all well pleased with its revival, and an early day was named and agreed to, provided Mr. Crawford should be disengaged: the young ladies did not forget that stipulation, and though Mrs. Norris would willingly have answered for his being so, they would neither authorise the liberty nor run the risk; and at last, on a hint from Miss Bertram, Mr. Rushworth discovered that the properest thing to be done was for him to walk down to the Parsonage directly, and call on Mr. Crawford, and inquire whether Wednesday would suit him or not.

Before his return Mrs. Grant and Miss Crawford came in. Having been out some time, and taken a different route to the house, they had not met him. Comfortable hopes, however, were given that he would find Mr. Crawford at home. The Sotherton scheme was mentioned of course. It was hardly possible, indeed, that anything else should be talked of, for Mrs. Norris was in high spirits about it; and Mrs. Rushworth, a well-meaning, civil, prosing, pompous woman, who thought nothing of consequence, but as it related to her own and her son's concerns, had not yet given over pressing Lady Bertram to be of the party. Lady Bertram constantly declined it; but her placid manner of refusal made Mrs. Rushworth still think she wished to come, till Mrs. Norris's more numerous words and louder tone convinced her of the truth.

"The fatigue would be too much for my sister, a great deal too much, I assure you, my dear Mrs. Rushworth. Ten miles there, and ten back, you know. You must excuse my sister on this occasion, and accept of our two dear girls and myself without her. Sotherton is the only place that could give her a wishto go so far, but it cannot be, indeed. She will have a companion in Fanny Price, you know, so it will all do very well; and as for Edmund, as he is not here to speak for himself, I will answer for his being most happy to join the party. He can go on horseback, you know."

Mrs. Rushworth being obliged to yield to Lady Bertram's staying at home, could only be sorry. "The loss of her ladyship's company would be a great drawback, and she should have been extremely happy to have seen the young lady too, Miss Price, who had never been at Sotherton yet, and it was a pity she should not see the place."

"You are very kind, you are all kindness, my dear madam," cried Mrs. Norris; "but as to Fanny, she will have opportunities in plenty of seeing Sotherton. She has time enough before her; and her going now is quite out of the question. Lady Bertram could not possibly spare her."

"Oh no! I cannot do without Fanny."

Mrs. Rushworth proceeded next, under the conviction that everybody must be wanting to see Sotherton, to include Miss Crawford in the invitation; and though Mrs. Grant, who had not been at the trouble of visiting Mrs. Rushworth, on her coming into the neighbourhood, civilly declined it on her own account, she was glad to secure any pleasure for her sister; and Mary, properly pressed and persuaded, was not long in accepting her share of the civility. Mr. Rushworth came back from the Parsonage successful; and Edmund made his appearance just in time to learn what had been settled for

Wednesday, to attend Mrs. Rushworth to her carriage, and walk half-way down the park with the two other ladies.

On his return to the breakfast-room, he found Mrs. Norris trying to make up her mind as to whether Miss Crawford's being of the party were desirable or not, or whether her brother's barouche would not be full without her. The Miss Bertrams laughed at the idea, assuring her that the barouche would hold four perfectly well, independent of the box, on which onemight go with him.

"But why is it necessary," said Edmund, "that Crawford's carriage, or his only, should be employed? Why is no use to be made of my mother's chaise? I could not, when the scheme was first mentioned the other day, understand why a visit from the family were not to be made in the carriage of the family." "What!" cried Julia: "go boxed up three in a postchaise in this weather, when we may have seats in a barouche! No, my dear Edmund, that will not quite do."

"Besides," said Maria, "I know that Mr. Crawford depends upon taking us. After what passed at first, he would claim it as a promise."

"And, my dear Edmund," added Mrs. Norris, "taking out twocarriages when onewill do, would be trouble for nothing; and, between ourselves, coachman is not very fond of the roads between this and Sotherton: he always complains bitterly of the narrow lanes scratching his carriage, and you know one should not like to have dear Sir Thomas, when he comes home, find all the varnish scratched off."

"That would not be a very handsome reason for using Mr. Crawford's," said Maria; "but the truth is, that Wilcox is a stupid old fellow, and does not know how to drive. I will answer for it that we shall find no inconvenience from narrow roads on Wednesday."

"There is no hardship, I suppose, nothing unpleasant," said Edmund, "in going on the barouche box."

"Unpleasant!" cried Maria: "oh dear! I believe it would be generally thought the favourite seat. There can be no comparison as to one's view of the country. Probably Miss Crawford will choose the barouche-box herself." "There can be no objection, then, to Fanny's going with you; there can be no doubt of your having room for her."

"Fanny!" repeated Mrs. Norris; "my dear Edmund, there is no idea of her going with us. She stays with her aunt. I told Mrs. Rushworth so. She is not expected." "You can have no reason, I imagine, madam," said he, addressing his mother, "for wishing Fanny notto be of the party, but as it relates to yourself, to your own comfort. If you could do without her, you would not wish to keep her at home?" "To be sure not, but I cannotdo without her."

"You can, if I stay at home with you, as I mean to do."

There was a general cry out at this. "Yes," he continued, "there is no necessity for my going, and I mean to stay at home. Fanny has a great desire to see Sotherton. I know she wishes it very much. She has not often a gratification of the kind, and I am sure, ma'am, you would be glad to give her the pleasure now?" "Oh yes! very glad, if your aunt sees no objection."

Mrs. Norris was very ready with the only objection which could remain—their having positively assured Mrs. Rushworth that Fanny could not go, and the very strange appearance there would consequently be in taking her, which seemed to her a difficulty quite impossible to be got over. It must have the strangest appearance! It would be something so very unceremonious, so bordering on disrespect for Mrs. Rushworth, whose own manners were such a pattern of good-breeding and attention, that she really did not feel equal to it. Mrs. Norris had no affection for Fanny, and no wish of procuring her pleasure at any time; but her opposition to Edmund now, arose more from partiality for her own scheme, because it washer own, than from anything else. She felt that she had arranged everything extremely well, and that any alteration must be for the worse. When Edmund, therefore, told her in reply, as he did when she would give him the hearing, that she need not distress herself on Mrs. Rushworth's account, because he had taken the opportunity, as he walked with her through the hall, of mentioning Miss Price as one who would probably be of the party, and had directly received a very sufficient invitation for his cousin, Mrs. Norris was too much vexed to submit with a very good grace, and would only say, "Very well, very well, just as you chuse, settle it your own way, I am sure I do not care about it."

"It seems very odd," said Maria, "that you should be staying at home instead of Fanny." "I am sure she ought to be very much obliged to you," added Julia, hastily leaving the room as she spoke, from a consciousness that she ought to offer to stay at home herself.

"Fanny will feel quite as grateful as the occasion requires," was Edmund's only reply, and the subject dropt.

Fanny's gratitude, when she heard the plan, was, in fact, much greater than her pleasure. She felt Edmund's kindness with all, and more than all, the sensibility which he, unsuspicious of her fond attachment, could be aware of; but that he should forego any enjoyment on her account gave her pain, and her own satisfaction in seeing Sotherton would be nothing without him.

The next meeting of the two Mansfield families produced another alteration in the plan, and one that was admitted with general approbation. Mrs. Grant offered herself as companion for the day to Lady Bertram in lieu of her son, and Dr. Grant was to join them at dinner. Lady Bertram was very well pleased to have it so, and the young ladies were in spirits again. Even Edmund was very thankful for an arrangement which restored him to his share of the party; and Mrs. Norris thought it an excellent plan, and had it at her tongue's end, and was on the point of proposing it, when Mrs. Grant spoke.

Wednesday was fine, and soon after breakfast the barouche arrived, Mr. Crawford driving his sisters; and as everybody was ready, there was nothing to be done but for Mrs. Grant to alight and the others to take their places. The place of all places, the envied seat, the post of honour, was unappropriated. To whose happy lot was it to fall? While each of the Miss Bertrams were meditating how best, and with the most appearance of obliging the others, to secure it, the matter was settled by Mrs. Grant's saying, as she stepped from the carriage, "As there are five of you, it will be better that one should sit with Henry; and as you were saying lately that you wished you could drive, Julia, I think this will be a good opportunity for you to take a lesson."

Happy Julia! Unhappy Maria! The former was on the barouche-box in a moment, the latter took her seat within, in gloom and mortification; and the carriage drove off amid the good wishes of the two remaining ladies, and the barking of Pug in his mistress's arms.

Their road was through a pleasant country; and Fanny, whose rides had never been extensive, was soon beyond her knowledge, and was very happy in observing all that was new, and admiring all that was pretty. She was not often invited to join in the conversation of the others, nor did she desire it. Her own thoughts and reflections were habitually her best companions; and, in observing the appearance of the country, the bearings of the roads, the difference of soil, the state of the harvest, the cottages, the cattle, the children, she found entertainment that could only have been heightened by having Edmund to speak to of what she felt. That was the only point of resemblance between her and the lady who sat by her: in everything but a value for Edmund, Miss Crawford was very unlike her. She had none of Fanny's delicacy of taste, of mind, of feeling; she saw Nature, inanimate Nature, with little observation; her attention was all for men and women, her talents for the light and lively. In looking back after Edmund, however, when there was any stretch of road behind them, or when he gained on them in ascending a considerable hill, they were united, and a "there he is" broke at the same moment from them both, more than once.

For the first seven miles Miss Bertram had very little real comfort: her prospect always ended in Mr. Crawford and her sister sitting side by side, full of conversation and merriment; and to see only his expressive profile as he turned with a smile to Julia, or to catch the laugh of the other, was a perpetual source of irritation, which her own sense of propriety could but just smooth over. When Julia looked back, it was with a countenance of delight, and whenever she spoke to them, it was in the highest spirits: "her view of the country was charming, she wished they could all see it," etc.; but her only offer of exchange was addressed to Miss Crawford, as they gained the summit of a long hill, and was not more inviting than this: "Here is a fine burst of country. I wish you had my seat, but I dare say you will not take it, let me press you ever so much;" and Miss Crawford could hardly answer before they were moving again at a good pace.

When they came within the influence of Sotherton associations, it was better for Miss Bertram, who might be said to have two strings to her bow. She had Rushworth feelings, and Crawford feelings, and in the vicinity of Sotherton the former had considerable effect. Mr. Rushworth's consequence was hers. She could not tell Miss Crawford that "those woods belonged to Sotherton," she could not carelessly observe that "she believed that it was now all Mr. Rushworth's property on each side of the road," without elation of heart; and it was a pleasure to increase with their approach to the capital freehold mansion, and ancient manorial residence of the family, with all its rights of court-leet and court-baron.

"Now we shall have no more rough road, Miss Crawford; our difficulties are over. The rest of the way is such as it ought to be. Mr. Rushworth has made it since he succeeded to the estate. Here begins the village. Those cottages are really a disgrace. The church spire is reckoned remarkably handsome. I am glad the church is not so close to the great house as often happens in old places. The annoyance of the bells must be terrible. There is the parsonage: a tidy-looking house, and I understand the clergyman and his wife are very decent people. Those are almshouses, built by some of the family.

To the right is the steward's house; he is a very respectable man. Now we are coming to the lodge-gates; but we have nearly a mile through the park still. It is not ugly, you see, at this end; there is some fine timber, but the situation of the house is dreadful. We go down hill to it for half a mile, and it is a pity, for it would not be an ill-looking place if it had a better approach."

Miss Crawford was not slow to admire; she pretty well guessed Miss Bertram's feelings, and made it a point of honour to promote her enjoyment to the utmost. Mrs. Norris was all delight and volubility; and even Fanny had something to say in admiration, and might be heard with complacency. Her eye was eagerly taking in everything within her reach; and after being at some pains to get a view of the house, and observing that "it was a sort of building which she could not look at but with respect," she added, "Now, where is the avenue? The house fronts the east, I perceive. The avenue, therefore, must be at the back of it. Mr. Rushworth talked of the west front."

"Yes, it is exactly behind the house; begins at a little distance, and ascends for half a mile to the extremity of the grounds. You may see something of it here— something of the more distant trees. It is oak entirely."

Miss Bertram could now speak with decided information of what she had known nothing about when Mr. Rushworth had asked her opinion; and her spirits were in as happy a flutter as vanity and pride could furnish, when they drove up to the spacious stone steps before the principal entrance.

Chapter IX

Mr. Rushworth was at the door to receive his fair lady; and the whole party were welcomed by him with due attention. In the drawing-room they were met with equal cordiality by the mother, and Miss Bertram had all the distinction with each that she could wish. After the business of arriving was over, it was first necessary to eat, and the doors were thrown open to admit them through one or two intermediate rooms into the appointed dining-parlour, where a collation was prepared with abundance and elegance. Much was said, and much was ate, and all went well. The particular object of the day was then considered. How would Mr. Crawford like, in what manner would he chuse, to take a survey of the grounds? Mr. Rushworth mentioned his curricle. Mr. Crawford suggested the greater desirableness of some carriage which might convey more than two. "To be depriving themselves of the advantage of other eyes and other judgments, might be an evil even beyond the loss of present pleasure."

Mrs. Rushworth proposed that the chaise should be taken

also; but this was scarcely received as an amendment: the young ladies neither smiled nor spoke. Her next proposition, of shewing the house to such of them as had not been there before, was more acceptable, for Miss Bertram was pleased to have its size displayed, and all were glad to be doing something. The whole party rose accordingly, and under Mrs. Rushworth's guidance were shewn through a number of rooms, all lofty, and many large, and amply furnished in the taste of fifty years back, with shining floors, solid mahogany, rich damask, marble, gilding, and carving, each handsome in its way. Of pictures there were abundance, and some few good, but the larger part were family portraits, no longer anything to anybody but Mrs. Rushworth, who had been at great pains to learn all that the housekeeper could teach, and was now almost equally well qualified to shew the house.

On the present occasion she addressed herself chiefly to Miss Crawford and Fanny, but there was no comparison in the willingness of their attention; for Miss Crawford, who had seen scores of great houses, and cared for none of them, had only the appearance of civilly listening, while Fanny, to whom everything was almost as interesting as it was new, attended with unaffected earnestness to all that Mrs. Rushworth could relate of the family in former times, its rise and grandeur, regal visits and loyal efforts, delighted to connect anything with history already known, or warm her imagination with scenes of the past. The situation of the house excluded the possibility of much prospect from any of the rooms; and while Fanny and some of the others were attending Mrs. Rushworth, Henry Crawford was looking grave and shaking his head at the windows. Every room on the west front looked across a lawn to the beginning of the avenue immediately beyond tall iron palisades and gates.

Having visited many more rooms than could be supposed to be of any other use than to contribute to the window-tax, and find employment for housemaids, "Now," said Mrs. Rushworth, "we are coming to the chapel, which properly we ought to enter from above, and look down upon; but as we are quite among friends, I will take you in this way, if you will excuse me." They entered. Fanny's imagination had prepared her for something grander than a mere spacious, oblong room, fitted up for the purpose of devotion: with nothing more striking or more solemn than the profusion of mahogany, and the crimson velvet cushions appearing over the ledge of the family gallery above. "I am disappointed," said she, in a low voice, to Edmund. "This is not my idea of a chapel. There is nothing awful here, nothing melancholy, nothing grand. Here are no aisles, no arches, no inscriptions, no banners. No banners, cousin, to be 'blown by the night wind of heaven.' No signs that a 'Scottish monarch sleeps below.'""You forget, Fanny, how lately all this has been built, and for how confined a purpose, compared with the old chapels of castles and monasteries. It was only for the private use of the family. They have been buried, I suppose, in the parish church. Thereyou must look for the banners and the achievements."

"It was foolish of me not to think of all that; but I am disappointed." Mrs. Rushworth began her relation. "This chapel was fitted up as you see it, in James the Second's time. Before that period, as I understand, the pews were only wainscot; and there is some reason to think that the linings and cushions of the pulpit and family seat were only purple cloth; but this is not quite certain. It is a handsome chapel, and was formerly in constant use both morning and evening. Prayers were always read in it by the domestic chaplain, within the memory of many; but the late Mr. Rushworth left it off."

"Every generation has its improvements," said Miss Crawford, with a smile, to Edmund. Mrs. Rushworth was gone to repeat her lesson to Mr. Crawford; and Edmund, Fanny, and Miss Crawford remained in a cluster together.

"It is a pity," cried Fanny, "that the custom should have been discontinued. It was a valuable part of former times. There is something in a chapel and chaplain so much in character with a great house, with one's ideas of what such a household should be! A whole family assembling regularly for the purpose of prayer is fine!" "Very fine indeed," said Miss Crawford, laughing. "It must do the heads of the family a great deal of good to force all the poor housemaids and footmen to leave business and pleasure, and say their prayers here twice a day, while they are inventing excuses themselves for staying away." "Thatis hardly Fanny's idea of a family assembling," said Edmund. "If the master and mistress do notattend themselves, there must be more harm than good in the custom." "At any rate, it is safer to leave people to their own devices on such subjects. Everybody likes to go their own way—to chuse their own time and manner of devotion. The obligation of attendance, the formality, the restraint, the length of time—altogether it is a formidable thing, and what nobody likes; and if the good people who used to kneel and gape in that gallery could have foreseen that the time would ever come when men and women might lie another ten minutes in bed, when they woke with a headache, without danger of reprobation, because chapel was missed, they would have jumped with joy and envy. Cannot you imagine with what unwilling feelings the former belles of the house of Rushworth did many a time repair to this chapel? The young Mrs. Eleanors and Mrs. Bridgets— starched up into seeming piety, but with heads full of something very different—especially if the poor chaplain were not worth looking at—and, in those days, I fancy parsons were very inferior even to what they are now."

For a few moments she was unanswered. Fanny coloured and looked at Edmund, but felt too angry for speech; and he needed a little recollection before he could say, "Your lively mind can hardly be serious even on serious subjects. You have given us an amusing sketch, and human nature cannot say it was not so. We must all feel attimesthe difficulty of fixing our thoughts as we could wish; but if you are supposing it a frequent thing, that is to say, a weakness grown into a habit from neglect, what could be expected from the privatedevotions of such persons? Do you think the minds which are suffered, which are indulged in wanderings in a chapel, would be more collected in a closet?"

"Yes, very likely. They would have two chances at least in their favour. There would be less to distract the attention from without, and it would not be tried so long."

"The mind which does not struggle against itself under onecircumstance, would find objects to distract it in the other, I believe; and the influence of the place and of example may often rouse better feelings than are begun with. The greater length of the service, however, I admit to be sometimes too hard a stretch upon the mind. One wishes it were not so; but I have not yet left Oxford long enough to forget what chapel prayers are."

While this was passing, the rest of the party being scattered about the chapel, Julia called Mr. Crawford's attention to her sister, by saying, "Do look at Mr. Rushworth and Maria, standing side by side, exactly as if the ceremony were going to be performed. Have not they completely the air of it?"

Mr. Crawford smiled his acquiescence, and stepping forward to Maria, said, in a voice which she only could hear, "I do not like to see Miss Bertram so near the altar."

Starting, the lady instinctively moved a step or two, but recovering herself in a moment, affected to laugh, and asked him, in a tone not much louder, "If he would give her away?"

"I am afraid I should do it very awkwardly," was his reply, with a look of meaning.

Julia, joining them at the moment, carried on the joke.

"Upon my word, it is really a pity that it should not take place directly, if we had but a proper licence, for here we are altogether, and nothing in the world could be more snug and pleasant." And she talked and laughed about it with so little caution as to catch the comprehension of Mr. Rushworth and his mother, and expose her sister to the whispered gallantries of her lover, while Mrs. Rushworth spoke with proper smiles and dignity of its being a most happy event to her whenever it took place.

"If Edmund were but in orders!" cried Julia, and running to where he stood with Miss Crawford and Fanny: "My dear Edmund, if you were but in orders now, you might perform the ceremony directly. How unlucky that you are not ordained; Mr. Rushworth and Maria are quite ready."

Miss Crawford's countenance, as Julia spoke, might have

amused a disinterested observer. She looked almost aghast under the new idea she was receiving. Fanny pitied her. "How distressed she will be at what she said just now," passed across her mind.

"Ordained!" said Miss Crawford; "what, are you to be a clergyman?" "Yes; I shall take orders soon after my father's return— probably at Christmas."

Miss Crawford, rallying her spirits, and recovering her complexion, replied only, "If I had known this before, I would have spoken of the cloth with more respect," and turned the subject. The chapel was soon afterwards left to the silence and stillness which reigned in it, with few interruptions, throughout the year. Miss Bertram, displeased with her sister, led the way, and all seemed to feel that they had been there long enough.

The lower part of the house had been now entirely shewn, and Mrs. Rushworth, never weary in the cause, would have proceeded towards the principal staircase, and taken them through all the rooms above, if her son had not interposed with a doubt of there being time enough. "For if," said he, with the sort of self-evident proposition which many a clearer head does not always avoid, "we are toolong going over the house, we shall not have time for what is to be done out of doors. It is past two, and we are to dine at five."

Mrs. Rushworth submitted; and the question of surveying the grounds, with the who and the how, was likely to be more fully agitated, and Mrs. Norris was beginning to arrange by what junction of carriages and horses most could be done, when the young people, meeting with an outward door, temptingly open on a flight of steps which led immediately to turf and shrubs, and all the sweets of pleasure-grounds, as by one impulse, one wish for air and liberty, all walked out.

"Suppose we turn down here for the present," said Mrs. Rushworth, civilly taking the hint and following them. "Here are the greatest number of our plants, and here are the curious pheasants."

"Query," said Mr. Crawford, looking round him, "whether we may not find something to employ us here before we go farther? I see walls of great promise. Mr. Rushworth, shall we summon a council on this lawn?"

"James," said Mrs. Rushworth to her son, "I believe the wilderness will be new to all the party. The Miss Bertrams have never seen the wilderness yet."

No objection was made, but for some time there seemed no inclination to move in any plan, or to any distance. All were attracted at first by the plants or the pheasants, and all dispersed about in happy independence. Mr. Crawford was the first to move forward to examine the capabilities of that end of the house. The lawn, bounded on each side by a high wall, contained beyond the first planted area a bowling-green, and beyond the bowling-green a long terrace walk, backed by iron palisades, and commanding a view over them into the tops of the trees of the wilderness immediately adjoining. It was a good spot for fault-finding.

Mr. Crawford was soon followed by Miss Bertram and Mr. Rushworth; and when, after a little time, the others began to form into parties, these three were found in busy consultation on the terrace by Edmund, Miss Crawford, and Fanny, who seemed as naturally to unite, and who, after a short participation of their regrets and difficulties, left them and walked on. The remaining three, Mrs. Rushworth, Mrs. Norris, and Julia, were still far behind; for Julia, whose happy star no longer prevailed, was obliged to keep by the side of Mrs. Rushworth, and restrain her impatient feet to that lady's slow pace, while her aunt, having fallen in with the housekeeper, who was come out to feed the pheasants, was lingering behind in gossip with her.

Poor Julia, the only one out of the nine not tolerably satisfied with their lot, was now in a state of complete penance, and as different from the Julia of the barouche-box as could well be imagined. The politeness which she had been brought up to practise as a duty made it impossible for her to escape; while the want of that higher species of self-command, that just consideration of others, that knowledge of her own heart, that principle of right, which had not formed any essential part of her education, made her miserable under it.

"This is insufferably hot," said Miss Crawford, when they had taken one turn on the terrace, and were drawing a second time to the door in the middle which opened to the wilderness. "Shall any of us object to being comfortable? Here is a nice little wood, if one can but get into it. What happiness if the door should not be locked! but of course it is; for in these great places the gardeners are the only people who can go where they like."

The door, however, proved not to be locked, and they were all agreed in turning joyfully through it, and leaving the unmitigated glare of day behind. A considerable flight of steps landed them in the wilderness, which was a planted wood of about two acres, and though chiefly of larch and laurel, and beech cut down, and though laid out with too much regularity, was darkness and shade, and natural beauty, compared with the bowling-green and the terrace. They all felt the refreshment of it, and for some time could only walk and admire. At length, after a short pause, Miss Crawford began with, "So you are to be a clergyman, Mr. Bertram. This is rather a surprise to me."

"Why should it surprise you? You must suppose me designed for some profession, and might perceive that I am neither a lawyer, nor a soldier, nor a sailor."

"Very true; but, in short, it had not occurred to me. And you know there is generally an uncle or a grandfather to leave a fortune to the second son."

"A very praiseworthy practice," said Edmund, "but not quite universal. I am one of the exceptions, and beingone, must do something for myself."

"But why are you to be a clergyman? I thought thatwas always the lot of the youngest, where there were many to chuse before him." "Do you think the church itself never chosen, then?" "Neveris a black word. But yes, in the neverof conversation, which means notveryoften, I do think it. For what is to be done in the church? Men love to distinguish themselves, and in either of the other lines distinction may be gained, but not in the church. A clergyman is nothing."

"The nothingof conversation has its gradations, I hope, as well as the never. A clergyman cannot be high in state or fashion. He must not head mobs, or set the ton in dress. But I cannot call that situation nothing which has the charge of all that is of the first importance to mankind, individually or collectively considered, temporally and eternally, which has the guardianship of religion and morals, and consequently of the manners which result from their influence. No one here can call the officenothing. If the man who holds it is so, it is by the neglect of his duty, by foregoing its just importance, and stepping out of his place to appear what he ought not to appear." "Youassign greater consequence to the clergyman than one has been used to hear given, or than I can quite comprehend. One does not see much of this influence and importance in society, and how can it be acquired where they are so seldom seen themselves? How can two sermons a week, even supposing them worth hearing, supposing the preacher to have the sense to prefer Blair's to his own, do all that you speak of? govern the conduct and fashion the manners of a large congregation for the rest of the week? One scarcely sees a clergyman out of his pulpit."

"Youare speaking of London, Iam speaking of the nation at large." "The metropolis, I imagine, is a pretty fair sample of the rest." "Not, I should hope, of the proportion of virtue to vice throughout the kingdom. We do not look in great cities for our best morality. It is not there that respectable people of any denomination can do most good; and it certainly is not there that the influence of the clergy can be most felt. A fine preacher is followed and admired; but it is not in fine preaching only that a good clergyman will be useful in his parish and his neighbourhood, where the parish and neighbourhood are of a size capable of knowing his private character, and observing his general conduct, which in London can rarely be the case. The clergy are lost there in the crowds of their parishioners. They are known to the largest part only as preachers.

And with regard to their influencing public manners, Miss Crawford must not misunderstand me, or suppose I mean to call them the arbiters of good-breeding, the regulators of refinement and courtesy, the masters of the ceremonies of life.

The mannersI speak of might rather be called conduct, perhaps, the result of good principles; the effect, in short, of those doctrines which it is their duty to teach and recommend; and it will, I believe, be everywhere found, that as the clergy are, or are not what they ought to be, so are the rest of the nation." "Certainly," said Fanny, with gentle earnestness.

"There," cried Miss Crawford, "you have quite convinced Miss Price already."

"I wish I could convince Miss Crawford too."

"I do not think you ever will," said she, with an arch smile; "I am just as much surprised now as I was at first that you should intend to take orders. You really are fit for something better. Come, do change your mind. It is not too late. Go into the law."

"Go into the law! With as much ease as I was told to go into this wilderness."

"Now you are going to say something about law being the worst wilderness of the two, but I forestall you; remember, I have forestalled you."

"You need not hurry when the object is only to prevent my saying a bonmot, for there is not the least wit in my nature. I am a very matter-of-fact, plain-spoken being, and may blunder on the borders of a repartee for half an hour together without striking it out."

A general silence succeeded. Each was thoughtful. Fanny made the first interruption by saying, "I wonder that I should be tired with only walking in this sweet wood; but the next time we come to a seat, if it is not disagreeable to you, I should be glad to sit down for a little while."

"My dear Fanny," cried Edmund, immediately drawing her arm within his, "how thoughtless I have been! I hope you are not very tired. Perhaps," turning to Miss Crawford, "my other companion may do me the honour of taking an arm."

"Thank you, but I am not at all tired." She took it, however, as she spoke, and the gratification of having her do so, of feeling such a connexion for the first time, made him a little forgetful of Fanny. "You scarcely touch me," said he. "You do not make me of any use. What a difference in the weight of a woman's arm from that of a man! At Oxford I have been a good deal used to have a man lean on me for the length of a street, and you are only a fly in the comparison."

"I am really not tired, which I almost wonder at; for we must have walked at least a mile in this wood. Do not you think we have?" "Not half a mile," was his sturdy answer; for he was not yet so much in love as to measure distance, or reckon time, with feminine lawlessness.

"Oh! you do not consider how much we have wound about. We have taken such a very serpentine course, and the wood itself must be half a mile long in a straight line, for we have never seen the end of it yet since we left the first great path."

"But if you remember, before we left that first great path, we saw directly to the end of it. We looked down the whole vista, and saw it closed by iron gates, and it could not have been more than a furlong in length."

"Oh! I know nothing of your furlongs, but I am sure it is a very long wood, and that we have been winding in and out ever since we came into it; and therefore, when I say that we have walked a mile in it, I must speak within compass."

"We have been exactly a quarter of an hour here," said Edmund, taking out his watch. "Do you think we are walking four miles an hour?"

"Oh! do not attack me with your watch. A watch is always too fast or too slow. I cannot be dictated to by a watch."

A few steps farther brought them out at the bottom of the very walk they had been talking of; and standing back, well shaded and sheltered, and looking over a ha-ha into the park, was a comfortable-sized bench, on which they all sat down.

"I am afraid you are very tired, Fanny," said Edmund, observing her; "why would not you speak sooner? This will be a bad day's amusement for you if you are to be knocked up. Every sort of exercise fatigues her so soon, Miss Crawford, except riding."

"How abominable in you, then, to let me engross her horse as I did all last week! I am ashamed of you and of myself, but it shall never happen again." "Yourattentiveness and consideration makes me more sensible of my own neglect. Fanny's interest seems in safer hands with you than with me."

"That she should be tired now, however, gives me no surprise; for there is nothing in the course of one's duties so fatiguing as what we have been doing this morning: seeing a great house, dawdling from one room to another, straining one's eyes and one's attention, hearing what one does not understand, admiring what one does not care for. It is generally allowed to be the greatest bore in the world, and Miss Price has found it so, though she did not know it."

"I shall soon be rested," said Fanny; "to sit in the shade on a fine day, and look upon verdure, is the most perfect refreshment."

After sitting a little while Miss Crawford was up again. "I must move," said she; "resting fatigues me. I have looked across the ha-ha till I am weary. I must go and look through that iron gate at the same view, without being able to see it so well."

Edmund left the seat likewise. "Now, Miss Crawford, if you will look up the walk, you will convince yourself that it cannot be half a mile long, or half half a mile."

"It is an immense distance," said she; "I see thatwith a glance."

He still reasoned with her, but in vain. She would not calculate, she would not compare. She would only smile and assert. The greatest degree of rational consistency could not have been more engaging, and they talked with mutual satisfaction. At last it was agreed that they should endeavour to determine the dimensions of the wood by walking a little more about it.

They would go to one end of it, in the line they were then in— for there was a straight green walk along the bottom by the side of the ha-ha—and perhaps turn a little way in some other direction, if it seemed likely to assist them, and be back in a few minutes. Fanny said she was rested, and would have moved too, but this was not suffered. Edmund urged her remaining where she was with an earnestness which she could not resist, and she was left on the bench to think with pleasure of her cousin's care, but with great regret that she was not stronger. She watched them till they had turned the corner, and listened till all sound of them had ceased.

Chapter X

A quarter of an hour, twenty minutes, passed away, and Fanny was still thinking of Edmund, Miss Crawford, and herself, without interruption from any one. She began to be surprised at being left so long, and to listen with an anxious desire of hearing their steps and their voices again. She listened, and at length she heard; she heard voices and feet approaching; but she had just satisfied herself that it was not those she wanted, when Miss Bertram, Mr. Rushworth, and Mr. Crawford issued from the same path which she had trod herself, and were before her.

"Miss Price all alone" and "My dear Fanny, how comes this?" were the first salutations. She told her story. "Poor dear Fanny," cried her cousin, "how ill you have been used by them! You had better have staid with us."

Then seating herself with a gentleman on each side, she resumed the conversation which had engaged them before, and discussed the possibility of improvements with much animation. Nothing was fixed on; but Henry Crawford was full of ideas and projects, and, generally speaking, whatever he proposed was immediately approved, first by her, and then by Mr. Rushworth, whose principal business seemed to be to hear the others, and who scarcely risked an original thought of his own beyond a wish that they had seen his friend Smith's place.

After some minutes spent in this way, Miss Bertram, observing the iron gate, expressed a wish of passing through it into the park, that their views and their plans might be more comprehensive. It was the very thing of all others to be wished, it was the best, it was the only way of proceeding with any advantage, in Henry Crawford's opinion; and he directly saw a knoll not half a mile off, which would give them exactly the requisite command of the house. Go therefore they must to that knoll, and through that gate; but the gate was locked. Mr.

Rushworth wished he had brought the key; he had been very near thinking whether he should not bring the key; he was determined he would never come without the key again; but still this did not remove the present evil. They could not get through; and as Miss Bertram's inclination for so doing did by no means lessen, it ended in Mr. Rushworth's declaring outright that he would go and fetch the key. He set off accordingly.

"It is undoubtedly the best thing we can do now, as we are so far from the house already," said Mr. Crawford, when he was gone.

"Yes, there is nothing else to be done. But now, sincerely, do not you find the place altogether worse than you expected?"

"No, indeed, far otherwise. I find it better, grander, more complete in its style, though that style may not be the best. And to tell you the truth," speaking rather lower, "I do not think that Ishall ever see Sotherton again with so much pleasure as I do now. Another summer will hardly improve it to me."

After a moment's embarrassment the lady replied, "You are too much a man of the world not to see with the eyes of the world. If other people think Sotherton improved, I have no doubt that you will."

"I am afraid I am not quite so much the man of the world as might be good for me in some points. My feelings are not quite so evanescent, nor my memory of the past under such easy dominion as one finds to be the case with men of the world."

This was followed by a short silence. Miss Bertram began again. "You seemed to enjoy your drive here very much this morning. I was glad to see you so well entertained. You and Julia were laughing the whole way."

"Were we? Yes, I believe we were; but I have not the least recollection at what. Oh! I believe I was relating to her some ridiculous stories of an old Irish groom of my uncle's. Your sister loves to laugh."

"You think her more light-hearted than I am?"

"More easily amused," he replied; "consequently, you

know," smiling, "better company. I could not have hoped to entertain you with Irish anecdotes during a ten miles' drive." "Naturally, I believe, I am as lively as Julia, but I have more to think of now."

"You have, undoubtedly; and there are situations in which very high spirits would denote insensibility. Your prospects, however, are too fair to justify want of spirits. You have a very smiling scene before you."

"Do you mean literally or figuratively? Literally, I conclude. Yes, certainly, the sun shines, and the park looks very cheerful. But unluckily that iron gate, that ha-ha, give me a feeling of restraint and hardship. 'I cannot get out,' as the starling said." As she spoke, and it was with expression, she walked to the gate: he followed her. "Mr. Rushworth is so long fetching this key!"

"And for the world you would not get out without the key and without Mr. Rushworth's authority and protection, or I think you might with little difficulty pass round the edge of the gate, here, with my assistance; I think it might be done, if you really wished to be more at large, and could allow yourself to think it not prohibited."

"Prohibited! nonsense! I certainly can get out that way, and I will. Mr. Rushworth will be here in a moment, you know; we shall not be out of sight."

"Or if we are, Miss Price will be so good as to tell him that he will find us near that knoll: the grove of oak on the knoll." Fanny, feeling all this to be wrong, could not help making an effort to prevent it. "You will hurt yourself, Miss Bertram," she cried; "you will certainly hurt yourself against those spikes; you will tear your gown; you will be in danger of slipping into the ha-ha. You had better not go."

Her cousin was safe on the other side while these words were spoken, and, smiling with all the good-humour of success, she said, "Thank you, my dear Fanny, but I and my gown are alive and well, and so good-bye."

Fanny was again left to her solitude, and with no increase of pleasant feelings, for she was sorry for almost all that she had seen and heard, astonished at Miss Bertram, and angry with Mr. Crawford. By taking a circuitous route, and, as it appeared to her, very unreasonable direction to the knoll, they were soon beyond her eye; and for some minutes longer she remained without sight or sound of any companion. She seemed to have the little wood all to herself. She could almost have thought that Edmund and Miss Crawford had left it, but that it was impossible for Edmund to forget her so entirely. She was again roused from disagreeable musings by sudden footsteps: somebody was coming at a quick pace down the principal walk. She expected Mr. Rushworth, but it was Julia, who, hot and out of breath, and with a look of disappointment, cried out on seeing her, "Heyday! Where are the others? I thought Maria and Mr. Crawford were with you."

Fanny Explained: "A pretty trick, upon my word! I cannot see them anywhere," looking eagerly into the park. "But they cannot be very far off, and I think I am equal to as much as Maria, even without help."

"But, Julia, Mr. Rushworth will be here in a moment with the key. Do wait for Mr. Rushworth."

"Not I, indeed. I have had enough of the family for one morning. Why, child, I have but this moment escaped from his horrible mother. Such a penance as I have been enduring, while you were sitting here so composed and so happy! It might have been as well, perhaps, if you had been in my place, but you always contrive to keep out of these scrapes."

This was a most unjust reflection, but Fanny could allow for it, and let it pass: Julia was vexed, and her temper was hasty; but she felt that it would not last, and therefore, taking no notice, only asked her if she had not seen Mr. Rushworth.

"Yes, yes, we saw him. He was posting away as if upon life and death, and could but just spare time to tell us his errand, and where you all were."

"It is a pity he should have so much trouble for nothing."

"Thatis Miss Maria's concern. I am not obliged to punish myself for hersins. The mother I could not avoid, as long as my tiresome aunt was dancing about with the housekeeper, but the son I canget away from." And she immediately scrambled across the fence, and walked away, not attending to Fanny's last question of whether she had seen anything of Miss Crawford and Edmund. The sort of dread in which Fanny now sat of seeing Mr. Rushworth prevented her thinking so much of their continued absence, however, as she might have done. She felt that he had been very ill-used, and was quite unhappy in having to communicate what had passed. He joined her within five minutes after Julia's exit; and though she made the best of the story, he was evidently mortified and displeased in no common degree. At first he scarcely said anything; his looks only expressed his extreme surprise and vexation, and he walked to the gate and stood there, without seeming to know what to do.

"They desired me to stay—my cousin Maria charged me to say that you would find them at that knoll, or thereabouts."

"I do not believe I shall go any farther," said he sullenly; "I see nothing of them. By the time I get to the knoll they may be gone somewhere else. I have had walking enough."

And he sat down with a most gloomy countenance by Fanny. "I am very sorry," said she; "it is very unlucky." And she longed to be able to say something more to the purpose.

After an interval of silence, "I think they might as well have staid for me," said he.

"Miss Bertram thought you would follow her."

"I should not have had to follow her if she had staid."

This could not be denied, and Fanny was silenced. After another pause, he went on—"Pray, Miss Price, are you such a great admirer of this Mr. Crawford as some people are? For my part, I can see nothing in him."

"I do not think him at all handsome."

"Handsome! Nobody can call such an undersized man handsome. He is not five foot nine. I should not wonder if he is not more than five foot eight. I think he is an ill-looking fellow. In my opinion, these Crawfords are no addition at all. We did very well without them."

A small sigh escaped Fanny here, and she did not know how to contradict him. "If I had made any difficulty about fetching the key, there might have been some excuse, but I went the very moment she said she wanted it."

"Nothing could be more obliging than your manner, I am sure, and I dare say you walked as fast as you could; but still it is some distance, you know, from this spot to the house, quite into the house; and when people are waiting, they are bad judges of time, and every half minute seems like five."

He got up and walked to the gate again, and "wished he had had the key about him at the time." Fanny thought she discerned in his standing there an indication of relenting, which encouraged her to another attempt, and she said, therefore, "It is a pity you should not join them. They expected to have a better view of the house from that part of the park, and will be thinking how it may be improved; and nothing of that sort, you know, can be settled without you."

She found herself more successful in sending away than in retaining a companion. Mr. Rushworth was worked on. "Well," said he, "if you really think I had better go: it would be foolish to bring the key for nothing." And letting himself out, he walked off without farther ceremony.

Fanny's thoughts were now all engrossed by the two who had left her so long ago, and getting quite impatient, she resolved to go in search of them. She followed their steps along the bottom walk, and had just turned up into another, when the voice and the laugh of Miss Crawford once more caught her ear; the sound approached, and a few more windings brought them before her. They were just returned into the wilderness from the park, to which a sidegate, not fastened, had tempted them very soon after their leaving her, and they had been across a portion of the park into the very avenue which Fanny had been hoping the whole morning to reach at last, and had been sitting down under one of the trees. This was their history. It was evident that they had been spending their time pleasantly, and were not aware of the length of their absence. Fanny's best consolation was in being assured that Edmund had wished for her very much, and that he should certainly have come back for her, had she not been tired already; but this was not quite sufficient to do away with the pain of having been left a whole hour, when he had talked of only a few minutes, nor to banish the sort of curiosity she felt to know what they had been conversing about all that time; and the result of the whole was to her disappointment and depression, as they prepared by general agreement to return to the house.

On reaching the bottom of the steps to the terrace, Mrs. Rushworth and Mrs. Norris presented themselves at the top, just ready for the wilderness, at the end of an hour and a half from their leaving the house. Mrs. Norris had been too well employed to move faster. Whatever cross-accidents had occurred to intercept the pleasures of her nieces, she had found a morning of complete enjoyment; for the housekeeper, after a great many courtesies on the subject of pheasants, had taken her to the dairy, told her all about their cows, and given her the receipt for a famous cream cheese; and since Julia's leaving them they had been met by the gardener, with whom she had made a most satisfactory acquaintance, for she had set him right as to his grandson's illness, convinced him that it was an ague, and promised him a charm for it; and he, in return, had shewn her all his choicest nursery of plants, and actually presented her with a very curious specimen of heath.

On this rencontrethey all returned to the house together, there to lounge away the time as they could with sofas, and chit-chat, and Quarterly Reviews, till the return of the others, and the arrival of dinner. It was late before the Miss Bertrams and the two gentlemen came in, and their ramble did not appear to have been more than partially agreeable, or at all productive of anything useful with regard to the object of the day. By their own accounts they had been all walking after each other, and the junction which had taken place at last seemed, to Fanny's observation, to have been as much too late for re-establishing harmony, as it confessedly had been for determining on any alteration. She felt, as she looked at Julia and Mr. Rushworth, that hers was not the only dissatisfied bosom amongst them: there was gloom on the face of each. Mr. Crawford and Miss Bertram were much more gay, and she thought that he was taking particular pains, during dinner, to do away any little resentment of the other two, and restore general good-humour.

Dinner was soon followed by tea and coffee, a ten miles' drive home allowed no waste of hours; and from the time of their sitting down to table, it was a quick succession of busy nothings till the carriage came to the door, and Mrs. Norris, having fidgeted about, and obtained a few pheasants' eggs and a cream cheese from the housekeeper, and made abundance of civil speeches to Mrs. Rushworth, was ready to lead the way. At the same moment Mr. Crawford, approaching Julia, said, "I hope I am not to lose my companion, unless she is afraid of the evening air in so exposed a seat."

The request had not been foreseen, but was very graciously received, and Julia's day was likely to end almost as well as it began. Miss Bertram had made up her mind to something different, and was a little disappointed; but her conviction of being really the one preferred comforted her under it, and enabled her to receive Mr. Rushworth's parting attentions as she ought.

He was certainly better pleased to hand her into the barouche than to assist her in ascending the box, and his complacency seemed confirmed by the arrangement. "Well, Fanny, this has been a fine day for you, upon my word," said Mrs. Norris, as they drove through the park. "Nothing but pleasure from beginning to end! I am sure you ought to be very much obliged to your aunt Bertram and me for contriving to let you go. A pretty good day's amusement you have had!"

Maria was just discontented enough to say directly, "I think youhave done pretty well yourself, ma'am. Your lap seems full of good things, and here is a basket of something between us which has been knocking my elbow unmercifully."

"My dear, it is only a beautiful little heath, which that nice old gardener would make me take; but if it is in your way, I will have it in my lap directly. There, Fanny, you shall carry that parcel for me; take great care of it: do not let it fall; it is a cream cheese, just like the excellent one we had at dinner. Nothing would satisfy that good old Mrs. Whitaker, but my taking one of the cheeses. I stood out as long as I could, till the tears almost came into her eyes, and I knew it was just the sort that my sister would be delighted with. That Mrs.

Whitaker is a treasure! She was quite shocked when I asked her whether wine was allowed at the second table, and she has turned away two housemaids for wearing white gowns. Take care of the cheese, Fanny. Now I can manage the other parcel and the basket very well."

"What else have you been spunging?" said Maria, half-pleased that Sotherton should be so complimented. "Spunging, my dear! It is nothing but four of those beautiful pheasants' eggs, which Mrs. Whitaker would quite force upon me: she would not take a denial.

She said it must be such an amusement to me, as she understood I lived quite alone, to have a few living creatures of that sort; and so to be sure it will. I shall get the dairymaid to set them under the first spare hen, and if they come to good I can have them moved to my own house and borrow a coop; and it will be a great delight to me in my lonely hours to attend to them. And if I have good luck, your mother shall have some."

It was a beautiful evening, mild and still, and the drive was as pleasant as the serenity of Nature could make it; but when Mrs. Norris ceased speaking, it was altogether a silent drive to those within. Their spirits were in general exhausted; and to determine whether the day had afforded most pleasure or pain, might occupy the meditations of almost all.

Chapter XI

The day at Sotherton, with all its imperfections, afforded the Miss Bertrams much more agreeable feelings than were derived from the letters from Antigua, which soon afterwards reached Mansfield. It was much pleasanter to think of Henry Crawford than of their father; and to think of their father in England again within a certain period, which these letters obliged them to do, was a most unwelcome exercise.

November was the black month fixed for his return. Sir Thomas wrote of it with as much decision as experience and anxiety could authorise. His business was so nearly concluded as to justify him in proposing to take his passage in the September packet, and he consequently looked forward with the hope of being with his beloved family again early in November. Maria was more to be pitied than Julia; for to her the father brought a husband, and the return of the friend most solicitous for her happiness would unite her to the lover, on whom she had chosen that happiness should depend. It was a gloomy prospect, and all she could do was to throw a mist over it, and hope when the mist cleared away she should see something else. It would hardly be earlyin November, there were generally delays, a bad passage or something; that favouring somethingwhich everybody who shuts their eyes while they look, or their understandings while they reason, feels the comfort of. It would probably be the middle of November at least; the middle of November was three months off. Three months comprised thirteen weeks. Much might happen in thirteen weeks.

Sir Thomas would have been deeply mortified by a suspicion of half that his daughters felt on the subject of his return, and would hardly have found consolation in a knowledge of the interest it excited in the breast of another young lady. Miss Crawford, on walking up with her brother to spend the evening at Mansfield Park, heard the good news; and though seeming to have no concern in the affair beyond politeness, and to have vented all her feelings in a quiet congratulation, heard it with an attention not so easily satisfied. Mrs. Norris gave the particulars of the letters, and the subject was dropt; but after tea, as Miss Crawford was standing at an open window with Edmund and Fanny looking out on a twilight scene, while the Miss Bertrams, Mr. Rushworth, and Henry Crawford were all busy with candles at the pianoforte, she suddenly revived it by turning round towards the group, and saying, "How happy Mr. Rushworth looks! He is thinking of November."

Edmund looked round at Mr. Rushworth too, but had nothing to say. "Your father's return will be a very interesting event." "It will, indeed, after such an absence; an absence not only long, but including so many dangers."

"It will be the forerunner also of other interesting events: your sister's marriage, and your taking orders."

"Yes."

"Don't be affronted," said she, laughing, "but it does put me in mind of some of the old heathen heroes, who, after performing great exploits in a foreign land, offered sacrifices to the gods on their safe return."

"There is no sacrifice in the case," replied Edmund, with a serious smile, and glancing at the pianoforte again; "it is entirely her own doing."

"Oh yes I know it is. I was merely joking. She has done no more than what every young woman would do; and I have no doubt of her being extremely happy. My other sacrifice, of course, you do not understand."

"My taking orders, I assure you, is quite as voluntary as Maria's marrying."

"It is fortunate that your inclination and your father's convenience should accord so well. There is a very good living kept for you, I understand, hereabouts." "Which you suppose has biassed me?" "But thatI am sure it has not," cried Fanny.

"Thank you for your good word, Fanny, but it is more than I would affirm myself. On the contrary, the knowing that there was such a provision for me probably did bias me. Nor can I think it wrong that it should.

There was no natural disinclination to be overcome, and I see no reason why a man should make a worse clergyman for knowing that he will have a competence early in life. I was in safe hands. I hope I should not have been influenced myself in a wrong way, and I am sure my father was too conscientious to have allowed it. I have no doubt that I was biased, but I think it was blamelessly."

"It is the same sort of thing," said Fanny, after a short pause, "as for the son of an admiral to go into the navy, or the son of a general to be in the army, and nobody sees anything wrong in that. Nobody wonders that they should prefer the line where their friends can serve them best, or suspects them to be less in earnest in it than they appear."

"No, my dear Miss Price, and for reasons good. The profession, either navy or army, is its own justification. It has everything in its favour: heroism, danger, bustle, fashion.

Soldiers and sailors are always acceptable in society. Nobody can wonder that men are soldiers and sailors."

"But the motives of a man who takes orders with the certainty of preferment may be fairly suspected, you think?" said Edmund. "To be justified in your eyes, he must do it in the most complete uncertainty of any provision."

"What! take orders without a living! No; that is madness indeed; absolute madness." "Shall I ask you how the church is to be filled, if a man is neither to take orders with a living nor without? No; for you certainly would not know what to say. But I must beg some advantage to the clergyman from your own argument. As he cannot be influenced by those feelings which you rank highly as temptation and reward to the soldier and sailor in their choice of a profession, as heroism, and noise, and fashion, are all against him, he ought to be less liable to the suspicion of wanting sincerity or good intentions in the choice of his."

"Oh! no doubt he is very sincere in preferring an income ready made, to the trouble of working for one; and has the best intentions of doing nothing all the rest of his days but eat, drink, and grow fat. It is indolence, Mr. Bertram, indeed. Indolence and love of ease; a want of all laudable ambition, of taste for good company, or of inclination to take the trouble of being agreeable, which make men clergymen. A clergyman has nothing to do but be slovenly and selfish—read the newspaper, watch the weather, and quarrel with his wife. His curate does all the work, and the business of his own life is to dine." "There are such clergymen, no doubt, but I think they are not so common as to justify Miss Crawford in esteeming it their general character. I suspect that in this comprehensive and (may I say) commonplace censure, you are not judging from yourself, but from prejudiced persons, whose opinions you have been in the habit of hearing. It is impossible that your own observation can have given you much knowledge of the clergy. You can have been personally acquainted with very few of a set of men you condemn so conclusively. You are speaking what you have been told at your uncle's table."

"I speak what appears to me the general opinion; and

where an opinion is general, it is usually correct. Though Ihave not seen much of the domestic lives of clergymen, it is seen by too many to leave any deficiency of information." "Where any one body of educated men, of whatever denomination, are condemned indiscriminately, there must be a deficiency of information, or (smiling) of something else. Your uncle, and his brother admirals, perhaps knew little of clergymen beyond the chaplains whom, good or bad, they were always wishing away." "Poor William! He has met with great kindness from the chaplain of the Antwerp," was a tender apostrophe of Fanny's, very much to the purpose of her own feelings if not of the conversation.

"I have been so little addicted to take my opinions from my uncle," said Miss Crawford, "that I can hardly suppose—and since you push me so hard, I must observe, that I am not entirely without the means of seeing what clergymen are, being at this present time the guest of my own brother, Dr. Grant. And though Dr. Grant is most kind and obliging to me, and though he is really a gentleman, and, I dare say, a good scholar and clever, and often preaches good sermons, and is very respectable, Isee him to be an indolent, selfish bonvivant, who must have his palate consulted in everything; who will not stir a finger for the convenience of any one; and who, moreover, if the cook makes a blunder, is out of humour with his excellent wife. To own the truth, Henry and I were partly driven out this very evening by a disappointment about a green goose, which he could not get the better of. My poor sister was forced to stay and bear it."

"I do not wonder at your disapprobation, upon my word. It is a great defect of temper, made worse by a very faulty habit of self-indulgence; and to see your sister suffering from it must be exceedingly painful to such feelings as yours. Fanny, it goes against us. We cannot attempt to defend Dr. Grant."

"No," replied Fanny, "but we need not give up his profession for all that; because, whatever profession Dr. Grant had chosen, he would have taken a—not a good temper into it; and as he must, either in the navy or army, have had a great many more people under his command than he has now, I think more would have been made unhappy by him as a sailor or soldier than as a clergyman. Besides, I cannot but suppose that whatever there may be to wish otherwise in Dr. Grant would have been in a greater danger of becoming worse in a more active and worldly profession, where he would have had less time and obligation— where he might have escaped that knowledge of himself, the frequency, at least, of that knowledge which it is impossible he should escape as he is now. A man— a sensible man like Dr. Grant, cannot be in the habit of teaching others their duty every week, cannot go to church twice every Sunday, and preach such very good sermons in so good a manner as he does, without being the better for it himself. It must make him think; and I have no doubt that he oftener endeavours to restrain himself than he would if he had been anything but a clergyman."

"We cannot prove to the contrary, to be sure; but I wish you a better fate, Miss Price, than to be the wife of a man whose amiableness depends upon his own sermons; for though he may preach himself into a good-humour every Sunday, it will be bad enough to have him quarrelling about green geese from Monday morning till Saturday night."

"I think the man who could often quarrel with Fanny," said Edmund affectionately, "must be beyond the reach of any sermons." Fanny turned farther into the window; and Miss Crawford had only time to say, in a pleasant manner, "I fancy Miss Price has been more used to deserve praise than to hear it"; when, being earnestly invited by the Miss Bertrams to join in a glee, she tripped off to the instrument, leaving Edmund looking after her in an ecstasy of admiration of all her many virtues, from her obliging manners down to her light and graceful tread.

"There goes good-humour, I am sure," said he presently. "There goes a temper which would never give pain! How well she walks! and how readily she falls in with the inclination of others! joining them the moment she is asked. What a pity," he added, after an instant's reflection, "that she should have been in such hands!"

Fanny agreed to it, and had the pleasure of seeing him

continue at the window with her, in spite of the expected glee; and of having his eyes soon turned, like hers, towards the scene without, where all that was solemn, and soothing, and lovely, appeared in the brilliancy of an unclouded night, and the contrast of the deep shade of the woods. Fanny spoke her feelings. "Here's harmony!" said she; "here's repose! Here's what may leave all painting and all music behind, and what poetry only can attempt to describe! Here's what may tranquillise every care, and lift the heart to rapture! When I look out on such a night as this, I feel as if there could be neither wickedness nor sorrow in the world; and there certainly would be less of both if the sublimity of Nature were more attended to, and people were carried more out of themselves by contemplating such a scene."

"I like to hear your enthusiasm, Fanny. It is a lovely night, and they are much to be pitied who have not been taught to feel, in some degree, as you do; who have not, at least, been given a taste for Nature in early life. They lose a great deal."

"Youtaught me to think and feel on the subject, cousin."

"I had a very apt scholar. There's Arcturus looking very bright." "Yes, and the Bear. I wish I could see Cassiopeia."

"We must go out on the lawn for that. Should you be afraid?" "Not in the least. It is a great while since we have had any star-gazing."

"Yes; I do not know how it has happened." The glee began. "We will stay till this is finished, Fanny," said he, turning his back on the window; and as it advanced, she had the mortification of seeing him advance too, moving forward by gentle degrees towards the instrument, and when it ceased, he was close by the singers, among the most urgent in requesting to hear the glee again. Fanny sighed alone at the window till scolded away by Mrs. Norris's threats of catching cold.

Chapter XII

Sir Thomas was to return in November, and his eldest son had duties to call him earlier home. The approach of September brought tidings of Mr. Bertram, first in a letter to the gamekeeper and then in a letter to Edmund; and by the end of August he arrived himself, to be gay, agreeable, and gallant again as occasion served, or Miss Crawford demanded; to tell of races and Weymouth, and parties and friends, to which she might have listened six weeks before with some interest, and altogether to give her the fullest conviction, by the power of actual comparison, of her preferring his younger brother.

It was very vexatious, and she was heartily sorry for it; but so it was; and so far from now meaning to marry the elder, she did not even want to attract him beyond what the simplest claims of conscious beauty required: his lengthened absence from Mansfield, without anything but pleasure in view, and his own will to consult, made it perfectly clear that he did not care about her; and his indifference was so much more than equalled by her own, that were he now to step forth the owner of Mansfield Park, the Sir Thomas complete, which he was to be in time, she did not believe she could accept him.

The season and duties which brought Mr. Bertram back to Mansfield took Mr. Crawford into Norfolk. Everingham could not do without him in the beginning of September. He went for a fortnight—a fortnight of such dullness to the Miss Bertrams as ought to have put them both on their guard, and made even Julia admit, in her jealousy of her sister, the absolute necessity of distrusting his attentions, and wishing him not to return; and a fortnight of sufficient leisure, in the intervals of shooting and sleeping, to have convinced the gentleman that he ought to keep longer away, had he been more in the habit of examining his own motives, and of reflecting to what the indulgence of his idle vanity was tending; but, thoughtless and selfish from prosperity and bad example, he would not look beyond the present moment. The sisters, handsome, clever, and encouraging, were an amusement to his sated mind; and finding nothing in Norfolk to equal the social pleasures of Mansfield, he gladly returned to it at the time appointed, and was welcomed thither quite as gladly by those whom he came to trifle with further.

Maria, with only Mr. Rushworth to attend to her, and doomed to the repeated details of his day's sport, good or bad, his boast of his dogs, his jealousy of his neighbours, his doubts of their qualifications, and his zeal after poachers, subjects which will not find their way to female feelings without some talent on one side or some attachment on the other, had missed Mr. Crawford grievously; and Julia, unengaged and unemployed, felt all the right of missing him much more. Each sister believed herself the favourite. Julia might be justified in so doing by the hints of Mrs. Grant, inclined to credit what she wished, and Maria by the hints of Mr. Crawford himself. Everything returned into the same channel as before his absence; his manners being to each so animated and agreeable as to lose no ground with either, and just stopping short of the consistence, the steadiness, the solicitude, and the warmth which might excite general notice.

Fanny was the only one of the party who found anything to dislike; but since the day at Sotherton, she could never see Mr. Crawford with either sister without observation, and seldom without wonder or censure; and had her confidence in her own judgment been equal to her exercise of it in every other respect, had she been sure that she was seeing clearly, and judging candidly, she would probably have made some important communications to her usual confidant. As it was, however, she only hazarded a hint, and the hint was lost. "I am rather surprised," said she, "that Mr. Crawford should come back again so soon, after being here so long before, full seven weeks; for I had understood he was so very fond of change and moving about, that I thought something would certainly occur, when he was once gone, to take him elsewhere. He is used to much gayer places than Mansfield."

"It is to his credit," was Edmund's answer; "and I dare say it gives his sister pleasure. She does not like his unsettled habits.""What a favourite he is with my cousins!"

"Yes, his manners to women are such as must please. Mrs. Grant, I believe, suspects him of a preference for Julia; I have never seen much symptom of it, but I wish it may be so. He has no faults but what a serious attachment would remove." "If Miss Bertram were not engaged," said Fanny cautiously, "I could sometimes almost think that he admired her more than Julia." "Which is, perhaps, more in favour of his liking Julia best, than you, Fanny, may be aware; for I believe it often happens that a man, before he has quite made up his own mind, will distinguish the sister or intimate friend of the woman he is really thinking of more than the woman herself Crawford has too much sense to stay here if he found himself in any danger from Maria; and I am not at all afraid for her, after such a proof as she has given that her feelings are not strong." Fanny supposed she must have been mistaken, and meant to think differently in future; but with all that submission to Edmund could do, and all the help of the coinciding looks and hints which she occasionally noticed in some of the others, and which seemed to say that Julia was Mr. Crawford's choice, she knew not always what to think.

She was privy, one evening, to the hopes of her aunt Norris on the subject, as well as to her feelings, and the feelings of Mrs. Rushworth, on a point of some similarity, and could not help wondering as she listened; and glad would she have been not to be obliged to listen, for it was while all the other young people were dancing, and she sitting, most unwillingly, among the chaperons at the fire, longing for the re-entrance of her elder cousin, on whom all her own hopes of a partner then depended. It was Fanny's first ball, though without the preparation or splendour of many a young lady's first ball, being the thought only of the afternoon, built on the late acquisition of a violin player in the servants' hall, and the possibility of raising five couple with the help of Mrs. Grant and a new intimate friend of Mr. Bertram's just arrived on a visit. It had, however, been a very happy one to Fanny through four dances, and she was quite grieved to be losing even a quarter of an hour. While waiting and wishing, looking now at the dancers and now at the door, this dialogue between the two above-mentioned ladies was forced on her—

"I think, ma'am," said Mrs. Norris, her eyes directed towards Mr. Rushworth and Maria, who were partners for the second time, "we shall see some happy faces again now."

"Yes, ma'am, indeed," replied the other, with a stately simper, "there will be some satisfaction in looking on now, and I think it was rather a pity they should have been obliged to part. Young folks in their situation should be excused complying with the common forms. I wonder my son did not propose it." "I dare say he did, ma'am. Mr. Rushworth is never remiss. But dear Maria has such a strict sense of propriety, so much of that true delicacy which one seldom meets with nowadays, Mrs. Rushworth—that wish of avoiding particularity! Dear ma'am, only look at her face at this moment; how different from what it was the two last dances!"

Miss Bertram did indeed look happy, her eyes were sparkling with pleasure, and she was speaking with great animation, for Julia and her partner, Mr. Crawford, were close to her; they were all in a cluster together. How she had looked before, Fanny could not recollect, for she had been dancing with Edmund herself, and had not thought about her.

Mrs. Norris continued, "It is quite delightful, ma'am, to see young people so properly happy, so well suited, and so much the thing! I cannot but think of dear Sir Thomas's delight. And what do you say, ma'am, to the chance of another match? Mr. Rushworth has set a good example, and such things are very catching." Mrs. Rushworth, who saw nothing but her son, was quite at a loss. "The couple above, ma'am. Do you see no symptoms there?" "Oh dear! Miss Julia and Mr. Crawford. Yes, indeed, a very pretty match. What is his property?" "Four thousand a year."

"Very well. Those who have not more must be satisfied with what they have. Four thousand a year is a pretty estate, and he seems a very genteel, steady young man, so I hope Miss Julia will be very happy."

"It is not a settled thing, ma'am, yet. We only speak of it among friends. But I have very little doubt it willbe. He is growing extremely particular in his attentions."

Fanny could listen no farther. Listening and wondering were all suspended for a time, for Mr. Bertram was in the room again; and though feeling it would be a great honour to be asked by him, she thought it must happen. He came towards their little circle; but instead of asking her to dance, drew a chair near her, and gave her an account of the present state of a sick horse, and the opinion of the groom, from whom he had just parted. Fanny found that it was not to be, and in the modesty of her nature immediately felt that she had been unreasonable in expecting it. When he had told of his horse, he took a newspaper from the table, and looking over it, said in a languid way, "If you want to dance, Fanny, I will stand up with you." With more than equal civility the offer was declined; she did not wish to dance. "I am glad of it," said he, in a much brisker tone, and throwing down the newspaper again, "for I am tired to death. I only wonder how the good people can keep it up so long. They had need be allin love, to find any amusement in such folly; and so they are, I fancy. If you look at them you may see they are so many couple of lovers—all but Yates and Mrs. Grant—and, between ourselves, she, poor woman, must want a lover as much as any one of them.

A desperate dull life hers must be with the doctor," making a sly face as he spoke towards the chair of the latter, who proving, however, to be close at his elbow, made so instantaneous a change of expression and subject necessary, as Fanny, in spite of everything, could hardly help laughing at. "A strange business this in America, Dr. Grant! What is your opinion? I always come to you to know what I am to think of public matters."

"My dear Tom," cried his aunt soon afterwards, "as you are not dancing, I dare say you will have no objection to join us in a rubber; shall you?" Then leaving her seat, and coming to him to enforce the proposal, added in a whisper, "We want to make a table for Mrs. Rushworth, you know. Your mother is quite anxious about it, but cannot very well spare time to sit down herself, because of her fringe. Now, you and I and Dr. Grant will just do; and though weplay but half-crowns, you know, you may bet half-guineas with him."

"I should be most happy," replied he aloud, and jumping up with alacrity, "it would give me the greatest pleasure; but that I am this moment going to dance." Come, Fanny, taking her hand, "do not be dawdling any longer, or the dance will be over."

Fanny was led off very willingly, though it was impossible for her to feel much gratitude towards her cousin, or distinguish, as he certainly did, between the selfishness of another person and his own. "A pretty modest request upon my word," he indignantly exclaimed as they walked away. "To want to nail me to a card-table for the next two hours with herself and Dr. Grant, who are always quarrelling, and that poking old woman, who knows no more of whist than of algebra. I wish my good aunt would be a little less busy! And to ask me in such a way too! without ceremony, before them all, so as to leave me no possibility of refusing. Thatis what I dislike most particularly. It raises my spleen more than anything, to have the pretence of being asked, of being given a choice, and at the same time addressed in such a way as to oblige one to do the very thing, whatever it be! If I had not luckily thought of standing up with you I could not have got out of it. It is a great deal too bad. But when my aunt has got a fancy in her head, nothing can stop her."

Chapter XIII

The Honourable John Yates, this new friend, had not much to recommend him beyond habits of fashion and expense, and being the younger son of a lord with a tolerable independence; and Sir Thomas would probably have thought his introduction at Mansfield by no means desirable. Mr. Bertram's acquaintance with him had begun at Weymouth, where they had spent ten days together in the same society, and the friendship, if friendship it might be called, had been proved and perfected by Mr. Yates's being invited to take Mansfield in his way, whenever he could, and by his promising to come; and he did come rather earlier than had been expected, in consequence of the sudden breaking-up of a large party assembled for gaiety at the house of another friend, which he had left Weymouth to join.

He came on the wings of disappointment, and with his head full of acting, for it had been a theatrical party; and the play in which he had borne a part was within two days of representation, when the sudden death of one of the nearest connexions of the family had destroyed the scheme and dispersed the performers. To be so near happiness, so near fame, so near the long paragraph in praise of the private theatricals at Ecclesford, the seat of the Right Hon. Lord Ravenshaw, in Cornwall, which would of course have immortalised the whole party for at least a twelvemonth! and being so near, to lose it all, was an injury to be keenly felt, and Mr. Yates could talk of nothing else. Ecclesford and its theatre, with its arrangements and dresses, rehearsals and jokes, was his never-failing subject, and to boast of the past his only consolation.

Happily for him, a love of the theatre is so general, an itch for acting so strong among young people, that he could hardly out-talk the interest of his hearers. From the first casting of the parts to the epilogue it was all bewitching, and there were few who did not wish to have been a party concerned, or would have hesitated to try their skill. The play had been Lovers' Vows, and Mr. Yates was to have been Count Cassel. "A trifling part," said he, "and not at all to my taste, and such a one as I certainly would not accept again; but I was determined to make no difficulties. Lord Ravenshaw and the duke had appropriated the only two characters worth playing before I reached Ecclesford; and though Lord Ravenshaw offered to resign his to me, it was impossible to take it, you know. I was sorry for himthat he should have so mistaken his powers, for he was no more equal to the Baron—a little man with a weak voice, always hoarse after the first ten minutes. It must have injured the piece materially; but Iwas resolved to make no difficulties.

Sir Henry thought the duke not equal to Frederick, but that was because Sir Henry wanted the part himself; whereas it was certainly in the best hands of the two. I was surprised to see Sir Henry such a stick. Luckily the strength of the piece did not depend upon him. Our Agatha was inimitable, and the duke was thought very great by many. And upon the whole, it would certainly have gone off wonderfully."

"It was a hard case, upon my word"; and, "I do think you were very much to be pitied," were the kind responses of listening sympathy. "It is not worth complaining about; but to be sure the poor old dowager could not have died at a worse time; and it is impossible to help wishing that the news could have been suppressed for just the three days we wanted. It was but three days; and being only a grandmother, and all happening two hundred miles off, I think there would have been no great harm, and it was suggested, I know; but Lord Ravenshaw, who I suppose is one of the most correct men in England, would not hear of it." "An afterpiece instead of a comedy," said Mr. Bertram. "Lovers' Vows were at an end, and Lord and Lady Ravenshaw left to act My Grandmother by themselves. Well, the jointure may comfort him; and perhaps, between friends, he began to tremble for his credit and his lungs in the Baron, and was not sorry to withdraw; and to make youamends, Yates, I think we must raise a little theatre at Mansfield, and ask you to be our manager." This, though the thought of the moment, did not end with the moment; for the inclination to act was awakened, and in no one more strongly than in him who was now master of the house; and who, having so much leisure as to make almost any novelty a certain good, had likewise such a degree of lively talents and comic taste, as were exactly adapted to the novelty of acting. The thought returned again and again. "Oh for the Ecclesford theatre and scenery to try something with." Each sister could echo the wish; and Henry Crawford, to whom, in all the riot of his gratifications it was yet an untasted pleasure, was quite alive at the idea.

"I really believe," said he, "I could be fool enough at this moment to undertake any character that ever was written, from Shylock or Richard III down to the singing hero of a farce in his scarlet coat and cocked hat. I feel as if I could be anything or everything; as if I could rant and storm, or sigh or cut capers, in any tragedy or comedy in the English language. Let us be doing something. Be it only half a play, an act, a scene; what should prevent us? Not these countenances, I am sure," looking towards the Miss Bertrams; "and for a theatre, what signifies a theatre? We shall be only amusing ourselves. Any room in this house might suffice."

"We must have a curtain," said Tom Bertram; "a few yards of green baize for a curtain, and perhaps that may be enough."

"Oh, quite enough," cried Mr. Yates, "with only just a side wing or two run up, doors in flat, and three or four scenes to be let down; nothing more would be necessary on such a plan as this. For mere amusement among ourselves we should want nothing more."

"I believe we must be satisfied with less," said Maria. "There would not be time, and other difficulties would arise. We must rather adopt Mr. Crawford's views, and make the performance, not the theatre, our object. Many parts of our best plays are independent of scenery."

"Nay," said Edmund, who began to listen with alarm. "Let us do nothing by halves. If we are to act, let it be in a theatre completely fitted up with pit, boxes, and gallery, and let us have a play entire from beginning to end; so as it be a German play, no matter what, with a good tricking, shifting afterpiece, and a figure-dance, and a hornpipe, and a song between the acts. If we do not outdo Ecclesford, we do nothing."

"Now, Edmund, do not be disagreeable," said Julia. "Nobody loves a play better than you do, or can have gone much farther to see one." "True, to see real acting, good hardened real acting; but I would hardly walk from this room to the next to look at the raw efforts of those who have not been bred to the trade: a set of gentlemen and ladies, who have all the disadvantages of education and decorum to struggle through." After a short pause, however, the subject still continued, and was discussed with unabated eagerness, every one's inclination increasing by the discussion, and a knowledge of the inclination of the rest; and though nothing was settled but that Tom Bertram would prefer a comedy, and his sisters and Henry Crawford a tragedy, and that nothing in the world could be easier than to find a piece which would please them all, the resolution to act something or other seemed so decided as to make Edmund quite uncomfortable. He was determined to prevent it, if possible, though his mother, who equally heard the conversation which passed at table, did not evince the least disapprobation.

The same evening afforded him an opportunity of trying his strength. Maria, Julia, Henry Crawford, and Mr. Yates were in the billiard-room. Tom, returning from them into the drawing-room, where Edmund was standing thoughtfully by the fire, while Lady Bertram was on the sofa at a little distance, and Fanny close beside her arranging her work, thus began as he entered—"Such a horribly vile billiard-table as ours is not to be met with, I believe, above ground. I can stand it no longer, and I think, I may say, that nothing shall ever tempt me to it again; but one good thing I have just ascertained: it is the very room for a theatre, precisely the shape and length for it; and the doors at the farther end, communicating with each other, as they may be made to do in five minutes, by merely moving the bookcase in my father's room, is the very thing we could have desired, if we had sat down to wish for it; and my father's room will be an excellent greenroom. It seems to join the billiard-room on purpose." "You are not serious, Tom, in meaning to act?" said Edmund, in a low voice, as his brother approached the fire. "Not serious! never more so, I assure you. What is there to surprise you in it?"

"I think it would be very wrong. In a generallight, private theatricals are open to some objections, but as weare circumstanced, I must think it would be highly injudicious, and more than injudicious to attempt anything of the kind. It would shew great want of feeling on my father's account, absent as he is, and in some degree of constant danger; and it would be imprudent, I think, with regard to Maria, whose situation is a very delicate one, considering everything, extremely delicate."

"You take up a thing so seriously! as if we were going to act three times a week till my father's return, and invite all the country. But it is not to be a display of that sort. We mean nothing but a little amusement among ourselves, just to vary the scene, and exercise our powers in something new. We want no audience, no publicity. We may be trusted, I think, in chusing some play most perfectly unexceptionable; and I can conceive no greater harm or danger to any of us in conversing in the elegant written language of some respectable author than in chattering in words of our own. I have no fears and no scruples. And as to my father's being absent, it is so far from an objection, that I consider it rather as a motive; for the expectation of his return must be a very anxious period to my mother; and if we can be the means of amusing that anxiety, and keeping up her spirits for the next few weeks, I shall think our time very well spent, and so, I am sure, will he. It is a veryanxious period for her."

As he said this, each looked towards their mother. Lady Bertram, sunk back in one corner of the sofa, the picture of health, wealth, ease, and tranquillity, was just falling into a gentle doze, while Fanny was getting through the few difficulties of her work for her. Edmund smiled and shook his head. "By Jove! this won't do," cried Tom, throwing himself into a chair with a hearty laugh. "To be sure, my dear mother, your anxiety—I was unlucky there."

"What is the matter?" asked her ladyship, in the heavy tone of one half-roused; "I was not asleep."

"Oh dear, no, ma'am, nobody suspected you! Well, Edmund," he continued, returning to the former subject, posture, and voice, as soon as Lady Bertram began to nod again, "but thisI willmaintain, that we shall be doing no harm."

"I cannot agree with you; I am convinced that my father would totally disapprove it."

"And I am convinced to the contrary. Nobody is fonder of the exercise of talent in young people, or promotes it more, than my father, and for anything of the acting, spouting, reciting kind, I think he has always a decided taste. I am sure he encouraged it in us as boys. How many a time have we mourned over the dead body of Julius Caesar, and to be'dand not tobe'd, in this very room, for his amusement? And I am sure, mynamewasNorval, every evening of my life through one Christmas holidays."

"It was a very different thing. You must see the difference yourself. My father wished us, as schoolboys, to speak well, but he would never wish his grown-up daughters to be acting plays. His sense of decorum is strict."

"I know all that," said Tom, displeased. "I know my father

as well as you do; and I'll take care that his daughters do nothing to distress him. Manage your own concerns, Edmund, and I'll take care of the rest of the family."

"If you are resolved on acting," replied the persevering Edmund, "I must hope it will be in a very small and quiet way; and I think a theatre ought not to be attempted. It would be taking liberties with my father's house in his absence which could not be justified."

"For everything of that nature I will be answerable," said Tom, in a decided tone. "His house shall not be hurt. I have quite as great an interest in being careful of his house as you can have; and as to such alterations as I was suggesting just now, such as moving a bookcase, or unlocking a door, or even as using the billiard-room for the space of a week without playing at billiards in it, you might just as well suppose he would object to our sitting more in this room, and less in the breakfast-room, than we did before he went away, or to my sister's pianoforte being moved from one side of the room to the other. Absolute nonsense!"

"The innovation, if not wrong as an innovation, will be wrong as an expense." "Yes, the expense of such an undertaking would be prodigious! Perhaps it might cost a whole twenty pounds. Something of a theatre we must have undoubtedly, but it will be on the simplest plan: a green curtain and a little carpenter's work, and that's all; and as the carpenter's work may be all done at home by Christopher Jackson himself, it will be too absurd to talk of expense; and as long as Jackson is employed, everything will be right with Sir Thomas. Don't imagine that nobody in this house can see or judge but yourself.

Don't act yourself, if you do not like it, but don't expect to govern everybody else." "No, as to acting myself," said Edmund, "thatI absolutely protest against." Tom walked out of the room as he said it, and Edmund was left to sit down and stir the fire in thoughtful vexation. Fanny, who had heard it all, and borne Edmund company in every feeling throughout the whole, now ventured to say, in her anxiety to suggest some comfort, "Perhaps they may not be able to find any play to suit them. Your brother's taste and your sisters' seem very different." "I have no hope there, Fanny. If they persist in the scheme, they will find something. I shall speak to my sisters and try to dissuade them, and that is all I can do." "I should think my aunt Norris would be on your side."

"I dare say she would, but she has no influence with either Tom or my sisters that could be of any use; and if I cannot convince them myself, I shall let things take their course, without attempting it through her. Family squabbling is the greatest evil of all, and we had better do anything than be altogether by the ears."

His sisters, to whom he had an opportunity of speaking the next morning, were quite as impatient of his advice, quite as unyielding to his representation, quite as determined in the cause of pleasure, as Tom. Their mother had no objection to the plan, and they were not in the least afraid of their father's disapprobation. There could be no harm in what had been done in so many respectable families, and by so many women of the first consideration; and it must be scrupulousness run mad that could see anything to censure in a plan like theirs, comprehending only brothers and sisters and intimate friends, and which would never be heard of beyond themselves.

Julia didseem inclined to admit that Maria's situation might require particular caution and delicacy—but that could not extend to her— she was at liberty; and Maria evidently considered her engagement as only raising her so much more above restraint, and leaving her less occasion than Julia to consult either father or mother. Edmund had little to hope, but he was still urging the subject when Henry Crawford entered the room, fresh from the Parsonage, calling out, "No want of hands in our theatre, Miss Bertram. No want of understrappers: my sister desires her love, and hopes to be admitted into the company, and will be happy to take the part of any old duenna or tame confidante, that you may not like to do yourselves."

Maria gave Edmund a glance, which meant, "What say you now? Can we be wrong if Mary Crawford feels the same?" And Edmund, silenced, was obliged to acknowledge that the charm of acting might well carry fascination to the mind of genius; and with the ingenuity of love, to dwell more on the obliging, accommodating purport of the message than on anything else. The scheme advanced. Opposition was vain; and as to Mrs. Norris, he was mistaken in supposing she would wish to make any. She started no difficulties that were not talked down in five minutes by her eldest nephew and niece, who were all-powerful with her; and as the whole arrangement was to bring very little expense to anybody, and none at all to herself, as she foresaw in it all the comforts of hurry, bustle, and importance, and derived the immediate advantage of fancying herself obliged to leave her own house, where she had been living a month at her own cost, and take up her abode in theirs, that every hour might be spent in their service, she was, in fact, exceedingly delighted with the project.

Chapter XXIII

"But why should Mrs. Grant ask Fanny?" said Lady Bertram. "How came she to think of asking Fanny? Fanny never dines there, you know, in this sort of way. I cannot spare her, and I am sure she does not want to go. Fanny, you do not want to go, do you?"

"If you put such a question to her," cried Edmund, preventing his cousin's speaking, "Fanny will immediately say No; but I am sure, my dear mother, she would like to go; and I can see no reason why she should not."

"I cannot imagine why Mrs. Grant should think of asking her? She never did before. She used to ask your sisters now and then, but she never asked Fanny."

"If you cannot do without me, ma'am—" said Fanny, in a self-denying tone."But my mother will have my father with her all the evening."

"To be sure, so I shall."

"Suppose you take my father's opinion, ma'am."

"That's well thought of. So I will, Edmund. I will ask Sir Thomas, as soon as he comes in, whether I can do without her."

"As you please, ma'am, on that head; but I meant my father's opinion as to the proprietyof the invitation's being accepted or not; and I think he will consider it a right thing by Mrs. Grant, as well as by Fanny, that being the firstinvitation it should be accepted."

"I do not know. We will ask him. But he will be very much surprised that Mrs. Grant should ask Fanny at all." There was nothing more to be said, or that could be said to any purpose, till Sir Thomas were present; but the subject involving, as it did, her own evening's comfort for the morrow, was so much uppermost in Lady Bertram's mind, that half an hour afterwards, on his looking in for a minute in his way from his plantation to his dressing-room, she called him back again, when he had almost closed the door, with "Sir Thomas, stop a moment—I have something to say to you."

Her tone of calm languor, for she never took the trouble of raising her voice, was always heard and attended to; and Sir Thomas came back. Her story began; and Fanny immediately slipped out of the room; for to hear herself the subject of any discussion with her uncle was more than her nerves could bear. She was anxious, she knew— more anxious perhaps than she ought to be—for what was it after all whether she went or staid? but if her uncle were to be a great while considering and deciding, and with very grave looks, and those grave looks directed to her, and at last decide against her, she might not be able to appear properly submissive and indifferent. Her cause, meanwhile, went on well. It began, on Lady Bertram's part, with—"I have something to tell you that will surprise you. Mrs. Grant has asked Fanny to dinner."

"Well," said Sir Thomas, as if waiting more to accomplish the surprise. "Edmund wants her to go. But how can I spare her?" "She will be late," said Sir Thomas, taking out his watch; "but what is your difficulty?"

Edmund found himself obliged to speak and fill up the blanks in his mother's story. He told the whole; and she had only to add, "So strange! for Mrs. Grant never used to ask her."

"But is it not very natural," observed Edmund, "that Mrs. Grant should wish to procure so agreeable a visitor for her sister?"

"Nothing can be more natural," said Sir Thomas, after a

short deliberation; "nor, were there no sister in the case, could anything, in my opinion, be more natural. Mrs. Grant's shewing civility to Miss Price, to Lady Bertram's niece, could never want explanation. The only surprise I can feel is, that this should be the firsttime of its being paid. Fanny was perfectly right in giving only a conditional answer. She appears to feel as she ought. But as I conclude that she must wish to go, since all young people like to be together, I can see no reason why she should be denied the indulgence."

"But can I do without her, Sir Thomas?"

"Indeed I think you may."

"She always makes tea, you know, when my sister is not here." "Your sister, perhaps, may be prevailed on to spend the day with us, and I shall certainly be at home."

"Very well, then, Fanny may go, Edmund."

The good news soon followed her. Edmund knocked at her door in his way to his own.

"Well, Fanny, it is all happily settled, and without the smallest hesitation on your uncle's side. He had but one opinion. You are to go."

"Thank you, I am soglad," was Fanny's instinctive reply; though when she had turned from him and shut the door, she could not help feeling, "And yet why should I be glad? for am I not certain of seeing or hearing something there to pain me?"

In spite of this conviction, however, she was glad. Simple as such an engagement might appear in other eyes, it had novelty and importance in hers, for excepting the day at Sotherton, she had scarcely ever dined out before; and though now going only half a mile, and only to three people, still it was dining out, and all the little interests of preparation were enjoyments in themselves. She had neither sympathy nor assistance from those who ought to have entered into her feelings and directed her taste; for Lady Bertram never thought of being useful to anybody, and Mrs. Norris, when she came on the morrow, in consequence of an early call and invitation from Sir Thomas, was in a very ill humour, and seemed intent only on lessening her niece's pleasure, both present and future, as much as possible.

"Upon my word, Fanny, you are in high luck to meet with such attention and indulgence! You ought to be very much obliged to Mrs. Grant for thinking of you, and to your aunt for letting you go, and you ought to look upon it as something extraordinary; for I hope you are aware that there is no real occasion for your going into company in this sort of way, or ever dining out at all; and it is what you must not depend upon ever being repeated. Nor must you be fancying that the invitation is meant as any particular compliment to you; the compliment is intended to your uncle and aunt and me. Mrs. Grant thinks it a civility due to usto take a little notice of you, or else it would never have come into her head, and you may be very certain that, if your cousin Julia had been at home, you would not have been asked at all."

Mrs. Norris had now so ingeniously done away all Mrs. Grant's part of the favour, that Fanny, who found herself expected to speak, could only say that she was very much obliged to her aunt Bertram for sparing her, and that she was endeavouring to put her aunt's evening work in such a state as to prevent her being missed.

"Oh! depend upon it, your aunt can do very well without you, or you would not be allowed to go. Ishall be here, so you may be quite easy about your aunt. And I hope you will have a very agreeableday, and find it all mighty delightful. But I must observe that five is the very awkwardest of all possible numbers to sit down to table; and I cannot but be surprised that such an elegantlady as Mrs. Grant should not contrive better! And round their enormous great wide table, too, which fills up the room so dreadfully! Had the doctor been contented to take my dining-table when I came away, as anybody in their senses would have done, instead of having that absurd new one of his own, which is wider, literally wider than the dinner-table here, how infinitely better it would have been! and how much more he would have been respected! for people are never respected when they step out of their proper sphere. Remember that, Fanny. Five—only five to be sitting round that table. However, you will have dinner enough on it for ten, I dare say." Mrs. Norris fetched breath, and went on again.

"The nonsense and folly of people's stepping out of their rank and trying to appear above themselves, makes me think it right to give youa hint, Fanny, now that you are going into company without any of us; and I do beseech and entreat you not to be putting yourself forward, and talking and giving your opinion as if you were one of your cousins—as if you were dear Mrs. Rushworth or Julia. Thatwill never do, believe me. Remember, wherever you are, you must be the lowest and last; and though Miss Crawford is in a manner at home at the Parsonage, you are not to be taking place of her. And as to coming away at night, you are to stay just as long as Edmund chuses. Leave him to settle that."

"Yes, ma'am, I should not think of anything else."

"And if it should rain, which I think exceedingly likely, for I never saw it more threatening for a wet evening in my life, you must manage as well as you can, and not be expecting the carriage to be sent for you. I certainly do not go home to-night, and, therefore, the carriage will not be out on my account; so you must make up your mind to what may happen, and take your things accordingly."

Her niece thought it perfectly reasonable. She rated her own claims to comfort as low even as Mrs. Norris could; and when Sir Thomas soon afterwards, just opening the door, said, "Fanny, at what time would you have the carriage come round?" she felt a degree of astonishment which made it impossible for her to speak."My dear Sir Thomas!" cried Mrs. Norris, red with anger, "Fanny can walk." "Walk!" repeated Sir Thomas, in a tone of most unanswerable dignity, and coming farther into the room. "My niece walk to a dinner engagement at this time of the year! Will twenty minutes after four suit you?"

"Yes, sir," was Fanny's humble answer, given with the feelings almost of a criminal towards Mrs. Norris; and not bearing to remain with her in what might seem a state of triumph, she followed her uncle out of the room, having staid behind him only long enough to hear these words spoken in angry agitation—

"Quite unnecessary! a great deal too kind! But Edmund

goes; true, it is upon Edmund's account. I observed he was hoarse on Thursday night."

But this could not impose on Fanny. She felt that the carriage was for herself, and herself alone: and her uncle's consideration of her, coming immediately after such representations from her aunt, cost her some tears of gratitude when she was alone.

The coachman drove round to a minute; another minute brought down the gentleman; and as the lady had, with a most scrupulous fear of being late, been many minutes seated in the drawing-room, Sir Thomas saw them off in as good time as his own correctly punctual habits required.

"Now I must look at you, Fanny," said Edmund, with the kind smile of an affectionate brother, "and tell you how I like you; and as well as I can judge by this light, you look very nicely indeed. What have you got on?"

"The new dress that my uncle was so good as to give me on my cousin's marriage. I hope it is not too fine; but I thought I ought to wear it as soon as I could, and that I might not have such another opportunity all the winter. I hope you do not think me too fine."

"A woman can never be too fine while she is all in white. No, I see no finery about you; nothing but what is perfectly proper. Your gown seems very pretty. I like these glossy spots. Has not Miss Crawford a gown something the same?"

In approaching the Parsonage they passed close by the stable-yard and coach-house.

"Heyday!" said Edmund, "here's company, here's a carriage! who have they got to meet us?" And letting down the side-glass to distinguish, "'Tis Crawford's, Crawford's barouche, I protest! There are his own two men pushing it back into its old quarters. He is here, of course. This is quite a surprise, Fanny. I shall be very glad to see him."

There was no occasion, there was no time for Fanny to say how very differently she felt; but the idea of having such another to observe her was a great increase of the trepidation with which she performed the very awful ceremony of walking into the drawing-room.

In the drawing-room Mr. Crawford certainly was, having been just long enough arrived to be ready for dinner; and the smiles and pleased looks of the three others standing round him, shewed how welcome was his sudden resolution of coming to them for a few days on leaving Bath. A very cordial meeting passed between him and Edmund; and with the exception of Fanny, the pleasure was general; and even to herthere might be some advantage in his presence, since every addition to the party must rather forward her favourite indulgence of being suffered to sit silent and unattended to. She was soon aware of this herself; for though she must submit, as her own propriety of mind directed, in spite of her aunt Norris's opinion, to being the principal lady in company, and to all the little distinctions consequent thereon, she found, while they were at table, such a happy flow of conversation prevailing, in which she was not required to take any part—there was so much to be said between the brother and sister about Bath, so much between the two young men about hunting, so much of politics between Mr. Crawford and Dr. Grant, and of everything and all together between Mr. Crawford and Mrs. Grant, as to leave her the fairest prospect of having only to listen in quiet, and of passing a very agreeable day. She could not compliment the newly arrived gentleman, however, with any appearance of interest, in a scheme for extending his stay at Mansfield, and sending for his hunters from Norfolk, which, suggested by Dr. Grant, advised by Edmund, and warmly urged by the two sisters, was soon in possession of his mind, and which he seemed to want to be encouraged even by her to resolve on. Her opinion was sought as to the probable continuance of the open weather, but her answers were as short and indifferent as civility allowed. She could not wish him to stay, and would much rather not have him speak to her.

Her two absent cousins, especially Maria, were much in her thoughts on seeing him; but no embarrassing remembrance affected hisspirits. Here he was again on the same ground where all had passed before, and apparently as willing to stay and be happy without the Miss Bertrams, as if he had never known Mansfield in any other state. She heard them spoken of by him only in a general way, till they were all re-assembled in the drawing-room, when Edmund, being engaged apart in some matter of business with Dr. Grant, which seemed entirely to engross them, and Mrs. Grant occupied at the tea-table, he began talking of them with more particularity to his other sister. With a significant smile, which made Fanny quite hate him, he said, "So! Rushworth and his fair bride are at Brighton, I understand; happy man!"

"Yes, they have been there about a fortnight, Miss Price, have they not? And Julia is with them."

"And Mr. Yates, I presume, is not far off."

"Mr. Yates! Oh! we hear nothing of Mr. Yates. I do not imagine he figures much in the letters to Mansfield Park; do you, Miss Price? I think my friend Julia knows better than to entertain her father with Mr. Yates."

"Poor Rushworth and his two-and-forty speeches!" continued Crawford. "Nobody can ever forget them. Poor fellow! I see him now—his toil and his despair. Well, I am much mistaken if his lovely Maria will ever want him to make two-and-forty speeches to her"; adding, with a momentary seriousness, "She is too good for him— much too good." And then changing his tone again to one of gentle gallantry, and addressing Fanny, he said, "You were Mr. Rushworth's best friend. Your kindness and patience can never be forgotten, your indefatigable patience in trying to make it possible for him to learn his part— in trying to give him a brain which nature had denied— to mix up an understanding for him out of the superfluity of your own! Hemight not have sense enough himself to estimate your kindness, but I may venture to say that it had honour from all the rest of the party." Fanny coloured, and said nothing.

"It is as a dream, a pleasant dream!" he exclaimed, breaking forth again, after a few minutes' musing. "I shall always look back on our theatricals with exquisite pleasure. There was such an interest, such an animation, such a spirit diffused. Everybody felt it. We were all alive. There was employment, hope, solicitude, bustle, for every hour of the day.

Always some little objection, some little doubt, some little anxiety to be got over. I never was happier."

With silent indignation Fanny repeated to herself, "Never happier!—never happier than when doing what you must know was not justifiable!—never happier than when behaving so dishonourably and unfeelingly! Oh! what a corrupted mind!" "We were unlucky, Miss Price," he continued, in a lower tone, to avoid the possibility of being heard by Edmund, and not at all aware of her feelings, "we certainly were very unlucky. Another week, only one other week, would have been enough for us. I think if we had had the disposal of events—if Mansfield Park had had the government of the winds just for a week or two, about the equinox, there would have been a difference. Not that we would have endangered his safety by any tremendous weather— but only by a steady contrary wind, or a calm. I think, Miss Price, we would have indulged ourselves with a week's calm in the Atlantic at that season."

He seemed determined to be answered; and Fanny, averting her face, said, with a firmer tone than usual, "As far as Iam concerned, sir, I would not have delayed his return for a day. My uncle disapproved it all so entirely when he did arrive, that in my opinion everything had gone quite far enough." She had never spoken so much at once to him in her life before, and never so angrily to any one; and when her speech was over, she trembled and blushed at her own daring. He was surprised; but after a few moments' silent consideration of her, replied in a calmer, graver tone, and as if the candid result of conviction, "I believe you are right. It was more pleasant than prudent. We were getting too noisy." And then turning the conversation, he would have engaged her on some other subject, but her answers were so shy and reluctant that he could not advance in any. Miss Crawford, who had been repeatedly eyeing Dr. Grant and Edmund, now observed, "Those gentlemen must have some very interesting point to discuss."

"The most interesting in the world," replied her brother—"how to make money; how to turn a good income into a better. Dr. Grant is giving Bertram instructions about the living he is to step into so soon. I find he takes orders in a few weeks. They were at it in the dining-parlour. I am glad to hear Bertram will be so well off. He will have a very pretty income to make ducks and drakes with, and earned without much trouble. I apprehend he will not have less than seven hundred a year. Seven hundred a year is a fine thing for a younger brother; and as of course he will still live at home, it will be all for his menusplaisirs; and a sermon at Christmas and Easter, I suppose, will be the sum total of sacrifice."

His sister tried to laugh off her feelings by saying, "Nothing amuses me more than the easy manner with which everybody settles the abundance of those who have a great deal less than themselves. You would look rather blank, Henry, if your menusplaisirswere to be limited to seven hundred a year." "Perhaps I might; but all thatyou know is entirely comparative. Birthright and habit must settle the business. Bertram is certainly well off for a cadet of even a baronet's family. By the time he is four or five and twenty he will have seven hundred a year, and nothing to do for it."

Miss Crawford couldhave said that there would be a something to do and to suffer for it, which she could not think lightly of; but she checked herself and let it pass; and tried to look calm and unconcerned when the two gentlemen shortly afterwards joined them. "Bertram," said Henry Crawford, "I shall make a point of coming to Mansfield to hear you preach your first sermon. I shall come on purpose to encourage a young beginner. When is it to be? Miss Price, will not you join me in encouraging your cousin? Will not you engage to attend with your eyes steadily fixed on him the whole time— as I shall do—not to lose a word; or only looking off just to note down any sentence preeminently beautiful? We will provide ourselves with tablets and a pencil. When will it be? You must preach at Mansfield, you know, that Sir Thomas and Lady Bertram may hear you."

"I shall keep clear of you, Crawford, as long as I can," said Edmund; "for you would be more likely to disconcert me, and I should be more sorry to see you trying at it than almost any other man."

"Will he not feel this?" thought Fanny. "No, he can feel nothing as he ought."

The party being now all united, and the chief talkers attracting each other, she remained in tranquillity; and as a whist-table was formed after tea—formed really for the amusement of Dr. Grant, by his attentive wife, though it was not to be supposed so—and Miss Crawford took her harp, she had nothing to do but to listen; and her tranquillity remained undisturbed the rest of the evening, except when Mr. Crawford now and then addressed to her a question or observation, which she could not avoid answering. Miss Crawford was too much vexed by what had passed to be in a humour for anything but music. With that she soothed herself and amused her friend.

The assurance of Edmund's being so soon to take orders, coming upon her like a blow that had been suspended, and still hoped uncertain and at a distance, was felt with resentment and mortification. She was very angry with him. She had thought her influence more. She hadbegun to think of him; she felt that she had, with great regard, with almost decided intentions; but she would now meet him with his own cool feelings. It was plain that he could have no serious views, no true attachment, by fixing himself in a situation which he must know she would never stoop to. She would learn to match him in his indifference: She would henceforth admit his attentions without any idea beyond immediate amusement. If hecould so command his affections, hersshould do her no harm.

Chapter XLV

At about the week's end from his return to Mansfield, Tom's immediate danger was over, and he was so far pronounced safe as to make his mother perfectly easy; for being now used to the sight of him in his suffering, helpless state, and hearing only the best, and never thinking beyond what she heard, with no disposition for alarm and no aptitude at a hint, Lady Bertram was the happiest subject in the world for a little medical imposition. The fever was subdued; the fever had been his complaint; of course he would soon be well again. Lady Bertram could think nothing less, and Fanny shared her aunt's security, till she received a few lines from Edmund, written purposely to give her a clearer idea of his brother's situation, and acquaint her with the apprehensions which he and his father had imbibed from the physician with respect to some strong hectic symptoms, which seemed to seize the frame on the departure of the fever. They judged it best that Lady Bertram should not be harassed by alarms which, it was to be hoped, would prove unfounded; but there was no reason why Fanny should not know the truth. They were apprehensive for his lungs.

A very few lines from Edmund shewed her the patient and the sickroom in a juster and stronger light than all Lady Bertram's sheets of paper could do. There was hardly any one in the house who might not have described, from personal observation, better than herself; not one who was not more useful at times to her son. She could do nothing but glide in quietly and look at him; but when able to talk or be talked to, or read to, Edmund was the companion he preferred. His aunt worried him by her cares, and Sir Thomas knew not how to bring down his conversation or his voice to the level of irritation and feebleness. Edmund was all in all. Fanny would certainly believe him so at least, and must find that her estimation of him was higher than ever when he appeared as the attendant, supporter, cheerer of a suffering brother. There was not only the debility of recent illness to assist: there was also, as she now learnt, nerves much affected, spirits much depressed to calm and raise, and her own imagination added that there must be a mind to be properly guided.

The family were not consumptive, and she was more inclined to hope than fear for her cousin, except when she thought of Miss Crawford; but Miss Crawford gave her the idea of being the child of good luck, and to her selfishness and vanity it would be good luck to have Edmund the only son.

Even in the sick chamber the fortunate Mary was not forgotten. Edmund's letter had this postscript. "On the subject of my last, I had actually begun a letter when called away by

Tom's illness, but I have now changed my mind, and fear to trust the influence of friends. When Tom is better, I shall go."

Such was the state of Mansfield, and so it continued, with scarcely any change, till Easter. A line occasionally added by Edmund to his mother's letter was enough for Fanny's information. Tom's amendment was alarmingly slow.

Easter came particularly late this year, as Fanny had most sorrowfully considered, on first learning that she had no chance of leaving Portsmouth till after it. It came, and she had yet heard nothing of her return—nothing even of the going to London, which was to precede her return. Her aunt often expressed a wish for her, but there was no notice, no message from the uncle on whom all depended. She supposed he could not yet leave his son, but it was a cruel, a terrible delay to her. The end of April was coming on; it would soon be almost three months, instead of two, that she had been absent from them all, and that her days had been passing in a state of penance, which she loved them too well to hope they would thoroughly understand; and who could yet say when there might be leisure to think of or fetch her?

Her eagerness, her impatience, her longings to be with them, were such as to bring a line or two of Cowper's Tirocinium for ever before her. "With what intense desire she wants her home," was continually on her tongue, as the truest description of a yearning which she could not suppose any schoolboy's bosom to feel more keenly.

When she had been coming to Portsmouth, she had loved to call it her home, had been fond of saying that she was going home; the word had been very dear to her, and so it still was, but it must be applied to Mansfield. Thatwas now the home. Portsmouth was Portsmouth; Mansfield was home. They had been long so arranged in the indulgence of her secret meditations, and nothing was more consolatory to her than to find her aunt using the same language: "I cannot but say I much regret your being from home at this distressing time, so very trying to my spirits. I trust and hope, and sincerely wish you may never be absent from home so long again," were most delightful sentences to her. Still, however, it was her private regale. Delicacy to her parents made her careful not to betray such a preference of her uncle's house. It was always: "When I go back into Northamptonshire, or when I return to Mansfield, I shall do so and so." For a great while it was so, but at last the longing grew stronger, it overthrew caution, and she found herself talking of what she should do when she went home before she was aware. She reproached herself, coloured, and looked fearfully towards her father and mother. She need not have been uneasy. There was no sign of displeasure, or even of hearing her. They were perfectly free from any jealousy of Mansfield. She was as welcome to wish herself there as to be there. It was sad to Fanny to lose all the pleasures of spring. She had not known before what pleasures she hadto lose in passing March and April in a town. She had not known before how much the beginnings and progress of vegetation had delighted her. What animation, both of body and mind, she had derived from watching the advance of that season which cannot, in spite of its capriciousness, be unlovely, and seeing its increasing beauties from the earliest flowers in the warmest divisions of her aunt's garden, to the opening of leaves of her uncle's plantations, and the glory of his woods.

To be losing such pleasures was no trifle; to be losing them, because she was in the midst of closeness and noise, to have confinement, bad air, bad smells, substituted for liberty, freshness, fragrance, and verdure, was infinitely worse: but even these incitements to regret were feeble, compared with what arose from the conviction of being missed by her best friends, and the longing to be useful to those who were wanting her!

Could she have been at home, she might have been of service to every creature in the house. She felt that she must have been of use to all. To all she must have saved some trouble of head or hand; and were it only in supporting the spirits of her aunt Bertram, keeping her from the evil of solitude, or the still greater evil of a restless, officious companion, too apt to be heightening danger in order to enhance her own importance, her being there would have been a general good. She loved to fancy how she could have read to her aunt, how she could have talked to her, and tried at once to make her feel the blessing of what was, and prepare her mind for what might be; and how many walks up and down stairs she might have saved her, and how many messages she might have carried. It astonished her that Tom's sisters could be satisfied with remaining in London at such a time, through an illness which had now, under different degrees of danger, lasted several weeks. Theymight return to Mansfield when they chose; travelling could be no difficulty to them, and she could not comprehend how both could still keep away. If Mrs. Rushworth could imagine any interfering obligations, Julia was certainly able to quit London whenever she chose. It appeared from one of her aunt's letters that Julia had offered to return if wanted, but this was all. It was evident that she would rather remain where she was.

Fanny was disposed to think the influence of London very much at war with all respectable attachments. She saw the proof of it in Miss Crawford, as well as in her cousins; herattachment to Edmund had been respectable, the most respectable part of her character; her friendship for herself had at least been blameless. Where was either sentiment now? It was so long since Fanny had had any letter from her, that she had some reason to think lightly of the friendship which had been so dwelt on. It was weeks since she had heard anything of Miss Crawford or of her other connexions in town, except through Mansfield, and she was beginning to suppose that she might never know whether Mr. Crawford had gone into Norfolk again or not till they met, and might never hear from his sister any more this spring, when the following letter was received to revive old and create some new sensations—

"Forgive me, my dear Fanny, as soon as you can, for my long silence, and behave as if you could forgive me directly. This is my modest request and expectation, for you are so good, that I depend upon being treated better than I deserve, and I write now to beg an immediate answer. I want to know the state of things at Mansfield Park, and you, no doubt, are perfectly able to give it. One should be a brute not to feel for the distress they are in; and from what I hear, poor Mr. Bertram has a bad chance of ultimate recovery. I thought little of his illness at first. I looked upon him as the sort of person to be made a fuss with, and to make a fuss himself in any trifling disorder, and was chiefly concerned for those who had to nurse him; but now it is confidently asserted that he is really in a decline, that the symptoms are most alarming, and that part of the family, at least, are aware of it. If it be so, I am sure you must be included in that part, that discerning part, and therefore entreat you to let me know how far I have been rightly informed.

I need not say how rejoiced I shall be to hear there has been any mistake, but the report is so prevalent that I confess I cannot help trembling. To have such a fine young man cut off in the flower of his days is most melancholy. Poor Sir Thomas will feel it dreadfully. I really am quite agitated on the subject. Fanny, Fanny, I see you smile and look cunning, but, upon my honour, I never bribed a physician in my life. Poor young man! If he is to die, there will be twopoor young men less in the world; and with a fearless face and bold voice would I say to any one, that wealth and consequence could fall into no hands more deserving of them. It was a foolish precipitation last Christmas, but the evil of a few days may be blotted out in part. Varnish and gilding hide many stains. It will be but the loss of the Esquire after his name. With real affection, Fanny, like mine, more might be overlooked. Write to me by return of post, judge of my anxiety, and do not trifle with it. Tell me the real truth, as you have it from the fountainhead. And now, do not trouble yourself to be ashamed of either my feelings or your own.

Believe me, they are not only natural, they are philanthropic and virtuous. I put it to your conscience, whether 'Sir Edmund' would not do more good with all the Bertram property than any other possible 'Sir.' Had the Grants been at home I would not have troubled you, but you are now the only one I can apply to for the truth, his sisters not being within my reach. Mrs. R. has been spending the Easter with the Aylmers at Twickenham (as to be sure you know), and is not yet returned; and Julia is with the cousins who live near

Bedford Square, but I forget their name and street. Could I immediately apply to either, however, I should still prefer you, because it strikes me that they have all along been so unwilling to have their own amusements cut up, as to shut their eyes to the truth. I suppose Mrs. R.'s Easter holidays will not last much longer; no doubt they are thorough holidays to her. The Aylmers are pleasant people; and her husband away, she can have nothing but enjoyment. I give her credit for promoting his going dutifully down to Bath, to fetch his mother; but how will she and the dowager agree in one house? Henry is not at hand, so I have nothing to say from him. Do not you think Edmund would have been in town again long ago, but for this illness?— Yours ever, Mary."

"I had actually begun folding my letter when Henry walked in, but he brings no intelligence to prevent my sending it. Mrs. R. knows a decline is apprehended; he saw her this morning: she returns to Wimpole Street to-day; the old lady is come. Now do not make yourself uneasy with any queer fancies because he has been spending a few days at Richmond. He does it every spring. Be assured he cares for nobody but you. At this very moment he is wild to see you, and occupied only in contriving the means for doing so, and for making his pleasure conduce to yours. In proof, he repeats, and more eagerly, what he said at Portsmouth about our conveying you home, and I join him in it with all my soul. Dear Fanny, write directly, and tell us to come. It will do us all good. He and I can go to the Parsonage, you know, and be no trouble to our friends at Mansfield Park. It would really be gratifying to see them all again, and a little addition of society might be of infinite use to them; and as to yourself, you must feel yourself to be so wanted there, that you cannot in conscience— conscientious as you are— keep away, when you have the means of returning. I have not time or patience to give half Henry's messages; be satisfied that the spirit of each and every one is unalterable affection."

Fanny's disgust at the greater part of this letter, with her extreme reluctance to bring the writer of it and her cousin Edmund together, would have made her (as she felt) incapable of judging impartially whether the concluding offer might be accepted or not. To herself, individually, it was most tempting. To be finding herself, perhaps within three days, transported to Mansfield, was an image of the greatest felicity, but it would have been a material drawback to be owing such felicity to persons in whose feelings and conduct, at the present moment, she saw so much to condemn: the sister's feelings, the brother's conduct, hercold-hearted ambition, histhoughtless vanity. To have him still the acquaintance, the flirt perhaps, of Mrs. Rushworth! She was mortified.

She had thought better of him. Happily, however, she was not left to weigh and decide between opposite inclinations and doubtful notions of right; there was no occasion to determine whether she ought to keep Edmund and Mary asunder or not. She had a rule to apply to, which settled everything. Her awe of her uncle, and her dread of taking a liberty with him, made it instantly plain to her what she had to do. She must absolutely decline the proposal.

If he wanted, he would send for her; and even to offer an early return was a presumption which hardly anything would have seemed to justify. She thanked Miss Crawford, but gave a decided negative. "Her uncle, she understood, meant to fetch her; and as her cousin's illness had continued so many weeks without her being thought at all necessary, she must suppose her return would be unwelcome at present, and that she should be felt an encumbrance."

Her representation of her cousin's state at this time was exactly according to her own belief of it, and such as she supposed would convey to the sanguine mind of her correspondent the hope of everything she was wishing for. Edmund would be forgiven for being a clergyman, it seemed, under certain conditions of wealth; and this, she suspected, was all the conquest of prejudice which he was so ready to congratulate himself upon. She had only learnt to think nothing of consequence but money.

CHAPTER XLVI

As Fanny could not doubt that her answer was conveying a real disappointment, she was rather in expectation, from her knowledge of Miss Crawford's temper, of being urged again; and though no second letter arrived for the space of a week, she had still the same feeling when it did come. On receiving it, she could instantly decide on its containing little writing, and was persuaded of its having the air of a letter of haste and business.

Its object was unquestionable; and two moments were enough to start the probability of its being merely to give her notice that they should be in Portsmouth that very day, and to throw her into all the agitation of doubting what she ought to do in such a case. If two moments, however, can surround with difficulties, a third can disperse them; and before she had opened the letter, the possibility of Mr. and Miss Crawford's having applied to her uncle and obtained his permission was giving her ease. This was the letter—

"A most scandalous, ill-natured rumour has just reached me, and I write, dear Fanny, to warn you against giving the least credit to it, should it spread into the country. Depend upon it, there is some mistake, and that a day or two will clear it up; at any rate, that Henry is blameless, and in spite of a moment's etourderie, thinks of nobody but you. Say not a word of it; hear nothing, surmise nothing, whisper nothing till I write again. I am sure it will be all hushed up, and nothing proved but Rushworth's folly. If they are gone, I would lay my life they are only gone to Mansfield Park, and Julia with them. But why would not you let us come for you? I wish you may not repent it.—Yours, etc."

Fanny stood aghast. As no scandalous, ill-natured rumour had reached her, it was impossible for her to understand much of this strange letter. She could only perceive that it must relate to Wimpole Street and Mr. Crawford, and only conjecture that something very imprudent had just occurred in that quarter to draw the notice of the world, and to excite her jealousy, in Miss Crawford's apprehension, if she heard it. Miss Crawford need not be alarmed for her. She was only sorry for the parties concerned and for Mansfield, if the report should spread so far; but she hoped it might not. If the Rushworths were gone themselves to Mansfield, as was to be inferred from what Miss

Crawford said, it was not likely that anything unpleasant should have preceded them, or at least should make any impression.

As to Mr. Crawford, she hoped it might give him a knowledge of his own disposition, convince him that he was not capable of being steadily attached to any one woman in the world, and shame him from persisting any longer in addressing herself.

It was very strange! She had begun to think he really loved her, and to fancy his affection for her something more than common; and his sister still said that he cared for nobody else. Yet there must have been some marked display of attentions to her cousin, there must have been some strong indiscretion, since her correspondent was not of a sort to regard a slight one. Very uncomfortable she was, and must continue, till she heard from Miss Crawford again. It was impossible to banish the letter from her thoughts, and she could not relieve herself by speaking of it to any human being. Miss Crawford need not have urged secrecy with so much warmth; she might have trusted to her sense of what was due to her cousin.

The next day came and brought no second letter. Fanny was disappointed. She could still think of little else all the morning; but, when her father came back in the afternoon with the daily newspaper as usual, she was so far from expecting any elucidation through such a channel that the subject was for a moment out of her head.

She was deep in other musing. The remembrance of her first evening in that room, of her father and his newspaper, came across her. No candle was now wanted. The sun was yet an hour and half above the horizon. She felt that she had, indeed, been three months there; and the sun's rays falling strongly into the parlour, instead of cheering, made her still more melancholy, for sunshine appeared to her a totally different thing in a town and in the country. Here, its power was only a glare: a stifling, sickly glare, serving but to bring forward stains and dirt that might otherwise have slept. There was neither health nor gaiety in sunshine in a town. She sat in a blaze of oppressive heat, in a cloud of moving dust, and her eyes could only wander from the walls, marked by her father's head, to the table cut and notched by her brothers, where stood the tea-board never thoroughly cleaned, the cups and saucers wiped in streaks, the milk a mixture of motes floating in thin blue, and the bread and butter growing every minute more greasy than even Rebecca's hands had first produced it. Her father read his newspaper, and her mother lamented over the ragged carpet as usual, while the tea was in preparation, and wished Rebecca would mend it; and Fanny was first roused by his calling out to her, after humphing and considering over a particular paragraph: "What's the name of your great cousins in town, Fan?"

A moment's recollection enabled her to say, "Rushworth, sir."

"And don't they live in Wimpole Street?"

"Yes, sir."

"Then, there's the devil to pay among them, that's all! There" (holding out the paper to her); "much good may such fine relations do you. I don't know what Sir Thomas may think of such matters; he may be too much of the courtier and fine gentleman to like his daughter the less. But, by G—! if she belonged to me, I'd give her the rope's end as long as I could stand over her. A little flogging for man and woman too would be the best way of preventing such things."

Fanny read to herself that "it was with infinite concern the newspaper had to announce to the world a matrimonial fracasin the family of Mr. R. of Wimpole Street; the beautiful Mrs. R., whose name had not long been enrolled in the lists of Hymen, and who had promised to become so brilliant a leader in the fashionable world, having quitted her husband's roof in company with the well-known and captivating Mr. C., the intimate friend and associate of Mr. R., and it was not known even to the editor of the newspaper whither they were gone."

"It is a mistake, sir," said Fanny instantly; "it must be a mistake, it cannot be true; it must mean some other people."

She spoke from the instinctive wish of delaying shame; she spoke with a resolution which sprung from despair, for she spoke what she did not, could not believe herself. It had been the shock of conviction as she read. The truth rushed on her; and how she could have spoken at all, how she could even have breathed, was afterwards matter of wonder to herself.

Mr. Price cared too little about the report to make her much answer. "It might be all a lie," he acknowledged; "but so many fine ladies were going to the devil nowadays that way, that there was no answering for anybody."

"Indeed, I hope it is not true," said Mrs. Price plaintively; "it would be so very shocking! If I have spoken once to Rebecca about that carpet, I am sure I have spoke at least a dozen times; have not I, Betsey? And it would not be ten minutes' work."

The horror of a mind like Fanny's, as it received the conviction of such guilt, and began to take in some part of the misery that must ensue, can hardly be described. At first, it was a sort of stupefaction; but every moment was quickening her perception of the horrible evil. She could not doubt, she dared not indulge a hope, of the paragraph being false. Miss Crawford's letter, which she had read so often as to make every line her own, was in frightful conformity with it. Her eager defence of her brother, her hope of its being hushedup, her evident agitation, were all of a piece with something very bad; and if there was a woman of character in existence, who could treat as a trifle this sin of the first magnitude, who would try to gloss it over, and desire to have it unpunished, she could believe Miss Crawford to be the woman! Now she could see her own mistake as to whowere gone, or saidto be gone. It was not Mr. and Mrs. Rushworth; it was Mrs. Rushworth and Mr. Crawford.

Fanny seemed to herself never to have been shocked before. There was no possibility of rest. The evening passed without a pause of misery, the night was totally sleepless. She passed only from feelings of sickness to shudderings of horror; and from hot fits of fever to cold. The event was so shocking, that there were moments even when her heart revolted from it as impossible: when she thought it could not be. A woman married only six months ago; a man professing himself devoted, even engagedto another; that other her near relation; the whole family, both families connected as they were by tie upon tie; all friends, all intimate together! It was too horrible a confusion of guilt, too gross a complication of evil, for human nature, not in a state of utter barbarism, to be capable of! yet her judgment told her it was so. Hisunsettled affections, wavering with his vanity, Maria'sdecided attachment, and no sufficient principle on either side, gave it possibility: Miss Crawford's letter stampt it a fact.

What would be the consequence? Whom would it not injure? Whose views might it not affect? Whose peace would it not cut up for ever? Miss Crawford, herself, Edmund; but it was dangerous, perhaps, to tread such ground. She confined herself, or tried to confine herself, to the simple, indubitable family misery which must envelop all, if it were indeed a matter of certified guilt and public exposure. The mother's sufferings, the father's; there she paused. Julia's, Tom's, Edmund's; there a yet longer pause. They were the two on whom it would fall most horribly. Sir Thomas's parental solicitude and high sense of honour and decorum, Edmund's upright principles, unsuspicious temper, and genuine strength of feeling, made her think it scarcely possible for them to support life and reason under such disgrace; and it appeared to her that, as far as this world alone was concerned, the greatest blessing to every one of kindred with Mrs. Rushworth would be instant annihilation.

Nothing happened the next day, or the next, to weaken her terrors. Two posts came in, and brought no refutation, public or private. There was no second letter to explain away the first from Miss Crawford; there was no intelligence from Mansfield, though it was now full time for her to hear again from her aunt. This was an evil omen. She had, indeed, scarcely the shadow of a hope to soothe her mind, and was reduced to so low and wan and trembling a condition, as no mother, not unkind, except Mrs. Price could have overlooked, when the third day did bring the sickening knock, and a letter was again put into her hands. It bore the London postmark, and came from Edmund.

"Dear Fanny,—You know our present wretchedness. May God support you under your share! We have been here two days, but there is nothing to be done. They cannot be traced.

You may not have heard of the last blow— Julia's elopement; she is gone to Scotland with Yates. She left London a few hours before we entered it. At any other time this would have been felt dreadfully. Now it seems nothing; yet it is an heavy aggravation. My father is not overpowered. More cannot be hoped. He is still able to think and act; and I write, by his desire, to propose your returning home. He is anxious to get you there for my mother's sake. I shall be at Portsmouth the morning after you receive this, and hope to find you ready to set off for Mansfield. My father wishes you to invite Susan to go with you for a few months. Settle it as you like; say what is proper; I am sure you will feel such an instance of his kindness at such a moment! Do justice to his meaning, however I may confuse it. You may imagine something of my present state. There is no end of the evil let loose upon us. You will see me early by the mail.— Yours, etc."

Never had Fanny more wanted a cordial. Never had she felt such a one as this letter contained. To-morrow! to leave Portsmouth to-morrow! She was, she felt she was, in the greatest danger of being exquisitely happy, while so many were miserable. The evil which brought such good to her! She dreaded lest she should learn to be insensible of it. To be going so soon, sent for so kindly, sent for as a comfort, and with leave to take Susan, was altogether such a combination of blessings as set her heart in a glow, and for a time seemed to distance every pain, and make her incapable of suitably sharing the distress even of those whose distress she thought of most. Julia's elopement could affect her comparatively but little; she was amazed and shocked; but it could not occupy her, could not dwell on her mind. She was obliged to call herself to think of it, and acknowledge it to be terrible and grievous, or it was escaping her, in the midst of all the agitating pressing joyful cares attending this summons to herself.

There is nothing like employment, active indispensable employment, for relieving sorrow. Employment, even melancholy, may dispel melancholy, and her occupations were hopeful. She had so much to do, that not even the horrible story of Mrs. Rushworth—now fixed to the last point of certainty could affect her as it had done before. She had not time to be miserable. Within twenty-four hours she was hoping to be gone; her father and mother must be spoken to, Susan prepared, everything got ready. Business followed business; the day was hardly long enough. The happiness she was imparting, too, happiness very little alloyed by the black communication which must briefly precede it—the joyful consent of her father and mother to Susan's going with her—the general satisfaction with which the going of both seemed regarded, and the ecstasy of Susan herself, was all serving to support her spirits.

The affliction of the Bertrams was little felt in the family. Mrs. Price talked of her poor sister for a few minutes, but how to find anything to hold Susan's clothes, because Rebecca took away all the boxes and spoilt them, was much more in her thoughts: and as for Susan, now unexpectedly gratified in the first wish of her heart, and knowing nothing personally of those who had sinned, or of those who were sorrowing—if she could help rejoicing from beginning to end, it was as much as ought to be expected from human virtue at fourteen.

As nothing was really left for the decision of Mrs. Price, or the good offices of Rebecca, everything was rationally and duly accomplished, and the girls were ready for the morrow. The advantage of much sleep to prepare them for their journey was impossible. The cousin who was travelling towards them could hardly have less than visited their agitated spirits—one all happiness, the other all varying and indescribable perturbation.

By eight in the morning Edmund was in the house. The girls heard his entrance from above, and Fanny went down. The idea of immediately seeing him, with the knowledge of what he must be suffering, brought back all her own first feelings. He so near her, and in misery. She was ready to sink as she entered the parlour. He was alone, and met her instantly; and she found herself pressed to his heart with only these words, just articulate, "My Fanny, my only sister; my only comfort now!" She could say nothing; nor for some minutes could he say more.

He turned away to recover himself, and when he spoke again, though his voice still faltered, his manner shewed the wish of self-command, and the resolution of avoiding any farther allusion. "Have you breakfasted? When shall you be ready? Does Susan go?" were questions following each other rapidly. His great object was to be off as soon as possible. When Mansfield was considered, time was precious; and the state of his own mind made him find relief only in motion. It was settled that he should order the carriage to the door in half an hour. Fanny answered for their having breakfasted and being quite ready in half an hour. He had already ate, and declined staying for their meal. He would walk round the ramparts, and join them with the carriage. He was gone again; glad to get away even from Fanny. He looked very ill; evidently suffering under violent emotions, which he was determined to suppress. She knew it must be so, but it was terrible to her.

The carriage came; and he entered the house again at the same moment, just in time to spend a few minutes with the family, and be a witness—but that he saw nothing— of the tranquil manner in which the daughters were parted with, and just in time to prevent their sitting down to the breakfast-table, which, by dint of much unusual activity, was quite and completely ready as the carriage drove from the door. Fanny's last meal in her father's house was in character with her first: she was dismissed from it as hospitably as she had been welcomed.

How her heart swelled with joy and gratitude as she passed the barriers of Portsmouth, and how Susan's face wore its broadest smiles, may be easily conceived. Sitting forwards, however, and screened by her bonnet, those smiles were unseen. The journey was likely to be a silent one. Edmund's deep sighs often reached Fanny. Had he been alone with her, his heart must have opened in spite of every resolution; but Susan's presence drove him quite into himself, and his attempts to talk on indifferent subjects could never be long supported.

Fanny watched him with never-failing solicitude, and sometimes catching his eye, revived an affectionate smile, which comforted her; but the first day's journey passed without her hearing a word from him on the subjects that were weighing him down. The next morning produced a little more. Just before their setting out from Oxford, while Susan was stationed at a window, in eager observation of the departure of a large family from the inn, the other two were standing by the fire; and Edmund, particularly struck by the alteration in Fanny's looks, and from his ignorance of the daily evils of her father's house, attributing an undue share of the change, attributing allto the recent event, took her hand, and said in a low, but very expressive tone, "No wonder— you must feel it—you must suffer. How a man who had once loved, could desert you! But yours—your regard was new compared with— —Fanny, think of me!"

The first division of their journey occupied a long day, and brought them, almost knocked up, to Oxford; but the second was over at a much earlier hour. They were in the environs of Mansfield long before the usual dinner-time, and as they approached the beloved place, the hearts of both sisters sank a little. Fanny began to dread the meeting with her aunts and Tom, under so dreadful a humiliation; and Susan to feel with some anxiety, that all her best manners, all her lately acquired knowledge of what was practised here, was on the point of being called into action. Visions of good and ill breeding, of old vulgarisms and new gentilities, were before her; and she was meditating much upon silver forks, napkins, and finger-glasses. Fanny had been everywhere awake to the difference of the country since February; but when they entered the Park her perceptions and her pleasures were of the keenest sort.

It was three months, full three months, since her quitting it, and the change was from winter to summer. Her eye fell everywhere on lawns and plantations of the freshest green; and the trees, though not fully clothed, were in that delightful state when farther beauty is known to be at hand, and when, while much is actually given to the sight, more yet remains for the imagination. Her enjoyment, however, was for herself alone. Edmund could not share it. She looked at him, but he was leaning back, sunk in a deeper gloom than ever, and with eyes closed, as if the view of cheerfulness oppressed him, and the lovely scenes of home must be shut out. It made her melancholy again; and the knowledge of what must be enduring there, invested even the house, modern, airy, and well situated as it was, with a melancholy aspect.

By one of the suffering party within they were expected with such impatience as she had never known before. Fanny had scarcely passed the solemn-looking servants, when Lady Bertram came from the drawing-room to meet her; came with no indolent step; and falling on her neck, said, "Dear Fanny! now I shall be comfortable."

Chapter XLVII

It had been a miserable party, each of the three believing themselves most miserable. Mrs. Norris, however, as most attached to Maria, was really the greatest sufferer. Maria was her first favourite, the dearest of all; the match had been her own contriving, as she had been wont with such pride of heart to feel and say, and this conclusion of it almost overpowered her. She was an altered creature, quieted, stupefied, indifferent to everything that passed. The being left with her sister and nephew, and all the house under her care, had been an advantage entirely thrown away; she had been unable to direct or dictate, or even fancy herself useful. When really touched by affliction, her active powers had been all benumbed; and neither Lady Bertram nor Tom had received from her the smallest support or attempt at support.

She had done no more for them than they had done for each other. They had been all solitary, helpless, and forlorn alike; and now the arrival of the others only established her superiority in wretchedness. Her companions were relieved, but there was no good for her. Edmund was almost as welcome to his brother as Fanny to her aunt; but Mrs. Norris, instead of having comfort from either, was but the more irritated by the sight of the person whom, in the blindness of her anger, she could have charged as the daemon of the piece. Had Fanny accepted Mr. Crawford this could not have happened.

Susan too was a grievance. She had not spirits to notice her in more than a few repulsive looks, but she felt her as a spy, and an intruder, and an indigent niece, and everything most odious. By her other aunt, Susan was received with quiet kindness. Lady Bertram could not give her much time, or many words, but she felt her, as Fanny's sister, to have a claim at Mansfield, and was ready to kiss and like her; and Susan was more than satisfied, for she came perfectly aware that nothing but ill-humour was to be expected from aunt Norris; and was so provided with happiness, so strong in that best of blessings, an escape from many certain evils, that she could have stood against a great deal more indifference than she met with from the others.

She was now left a good deal to herself, to get acquainted with the house and grounds as she could, and spent her days very happily in so doing, while those who might otherwise have attended to her were shut up, or wholly occupied each with the person quite dependent on them, at this time, for everything like comfort; Edmund trying to bury his own feelings in exertions for the relief of his brother's, and Fanny devoted to her aunt Bertram, returning to every former office with more than former zeal, and thinking she could never do enough for one who seemed so much to want her.

To talk over the dreadful business with Fanny, talk and lament, was all Lady Bertram's consolation. To be listened to and borne with, and hear the voice of kindness and sympathy in return, was everything that could be done for her. To be otherwise comforted was out of the question. The case admitted of no comfort. Lady Bertram did not think deeply, but, guided by Sir Thomas, she thought justly on all important points; and she saw, therefore, in all its enormity, what had happened, and neither endeavoured herself, nor required Fanny to advise her, to think little of guilt and infamy.

Her affections were not acute, nor was her mind tenacious. After a time, Fanny found it not impossible to direct her thoughts to other subjects, and revive some interest in the usual occupations; but whenever Lady Bertram wasfixed on the event, she could see it only in one light, as comprehending the loss of a daughter, and a disgrace never to be wiped off.

Fanny learnt from her all the particulars which had yet transpired. Her aunt was no very methodical narrator, but with the help of some letters to and from Sir Thomas, and what she already knew herself, and could reasonably combine, she was soon able to understand quite as much as she wished of the circumstances attending the story.

Mrs. Rushworth had gone, for the Easter holidays, to Twickenham, with a family whom she had just grown intimate with: a family of lively, agreeable manners, and probably of morals and discretion to suit, for to theirhouse Mr. Crawford had constant access at all times. His having been in the same neighbourhood Fanny already knew. Mr. Rushworth had been gone at this time to Bath, to pass a few days with his mother, and bring her back to town, and Maria was with these friends without any restraint, without even Julia; for Julia had removed from Wimpole Street two or three weeks before, on a visit to some relations of Sir Thomas; a removal which her father and mother were now disposed to attribute to some view of convenience on Mr. Yates's account. Very soon after the Rushworths' return to Wimpole Street, Sir Thomas had received a letter from an old and most particular friend in London, who hearing and witnessing a good deal to alarm him in that quarter, wrote to recommend Sir Thomas's coming to London himself, and using his influence with his daughter to put an end to the intimacy which was already exposing her to unpleasant remarks, and evidently making Mr. Rushworth uneasy. Sir Thomas was preparing to act upon this letter, without communicating its contents to any creature at Mansfield, when it was followed by another, sent express from the same friend, to break to him the almost desperate situation in which affairs then stood with the young people.

Mrs. Rushworth had left her husband's house: Mr. Rushworth had been in great anger and distress to him(Mr. Harding) for his advice; Mr. Harding feared there had been atleastvery flagrant indiscretion. The maidservant of Mrs. Rushworth, senior, threatened alarmingly. He was doing all in his power to quiet everything, with the hope of Mrs. Rushworth's return, but was so much counteracted in Wimpole Street by the influence of Mr. Rushworth's mother, that the worst consequences might be apprehended.

This dreadful communication could not be kept from the rest of the family. Sir Thomas set off, Edmund would go with him, and the others had been left in a state of wretchedness, inferior only to what followed the receipt of the next letters from London. Everything was by that time public beyond a hope. The servant of Mrs. Rushworth, the mother, had exposure in her power, and supported by her mistress, was not to be silenced. The two ladies, even in the short time they had been together, had disagreed; and the bitterness of the elder against her daughter-in-law might perhaps arise almost as much from the personal disrespect with which she had herself been treated as from sensibility for her son.

However that might be, she was unmanageable. But had she been less obstinate, or of less weight with her son, who was always guided by the last speaker, by the person who could get hold of and shut him up, the case would still have been hopeless, for Mrs. Rushworth did not appear again, and there was every reason to conclude her to be concealed somewhere with Mr. Crawford, who had quitted his uncle's house, as for a journey, on the very day of her absenting herself.

Sir Thomas, however, remained yet a little longer in town, in the hope of discovering and snatching her from farther vice, though all was lost on the side of character.

Hispresent state Fanny could hardly bear to think of. There was but one of his children who was not at this time a source of misery to him. Tom's complaints had been greatly heightened by the shock of his sister's conduct, and his recovery so much thrown back by it, that even Lady Bertram had been struck by the difference, and all her alarms were regularly sent off to her husband; and Julia's elopement, the additional blow which had met him on his arrival in London, though its force had been deadened at the moment, must, she knew, be sorely felt. She saw that it was. His letters expressed how much he deplored it. Under any circumstances it would have been an unwelcome alliance; but to have it so clandestinely formed, and such a period chosen for its completion, placed Julia's feelings in a most unfavourable light, and severely aggravated the folly of her choice. He called it a bad thing, done in the worst manner, and at the worst time; and though Julia was yet as more pardonable than Maria as folly than vice, he could not but regard the step she had taken as opening the worst probabilities of a conclusion hereafter like her sister's. Such was his opinion of the set into which she had thrown herself.

Fanny felt for him most acutely. He could have no comfort but in Edmund. Every other child must be racking his heart. His displeasure against herself she trusted, reasoning differently from Mrs. Norris, would now be done away. Sheshould be justified. Mr. Crawford would have fully acquitted her conduct in refusing him; but this, though most material to herself, would be poor consolation to Sir Thomas. Her uncle's displeasure was terrible to her; but what could her justification or her gratitude and attachment do for him? His stay must be on Edmund alone.

She was mistaken, however, in supposing that Edmund gave his father no present pain. It was of a much less poignant nature than what the others excited; but Sir Thomas was considering his happiness as very deeply involved in the offence of his sister and friend; cut off by it, as he must be, from the woman whom he had been pursuing with undoubted attachment and strong probability of success; and who, in everything but this despicable brother, would have been so eligible a connexion.

He was aware of what Edmund must be suffering on his own behalf, in addition to all the rest, when they were in town: he had seen or conjectured his feelings; and, having reason to think that one interview with Miss Crawford had taken place, from which Edmund derived only increased distress, had been as anxious on that account as on others to get him out of town, and had engaged him in taking Fanny home to her aunt, with a view to his relief and benefit, no less than theirs. Fanny was not in the secret of her uncle's feelings, Sir Thomas not in the secret of Miss Crawford's character. Had he been privy to her conversation with his son, he would not have wished her to belong to him, though her twenty thousand pounds had been forty.

That Edmund must be for ever divided from Miss

Crawford did not admit of a doubt with Fanny; and yet, till she knew that he felt the same, her own conviction was insufficient. She thought he did, but she wanted to be assured of it. If he would now speak to her with the unreserve which had sometimes been too much for her before, it would be most consoling; but thatshe found was not to be. She seldom saw him: never alone. He probably avoided being alone with her. What was to be inferred? That his judgment submitted to all his own peculiar and bitter share of this family affliction, but that it was too keenly felt to be a subject of the slightest communication. This must be his state. He yielded, but it was with agonies which did not admit of speech. Long, long would it be ere Miss Crawford's name passed his lips again, or she could hope for a renewal of such confidential intercourse as had been.

It waslong. They reached Mansfield on Thursday, and it was not till Sunday evening that Edmund began to talk to her on the subject. Sitting with her on Sunday evening—a wet Sunday evening—the very time of all others when, if a friend is at hand, the heart must be opened, and everything told; no one else in the room, except his mother, who, after hearing an affecting sermon, had cried herself to sleep, it was impossible not to speak; and so, with the usual beginnings, hardly to be traced as to what came first, and the usual declaration that if she would listen to him for a few minutes, he should be very brief, and certainly never tax her kindness in the same way again; she need not fear a repetition; it would be a subject prohibited entirely: he entered upon the luxury of relating circumstances and sensations of the first interest to himself, to one of whose affectionate sympathy he was quite convinced.

How Fanny listened, with what curiosity and concern, what pain and what delight, how the agitation of his voice was watched, and how carefully her own eyes were fixed on any object but himself, may be imagined. The opening was alarming. He had seen Miss Crawford. He had been invited to see her. He had received a note from Lady Stornaway to beg him to call; and regarding it as what was meant to be the last, last interview of friendship, and investing her with all the feelings of shame and wretchedness which Crawford's sister ought to have known, he had gone to her in such a state of mind, so softened, so devoted, as made it for a few moments impossible to Fanny's fears that it should be the last. But as he proceeded in his story, these fears were over. She had met him, he said, with a serious—certainly a serious— even an agitated air; but before he had been able to speak one intelligible sentence, she had introduced the subject in a manner which he owned had shocked him.

'I heard you were in town,' said she; 'I wanted to see you. Let us talk over this sad business. What can equal the folly of our two relations?' I could not answer, but I believe my looks spoke. She felt reproved. Sometimes how quick to feel! With a graver look and voice she then added, 'I do not mean to defend Henry at your sister's expense.' So she began, but how she went on, Fanny, is not fit, is hardly fit to be repeated to you. I cannot recall all her words. I would not dwell upon them if I could. Their substance was great anger at the follyof each. She reprobated her brother's folly in being drawn on by a woman whom he had never cared for, to do what must lose him the woman he adored; but still more the folly of poor Maria, in sacrificing such a situation, plunging into such difficulties, under the idea of being really loved by a man who had long ago made his indifference clear. Guess what I must have felt. To hear the woman whom— no harsher name than folly given! So voluntarily, so freely, so coolly to canvass it! No reluctance, no horror, no feminine, shall I say, no modest loathings? This is what the world does. For where, Fanny, shall we find a woman whom nature had so richly endowed? Spoilt, spoilt!"

After a little reflection, he went on with a sort of desperate calmness. "I will tell you everything, and then have done for ever. She saw it only as folly, and that folly stamped only by exposure. The want of common discretion, of caution: his going down to Richmond for the whole time of her being at Twickenham; her putting herself in the power of a servant; it was the detection, in short—oh, Fanny! it was the detection, not the offence, which she reprobated. It was the imprudence which had brought things to extremity, and obliged her brother to give up every dearer plan in order to fly with her."

He stopt. "And what," said Fanny (believing herself

required to speak), "what could you say?" "Nothing, nothing to be understood. I was like a man stunned. She went on, began to talk of you; yes, then she began to talk of you, regretting, as well she might, the loss of such a—. There she spoke very rationally. But she has always done justice to you. 'He has thrown away,' said she, 'such a woman as he will never see again. She would have fixed him; she would have made him happy for ever.' My dearest Fanny, I am giving you, I hope, more pleasure than pain by this retrospect of what might have been—but what never can be now. You do not wish me to be silent? If you do, give me but a look, a word, and I have done."

No look or word was given. "Thank God," said he. "We were all disposed to wonder, but it seems to have been the merciful appointment of Providence that the heart which knew no guile should not suffer. She spoke of you with high praise and warm affection; yet, even here, there was alloy, a dash of evil; for in the midst of it she could exclaim, 'Why would not she have him? It is all her fault. Simple girl! I shall never forgive her. Had she accepted him as she ought, they might now have been on the point of marriage, and Henry would have been too happy and too busy to want any other object. He would have taken no pains to be on terms with Mrs. Rushworth again. It would have all ended in a regular standing flirtation, in yearly meetings at Sotherton and Everingham.' Could you have believed it possible? But the charm is broken. My eyes are opened."

"Cruel!" said Fanny, "quite cruel. At such a moment to give way to gaiety, to speak with lightness, and to you! Absolute cruelty."

"Cruelty, do you call it? We differ there. No, hers is not a cruel nature. I do not consider her as meaning to wound my feelings. The evil lies yet deeper: in her total ignorance, unsuspiciousness of there being such feelings; in a perversion of mind which made it natural to her to treat the subject as she did. She was speaking only as she had been used to hear others speak, as she imagined everybody else would speak. Hers are not faults of temper. She would not voluntarily give unnecessary pain to any one, and though I may deceive myself, I cannot but think that for me, for my feelings, she would—

Hers are faults of principle, Fanny; of blunted delicacy and a corrupted, vitiated mind. Perhaps it is best for me, since it leaves me so little to regret. Not so, however. Gladly would I submit to all the increased pain of losing her, rather than have to think of her as I do. I told her so."

"Did you?"

"Yes; when I left her I told her so."

"How long were you together?"

"Five-and-twenty minutes. Well, she went on to say that what remained now to be done was to bring about a marriage between them. She spoke of it, Fanny, with a steadier voice than I can." He was obliged to pause more than once as he continued. "'We must persuade Henry to marry her,' said she; 'and what with honour, and the certainty of having shut himself out for ever from Fanny, I do not despair of it. Fanny he must give up. I do not think that even hecould now hope to succeed with one of her stamp, and therefore I hope we may find no insuperable difficulty. My influence, which is not small shall all go that way; and when once married, and properly supported by her own family, people of respectability as they are, she may recover her footing in society to a certain degree. In some circles, we know, she would never be admitted, but with good dinners, and large parties, there will always be those who will be glad of her acquaintance; and there is, undoubtedly, more liberality and candour on those points than formerly. What I advise is, that your father be quiet.

Do not let him injure his own cause by interference. Persuade him to let things take their course. If by any officious exertions of his, she is induced to leave Henry's protection, there will be much less chance of his marrying her than if she remain with him. I know how he is likely to be influenced. Let Sir Thomas trust to his honour and compassion, and it may all end well; but if he get his daughter away, it will be destroying the chief hold.'" After repeating this, Edmund was so much affected that Fanny, watching him with silent, but most tender concern, was almost sorry that the subject had been entered on at all. It was long before he could speak again. At last, "Now, Fanny," said he, "I shall soon have done.

I have told you the substance of all that she said. As soon

as I could speak, I replied that I had not supposed it possible, coming in such a state of mind into that house as I had done, that anything could occur to make me suffer more, but that she had been inflicting deeper wounds in almost every sentence. That though I had, in the course of our acquaintance, been often sensible of some difference in our opinions, on points, too, of some moment, it had not entered my imagination to conceive the difference could be such as she had now proved it. That the manner in which she treated the dreadful crime committed by her brother and my sister (with whom lay the greater seduction I pretended not to say), but the manner in which she spoke of the crime itself, giving it every reproach but the right; considering its ill consequences only as they were to be braved or overborne by a defiance of decency and impudence in wrong; and last of all, and above all, recommending to us a compliance, a compromise, an acquiescence in the continuance of the sin, on the chance of a marriage which, thinking as I now thought of her brother, should rather be prevented than sought; all this together most grievously convinced me that I had never understood her before, and that, as far as related to mind, it had been the creature of my own imagination, not Miss Crawford, that I had been too apt to dwell on for many months past.

That, perhaps, it was best for me; I had less to regret in sacrificing a friendship, feelings, hopes which must, at any rate, have been torn from me now. And yet, that I must and would confess that, could I have restored her to what she had appeared to me before, I would infinitely prefer any increase of the pain of parting, for the sake of carrying with me the right of tenderness and esteem. This is what I said, the purport of it; but, as you may imagine, not spoken so collectedly or methodically as I have repeated it to you. She was astonished, exceedingly astonished—more than astonished. I saw her change countenance. She turned extremely red. I imagined I saw a mixture of many feelings: a great, though short struggle; half a wish of yielding to truths, half a sense of shame, but habit, habit carried it.

She would have laughed if she could. It was a sort of laugh, as she answered, 'A pretty good lecture, upon my word.

Was it part of your last sermon? At this rate you will soon reform everybody at Mansfield and Thornton Lacey; and when I hear of you next, it may be as a celebrated preacher in some great society of Methodists, or as a missionary into foreign parts.' She tried to speak carelessly, but she was not so careless as she wanted to appear. I only said in reply, that from my heart I wished her well, and earnestly hoped that she might soon learn to think more justly, and not owe the most valuable knowledge we could any of us acquire, the knowledge of ourselves and of our duty, to the lessons of affliction, and immediately left the room. I had gone a few steps, Fanny, when I heard the door open behind me. 'Mr. Bertram,' said she. I looked back. 'Mr. Bertram,' said she, with a smile; but it was a smile ill-suited to the conversation that had passed, a saucy playful smile, seeming to invite in order to subdue me; at least it appeared so to me. I resisted; it was the impulse of the moment to resist, and still walked on. I have since, sometimes, for a moment, regretted that I did not go back, but I know I was right, and such has been the end of our acquaintance. And what an acquaintance has it been! How have I been deceived! Equally in brother and sister deceived! I thank you for your patience, Fanny. This has been the greatest relief, and now we will have done."

And such was Fanny's dependence on his words, that for five minutes she thought they haddone. Then, however, it all came on again, or something very like it, and nothing less than Lady Bertram's rousing thoroughly up could really close such a conversation. Till that happened, they continued to talk of Miss Crawford alone, and how she had attached him, and how delightful nature had made her, and how excellent she would have been, had she fallen into good hands earlier. Fanny, now at liberty to speak openly, felt more than justified in adding to his knowledge of her real character, by some hint of what share his brother's state of health might be supposed to have in her wish for a complete reconciliation. This was not an agreeable intimation. Nature resisted it for a while. It would have been a vast deal pleasanter to have had her more disinterested in her attachment; but his vanity was not of a strength to fight long against reason. He submitted to believe that Tom's illness had influenced her, only reserving for himself this consoling thought, that considering the many counteractions of opposing habits, she had certainly been moreattached to him than could have been expected, and for his sake been more near doing right. Fanny thought exactly the same; and they were also quite agreed in their opinion of the lasting effect, the indelible impression, which such a disappointment must make on his mind. Time would undoubtedly abate somewhat of his sufferings, but still it was a sort of thing which he never could get entirely the better of; and as to his ever meeting with any other woman who could— it was too impossible to be named but with indignation. Fanny's friendship was all that he had to cling to.

Chapter XLVIII

Let other pens dwell on guilt and misery. I quit such odious subjects as soon as I can, impatient to restore everybody, not greatly in fault themselves, to tolerable comfort, and to have done with all the rest.

My Fanny, indeed, at this very time, I havc the satisfaction of knowing, must have been happy in spite of everything. She must have been a happy creature in spite of all that she felt, or thought she felt, for the distress of those around her. She had sources of delight that must force their way. She was returned to Mansfield Park, she was useful, she was beloved; she was safe from Mr. Crawford; and when Sir Thomas came back she had every proof that could be given in his then melancholy state of spirits, of his perfect approbation and increased regard; and happy as all this must make her, she would still have been happy without any of it, for Edmund was no longer the dupe of Miss Crawford. It is true that Edmund was very far from happy himself. He was suffering from disappointment and regret, grieving over what was, and wishing for what could never be. She knew it was so, and was sorry; but it was with a sorrow so founded on satisfaction, so tending to ease, and so much in harmony with every dearest sensation, that there are few who might not have been glad to exchange their greatest gaiety for it.

Sir Thomas, poor Sir Thomas, a parent, and conscious of

errors in his own conduct as a parent, was the longest to suffer. He felt that he ought not to have allowed the marriage; that his daughter's sentiments had been sufficiently known to him to render him culpable in authorising it; that in so doing he had sacrificed the right to the expedient, and been governed by motives of selfishness and worldly wisdom. These were reflections that required some time to soften; but time will do almost everything; and though little comfort arose on Mrs. Rushworth's side for the misery she had occasioned, comfort was to be found greater than he had supposed in his other children. Julia's match became a less desperate business than he had considered it at first.

She was humble, and wishing to be forgiven; and Mr. Yates, desirous of being really received into the family, was disposed to look up to him and be guided. He was not very solid; but there was a hope of his becoming less trifling, of his being at least tolerably domestic and quiet; and at any rate, there was comfort in finding his estate rather more, and his debts much less, than he had feared, and in being consulted and treated as the friend best worth attending to. There was comfort also in Tom, who gradually regained his health, without regaining the thoughtlessness and selfishness of his previous habits.

He was the better for ever for his illness. He had suffered, and he had learned to think: two advantages that he had never known before; and the self-reproach arising from the deplorable event in Wimpole Street, to which he felt himself accessory by all the dangerous intimacy of his unjustifiable theatre, made an impression on his mind which, at the age of six-and-twenty, with no want of sense or good companions, was durable in its happy effects. He became what he ought to be: useful to his father, steady and quiet, and not living merely for himself.

Here was comfort indeed! and quite as soon as Sir Thomas could place dependence on such sources of good, Edmund was contributing to his father's ease by improvement in the only point in which he had given him pain before— improvement in his spirits. After wandering about and sitting under trees with Fanny all the summer evenings, he had so well talked his mind into submission as to be very tolerably cheerful again. These were the circumstances and the hopes which gradually brought their alleviation to Sir Thomas, deadening his sense of what was lost, and in part reconciling him to himself; though the anguish arising from the conviction of his own errors in the education of his daughters was never to be entirely done away.

Too late he became aware how unfavourable to the character of any young people must be the totally opposite treatment which Maria and Julia had been always experiencing at home, where the excessive indulgence and flattery of their aunt had been continually contrasted with his own severity. He saw how ill he had judged, in expecting to counteract what was wrong in Mrs. Norris by its reverse in himself; clearly saw that he had but increased the evil by teaching them to repress their spirits in his presence so as to make their real disposition unknown to him, and sending them for all their indulgences to a person who had been able to attach them only by the blindness of her affection, and the excess of her praise.

Here had been grievous mismanagement; but, bad as it was, he gradually grew to feel that it had not been the most direful mistake in his plan of education. Something must have been wanting within, or time would have worn away much of its ill effect. He feared that principle, active principle, had been wanting; that they had never been properly taught to govern their inclinations and tempers by that sense of duty which can alone suffice. They had been instructed theoretically in their religion, but never required to bring it into daily practice. To be distinguished for elegance and accomplishments, the authorised object of their youth, could have had no useful influence that way, no moral effect on the mind. He had meant them to be good, but his cares had been directed to the understanding and manners, not the disposition; and of the necessity of self-denial and humility, he feared they had never heard from any lips that could profit them. Bitterly did he deplore a deficiency which now he could scarcely comprehend to have been possible. Wretchedly did he feel, that with all the cost and care of an anxious and expensive education, he had brought up his daughters without their understanding their first duties, or his being acquainted with their character and temper.

The high spirit and strong passions of Mrs. Rushworth, especially, were made known to him only in their sad result. She was not to be prevailed on to leave Mr. Crawford. She hoped to marry him, and they continued together till she was obliged to be convinced that such hope was vain, and till the disappointment and wretchedness arising from the conviction rendered her temper so bad, and her feelings for him so like hatred, as to make them for a while each other's punishment, and then induce a voluntary separation.

She had lived with him to be reproached as the ruin of all his happiness in Fanny, and carried away no better consolation in leaving him than that she haddivided them. What can exceed the misery of such a mind in such a situation?

Mr. Rushworth had no difficulty in procuring a divorce; and so ended a marriage contracted under such circumstances as to make any better end the effect of good luck not to be reckoned on. She had despised him, and loved another; and he had been very much aware that it was so. The indignities of stupidity, and the disappointments of selfish passion, can excite little pity. His punishment followed his conduct, as did a deeper punishment the deeper guilt of his wife. Hewas released from the engagement to be mortified and unhappy, till some other pretty girl could attract him into matrimony again, and he might set forward on a second, and, it is to be hoped, more prosperous trial of the state: if duped, to be duped at least with good humour and good luck; while she must withdraw with infinitely stronger feelings to a retirement and reproach which could allow no second spring of hope or character.

Where she could be placed became a subject of most melancholy and momentous consultation. Mrs. Norris, whose attachment seemed to augment with the demerits of her niece, would have had her received at home and countenanced by them all. Sir Thomas would not hear of it; and Mrs. Norris's anger against Fanny was so much the greater, from considering herresidence there as the motive. She persisted in placing his scruples to heraccount, though Sir Thomas very solemnly assured her that, had there been no young woman in question, had there been no young person of either sex belonging to him, to be endangered by the society or hurt by the character of Mrs. Rushworth, he would never have offered so great an insult to the neighbourhood as to expect it to notice her. As a daughter, he hoped a penitent one, she should be protected by him, and secured in every comfort, and supported by every encouragement to do right, which their relative situations admitted; but farther than thathe could not go. Maria had destroyed her own character, and he would not, by a vain attempt to restore what never could be restored, by affording his sanction to vice, or in seeking to lessen its disgrace, be anywise accessory to introducing such misery in another man's family as he had known himself.

It ended in Mrs. Norris's resolving to quit Mansfield and devote herself to her unfortunate Maria, and in an establishment being formed for them in another country, remote and private, where, shut up together with little society, on one side no affection, on the other no judgment, it may be reasonably supposed that their tempers became their mutual punishment. Mrs. Norris's removal from Mansfield was the great supplementary comfort of Sir Thomas's life. His opinion of her had been sinking from the day of his return from Antigua: in every transaction together from that period, in their daily intercourse, in business, or in chat, she had been regularly losing ground in his esteem, and convincing him that either time had done her much disservice, or that he had considerably over-rated her sense, and wonderfully borne with her manners before. He had felt her as an hourly evil, which was so much the worse, as there seemed no chance of its ceasing but with life; she seemed a part of himself that must be borne for ever. To be relieved from her, therefore, was so great a felicity that, had she not left bitter remembrances behind her, there might have been danger of his learning almost to approve the evil which produced such a good.

She was regretted by no one at Mansfield. She had never been able to attach even those she loved best; and since Mrs. Rushworth's elopement, her temper had been in a state of such irritation as to make her everywhere tormenting. Not even

Fanny had tears for aunt Norris, not even when she was gone for ever. That Julia escaped better than Maria was owing, in some measure, to a favourable difference of disposition and circumstance, but in a greater to her having been less the darling of that very aunt, less flattered and less spoilt. Her beauty and acquirements had held but a second place. She had been always used to think herself a little inferior to Maria. Her temper was naturally the easiest of the two; her feelings, though quick, were more controllable, and education had not given her so very hurtful a degree of self-consequence.

She had submitted the best to the disappointment in Henry Crawford. After the first bitterness of the conviction of being slighted was over, she had been tolerably soon in a fair way of not thinking of him again; and when the acquaintance was renewed in town, and Mr. Rushworth's house became Crawford's object, she had had the merit of withdrawing herself from it, and of chusing that time to pay a visit to her other friends, in order to secure herself from being again too much attracted. This had been her motive in going to her cousin's. Mr. Yates's convenience had had nothing to do with it. She had been allowing his attentions some time, but with very little idea of ever accepting him; and had not her sister's conduct burst forth as it did, and her increased dread of her father and of home, on that event, imagining its certain consequence to herself would be greater severity and restraint, made her hastily resolve on avoiding such immediate horrors at all risks, it is probable that Mr. Yates would never have succeeded. She had not eloped with any worse feelings than those of selfish alarm. It had appeared to her the only thing to be done. Maria's guilt had induced Julia's folly.

Henry Crawford, ruined by early independence and bad domestic example, indulged in the freaks of a cold-blooded vanity a little too long. Once it had, by an opening undesigned and unmerited, led him into the way of happiness. Could he have been satisfied with the conquest of one amiable woman's affections, could he have found sufficient exultation in overcoming the reluctance, in working himself into the esteem and tenderness of Fanny Price, there would have been every probability of success and felicity for him. His affection had already done something. Her influence over him had already given him some influence over her. Would he have deserved more, there can be no doubt that more would have been obtained, especially when that marriage had taken place, which would have given him the assistance of her conscience in subduing her first inclination, and brought them very often together. Would he have persevered, and uprightly, Fanny must have been his reward, and a reward very voluntarily bestowed, within a reasonable period from Edmund's marrying Mary.

Had he done as he intended, and as he knew he ought, by going down to Everingham after his return from Portsmouth, he might have been deciding his own happy destiny. But he was pressed to stay for Mrs. Fraser's party; his staying was made of flattering consequence, and he was to meet Mrs. Rushworth there. Curiosity and vanity were both engaged, and the temptation of immediate pleasure was too strong for a mind unused to make any sacrifice to right: he resolved to defer his Norfolk journey, resolved that writing should answer the purpose of it, or that its purpose was unimportant, and staid. He saw Mrs. Rushworth, was received by her with a coldness which ought to have been repulsive, and have established apparent indifference between them for ever; but he was mortified, he could not bear to be thrown off by the woman whose smiles had been so wholly at his command: he must exert himself to subdue so proud a display of resentment; it was anger on Fanny's account; he must get the better of it, and make Mrs. Rushworth Maria Bertram again in her treatment of himself.

In this spirit he began the attack, and by animated perseverance had soon re-established the sort of familiar intercourse, of gallantry, of flirtation, which bounded his views; but in triumphing over the discretion which, though beginning in anger, might have saved them both, he had put himself in the power of feelings on her side more strong than he had supposed. She loved him; there was no withdrawing attentions avowedly dear to her. He was entangled by his own vanity, with as little excuse of love as possible, and without the smallest inconstancy of mind towards her cousin. To keep

Fanny and the Bertrams from a knowledge of what was passing became his first object. Secrecy could not have been more desirable for Mrs. Rushworth's credit than he felt it for his own. When he returned from Richmond, he would have been glad to see Mrs. Rushworth no more. All that followed was the result of her imprudence; and he went off with her at last, because he could not help it, regretting Fanny even at the moment, but regretting her infinitely more when all the bustle of the intrigue was over, and a very few months had taught him, by the force of contrast, to place a yet higher value on the sweetness of her temper, the purity of her mind, and the excellence of her principles.

That punishment, the public punishment of disgrace, should in a just measure attend hisshare of the offence is, we know, not one of the barriers which society gives to virtue. In this world the penalty is less equal than could be wished; but without presuming to look forward to a juster appointment hereafter, we may fairly consider a man of sense, like Henry Crawford, to be providing for himself no small portion of vexation and regret: vexation that must rise sometimes to self-reproach, and regret to wretchedness, in having so requited hospitality, so injured family peace, so forfeited his best, most estimable, and endeared acquaintance, and so lost the woman whom he had rationally as well as passionately loved. After what had passed to wound and alienate the two families, the continuance of the Bertrams and Grants in such close neighbourhood would have been most distressing; but the absence of the latter, for some months purposely lengthened, ended very fortunately in the necessity, or at least the practicability, of a permanent removal. Dr. Grant, through an interest on which he had almost ceased to form hopes, succeeded to a stall in Westminster, which, as affording an occasion for leaving Mansfield, an excuse for residence in London, and an increase of income to answer the expenses of the change, was highly acceptable to those who went and those who staid. Mrs. Grant, with a temper to love and be loved, must have gone with some regret from the scenes and people she had been used to; but the same happiness of disposition must in any place, and any society, secure her a great deal to enjoy, and she had again a home to offer Mary; and Mary had had enough of her own friends, enough of vanity, ambition, love, and disappointment in the course of the last half-year, to be in need of the true kindness of her sister's heart, and the rational tranquillity of her ways. They lived together; and when Dr. Grant had brought on apoplexy and death, by three great institutionary dinners in one week, they still lived together; for Mary, though perfectly resolved against ever attaching herself to a younger brother again, was long in finding among the dashing representatives, or idle heir-apparents, who were at the command of her beauty, and her 20,000, any one who could satisfy the better taste she had acquired at Mansfield, whose character and manners could authorise a hope of the domestic happiness she had there learned to estimate, or put Edmund Bertram sufficiently out of her head.

Edmund had greatly the advantage of her in this respect. He had not to wait and wish with vacant affections for an object worthy to succeed her in them. Scarcely had he done regretting Mary Crawford, and observing to Fanny how impossible it was that he should ever meet with such another woman, before it began to strike him whether a very different kind of woman might not do just as well, or a great deal better: whether Fanny herself were not growing as dear, as important to him in all her smiles and all her ways, as Mary Crawford had ever been; and whether it might not be a possible, an hopeful undertaking to persuade her that her warm and sisterly regard for him would be foundation enough for wedded love.

I purposely abstain from dates on this occasion, that every one may be at liberty to fix their own, aware that the cure of unconquerable passions, and the transfer of unchanging attachments, must vary much as to time in different people. I only entreat everybody to believe that exactly at the time when it was quite natural that it should be so, and not a week earlier, Edmund did cease to care about Miss Crawford, and became as anxious to marry Fanny as Fanny herself could desire.

With such a regard for her, indeed, as his had long been, a regard founded on the most endearing claims of innocence and helplessness, and completed by every recommendation of growing worth, what could be more natural than the change? Loving, guiding, protecting her, as he had been doing ever since her being ten years old, her mind in so great a degree formed by his care, and her comfort depending on his kindness, an object to him of such close and peculiar interest, dearer by all his own importance with her than any one else at Mansfield, what was there now to add, but that he should learn to prefer soft light eyes to sparkling dark ones. And being always with her, and always talking confidentially, and his feelings exactly in that favourable state which a recent disappointment gives, those soft light eyes could not be very long in obtaining the pre-eminence.

Having once set out, and felt that he had done so on this road to happiness, there was nothing on the side of prudence to stop him or make his progress slow; no doubts of her deserving, no fears of opposition of taste, no need of drawing new hopes of happiness from dissimilarity of temper. Her mind, disposition, opinions, and habits wanted no half-concealment, no self-deception on the present, no reliance on future improvement. Even in the midst of his late infatuation, he had acknowledged Fanny's mental superiority. What must be his sense of it now, therefore? She was of course only too good for him; but as nobody minds having what is too good for them, he was very steadily earnest in the pursuit of the blessing, and it was not possible that encouragement from her should be long wanting. Timid, anxious, doubting as she was, it was still impossible that such tenderness as hers should not, at times, hold out the strongest hope of success, though it remained for a later period to tell him the whole delightful and astonishing truth. His happiness in knowing himself to have been so long the beloved of such a heart, must have been great enough to warrant any strength of language in which he could clothe it to her or to himself; it must have been a delightful happiness. But there was happiness elsewhere which no description can reach. Let no one presume to give the feelings of a young woman on receiving the assurance of that affection of which she has scarcely allowed herself to entertain a hope.

Their own inclinations ascertained, there were no

difficulties behind, no drawback of poverty or parent. It was a match which Sir Thomas's wishes had even forestalled. Sick of ambitious and mercenary connexions, prizing more and more the sterling good of principle and temper, and chiefly anxious to bind by the strongest securities all that remained to him of domestic felicity, he had pondered with genuine satisfaction on the more than possibility of the two young friends finding their natural consolation in each other for all that had occurred of disappointment to either; and the joyful consent which met Edmund's application, the high sense of having realised a great acquisition in the promise of Fanny for a daughter, formed just such a contrast with his early opinion on the subject when the poor little girl's coming had been first agitated, as time is for ever producing between the plans and decisions of mortals, for their own instruction, and their neighbours' entertainment.

Fanny was indeed the daughter that he wanted. His charitable kindness had been rearing a prime comfort for himself. His liberality had a rich repayment, and the general goodness of his intentions by her deserved it. He might have made her childhood happier; but it had been an error of judgment only which had given him the appearance of harshness, and deprived him of her early love; and now, on really knowing each other, their mutual attachment became very strong. After settling her at Thornton Lacey with every kind attention to her comfort, the object of almost every day was to see her there, or to get her away from it. Selfishly dear as she had long been to Lady Bertram, she could not be parted with willingly by her. No happiness of son or niece could make her wish the marriage. But it was possible to part with her, because Susan remained to supply her place. Susan became the stationary niece, delighted to be so; and equally well adapted for it by a readiness of mind, and an inclination for usefulness, as Fanny had been by sweetness of temper, and strong feelings of gratitude. Susan could never be spared. First as a comfort to Fanny, then as an auxiliary, and last as her substitute, she was established at Mansfield, with every appearance of equal permanency.

Her more fearless disposition and happier nerves made

everything easy to her there. With quickness in understanding the tempers of those she had to deal with, and no natural timidity to restrain any consequent wishes, she was soon welcome and useful to all; and after Fanny's removal succeeded so naturally to her influence over the hourly comfort of her aunt, as gradually to become, perhaps, the most beloved of the two. In herusefulness, in Fanny's excellence, in William's continued good conduct and rising fame, and in the general well-doing and success of the other members of the family, all assisting to advance each other, and doing credit to his countenance and aid, Sir Thomas saw repeated, and for ever repeated, reason to rejoice in what he had done for them all, and acknowledge the advantages of early hardship and discipline, and the consciousness of being born to struggle and endure. With so much true merit and true love, and no want of fortune and friends, the happiness of the married cousins must appear as secure as earthly happiness can be.

Equally formed for domestic life, and attached to country pleasures, their home was the home of affection and comfort; and to complete the picture of good, the acquisition of Mansfield living, by the death of Dr. Grant, occurred just after they had been married long enough to begin to want an increase of income, and feel their distance from the paternal abode an inconvenience. On that event they removed to Mansfield; and the Parsonage there, which, under each of its two former owners, Fanny had never been able to approach but with some painful sensation of restraint or alarm, soon grew as dear to her heart, and as thoroughly perfect in her eyes, as everything else within the view and patronage of Mansfield Park had long been.

Chapter 6

Summary and Analysis

Summary

A young girl named Fanny Price comes to live with her wealthy uncle and aunt, Sir Thomas and Lady Bertram. Fanny's family is quite poor; her mother, unlike her sister Lady Bertram, married beneath her, and Fanny's father, a sailor, is disabled and drinks heavily. Fanny is abused by her other aunt, Mrs. Norris, a busybody who runs things at Mansfield Park, the Bertrams' estate. The Bertram daughters, Maria and Julia, are shallow, rather cruel girls, intent on marrying well and being fashionable. The elder son, Tom, is a roustabout and a drunk. Fanny finds solace only in the friendship of the younger son, Edmund, who is planning to be a clergyman. Fanny grows up shy and deferential, caught as she typically is between members of the Bertram family.

Sir Thomas leaves Mansfield Park for Antigua, where he owns plantations. In his absence, two new figures arrive at Mansfield: Henry and Mary Crawford, the brother and sister of the local minister's wife. Henry and Mary are attractive and cheerful, and they soon become indispensable members of the Mansfield circle. Henry flirts extensively with Maria, who is engaged to marry the boring but wealthy Rushworth. He also flirts with Julia when it suits his purposes. At first, Mary is interested in Tom, the older son and heir, but she soon realizes that he is boring and not really interested in her. She finds herself increasingly attracted to Edmund, although the prospect of marrying a clergyman does not appeal to her, and she is often cruel to him on this account. In the meantime,

Fanny has innocently fallen in love with Edmund, although she does not even admit this to herself. Yates, a visiting friend of Tom's, proposes that the group should put on a play. His idea is eagerly received by all except for Edmund and Fanny, who are horrified at the idea of acting. The play goes on anyways, however; Maria and Henry, as well as Mary and Edmund (who has been prevailed upon to take a role to avoid bringing in an outsider to play it), get to play some rather racy scenes with one another. When one of the women cannot make a rehearsal, Fanny is pressured to take a role. She is almost forced to give in when Sir Thomas makes a sudden entrance, having arrived from Antigua.

Sir Thomas is unhappy about the play and quickly puts a stop to the improprieties. Since Henry has not declared his love, Maria is married to Rushworth. She and Julia leave Mansfield Park for London. Relationships between the Crawfords and the Bertrams intensify. Edmund nearly proposes to Mary several times, but her condescension and amorality always stop him at the last minute. He confides his feelings to Fanny, who is secretly upset by them. In the meantime, on a lark, Henry has decided to woo Fanny. He is surprised to find himself sincerely in love with her. Fanny has become indispensable as a companion to her aunt and uncle, and on the occasion of her brother William's visit, they give a ball in her honor. Some time after the ball, Henry helps William get a promotion in the Navy. Using this as leverage, he proposes to Fanny, who is mortified and refuses. He continues to pursue her. Her uncle is disappointed that she has refused such a wealthy man, and, as an indirect result, she is sent to stay with her parents in their filthy house. Meanwhile, Edmund has been ordained and continues to debate over his relationship with Mary, to Fanny's dismay.

Henry comes to see Fanny at her parents' and renews his suit. He then leaves to take care of business on his estate. Fanny continues to receive letters from Mary encouraging her to take Henry's proposal. A series of events then happen in rapid succession: Tom Bertram falls dangerously ill as a result of his partying and nearly dies; Henry, who has gone not to his estate but to see friends, has run off with the married Maria; Julia, upset over her sister's rash act, elopes with Yates, Tom's friend. Fanny is recalled to Mansfield, bringing her younger sister Susan with her. Edmund has finally seen through Mary, who has admitted that she would like to see Tom die so that Edmund could be heir, and who has more or less condoned Henry and Maria's actions. He is heartbroken, but Fanny consoles him. Maria and Henry eventually split, and she goes to the Continent to live with the evil Mrs. Norris. Julia and Yates are reconciled to the family. Edmund finally comes to his senses and marries Fanny, and Susan takes her place with the Bertrams. Edmund, Fanny, and the rest of those at Mansfield live happily, while Henry, Mary, and Maria are cast out

Chapters 1-3

Summary

Some thirty years before the time of the narrative, and eleven years before the start of the events which are to be recounted, a young woman named Maria Ward married the wealthy and titled Sir Thomas Bertram of Mansfield Park. The new Lady Bertram became the talk of the neighborhood for her marriage; although her family was comfortable, they were not wealthy enough to see one of their daughters married to a baronet under normal circumstances. Hopes were high for her sisters, but one of them ended up marrying a clergyman, the Rev. Norris, and the other one a sailor, who was soon injured in the line of duty and came home to drink and father children. Mrs. Norris, the reverend's wife, lives near her sister Lady Bertram; Rev. Norris is the minister to the parish attached to Mansfield Park.

The two women have not heard from their third sister for many years, until, one day, a letter arrives informing them that she is about to give birth yet again and begging them to help see her older children placed in the world. Motivated by a sense of self-importance rather than any real family feeling, Mrs. Norris, Lady Bertram, and Sir Thomas decide to send for the wayward woman's oldest daughter, a girl of nine named

Fanny. After a discussion of the girl's proper "place" in the Bertram household, during which Mrs. Norris, ever the busybody, points out that she must be constantly reminded of her lower status, they decide that she will live with the Bertrams rather than the childless Mrs. Norris, who claims that she has no money and that her husband will be bothered by the presence of a child.

Fanny arrives at Mansfield Park and meets the family. Sir Thomas and Lady Bertram have four children: Tom, the heir, is 17; Edmund, who is to be a clergyman, is 16; Maria is 13; and Julia is 12. Fanny is quite shy and is frightened by brash Sir Thomas, neurotic Lady Bertram, and the spoiled children. The family is pleased with Fanny's modest looks and her retiring personality; she already seems to "know her place." Maria and Julia are not impressed with their new playmate, as she has no fancy dresses and does not speak French, nor is she interested in hearing their musical efforts.

Nevertheless, they are happy to have her around to use as a political third in their childish skirmishes. Mrs. Norris's constant harangues and the cruelties of the governess and the two girls soon wear Fanny down. One day, Edmund finds Fanny crying in the stairway. He comforts her, and the two become fast friends. Soon Fanny becomes almost happy at Mansfield Park, due in large part to the companionship of her cousin Edmund. Maria and Julia continue to see her as a second-class citizen, though; they are particularly puzzled that she does not want to learn drawing or music. Altogether, though, everyone is quite pleased with the young lady that Fanny is becoming. Sir Thomas also goes out of his way to help Fanny's beloved brother William, for whom he procures a spot in the Navy.

After Fanny has been at Mansfield Park for about five years, Mrs. Norris's husband dies. His position as parish minister was to have gone to Edmund, but Edmund is not of age yet and has not taken his orders as a priest. Normally, the position would go to a family friend to hold until Edmund was old enough, but Tom Bertram has been extravagant and contracted many debts, necessitating that the living (as parish positions are called in the 19th century) go to someone else. Dr. Grant comes with his wife to Mansfield to fill the position. Everyone expects that Mrs. Norris, now a widow, will take Fanny to live with her, but by her usual convoluted logic, she convinces the Bertrams, much to Fanny's relief, to keep the girl with them. The Grants soon settle into Mansfield society, despite Mrs. Norris's criticisms of their habits of household management.

About a year after the Grants' arrival, Sir Thomas finds it necessary to go to Antigua (an island in the Caribbean) to take care of some business matters concerning his plantation holdings there. He departs, taking Tom with him. Most of the inhabitants of Mansfield Park are secretly happy to see Sir Thomas go; his daughters view him as a stern master who thwarts their girlish pleasures, and Fanny is mostly afraid of him. When he leaves, she "grieve[s] because she could not grieve" sincerely at his departure; although he has told her to invite her brother William to visit Mansfield Park when his ship returns to England, he has also remarked that she herself has changed little over the last six years.

Analysis

The introductory chapters of this novel signify that *Mansfield Park* will take as its subject social mobility, which also happens to be the subject of all of Jane Austen's other novels and, for that matter, the subject of most of the novels written in the eighteenth and nineteenth centuries. There is a twist here, however. The marriage of Sir Thomas and Lady Bertram is the kind of event that would normally conclude one of Austen's novels: a beautiful but not economically suitable girl captures the heart and eventually the hand of a nobleman, while her younger sister "settles" for a nice clergyman with a comfortable living. Here we see for the first time the aftermath. Lady Bertram is a neurotic hypochondriac who sleeps most of the day, while Mrs. Norris is a busybody and one of the most excruciatingly annoying characters in all of fiction, truly a testament to Austen's wit and creative power. When Fanny comes to Mansfield Park, we see the true results of the social mobility of the previous generation. Although they want to help their sister's children out of a sense of self-importance and misguided *noblesse oblige,* Mrs. Norris and Lady Bertram do not want to see the rest of the family make the same jump in status they themselves have, particularly since Fanny, by virtue of her father's position in life, would be making a much greater leap. Those who have enjoyed the possibilities of social mobility have now become the most conservative, the zealous guardians of the class system. This is most evident in Mrs. Norris, who hasn't made it to the top herself but is the most interested in preserving the honor of Sir Thomas's family name, to continue to enjoy the glory of her own connection with Mansfield Park.

Fanny is a small child when she comes to Mansfield, though. Her initial moves along the social ladder will involve not marriage but the adoption of surrogate parents. Here she has something in common with the orphans of Dickens's novels, although, since she still has living parents, she cannot be the kind of social blank slate that Dickens' characters are. The insistence of Mrs. Norris and Sir Thomas that she must become enough of a sister that Edmund will not think of marrying her, but not enough to think herself the equal of the Bertram girls, points out the paradox. Fanny's attitude toward her adopted siblings by the end of the novel will speak to the relative success of her "adoption" as a Bertram.

The dissolute Tom Bertram is a symbol of the damaged state of both the British aristocracy in general and the Bertram family in particular. Having gotten himself heavily in debt keeping up with the fashions of the times, he has put the entire family in jeopardy. This jeopardy becomes quite literal when Sir Thomas is forced to undertake the hazardous journey to Antigua to manage his investments; perhaps if the family were not in such bad economic shape he would have sent a representative instead. The Antigua holdings have been the subject of much recent critical work on this novel. Upon Sir Thomas's return, questions are raised about the slave trade and other morally questionable aspects of the plantation business. While these questions are merely parlor conversation and are never hostile, they do remind the reader that it is slave labor that enables the Bertrams' lavish lifestyle. Austen shows an unusual (for her) awareness of current events in her references to these issues, and many have suggested that this book contains a submerged critique of slavery and the economic exploitation of the colonies by the British upper classes.

Chapters 4-8

Summary

The family flourishes in Sir Thomas's absence. Edmund takes over as leader of the family and proves to be just and kind. Maria and Julia are the toast of the neighborhood, and Mrs. Norris supervises their social outings and screens potential suitors. Lady Bertram rarely goes out, and Fanny becomes her companion and helpmate. Edmund once again does Fanny a great kindness, ignoring the objections of Mrs. Norris to get her a horse to ride for her health. Tom soon returns from Antigua; the business there has not gone well, and Sir Thomas will be staying longer than expected.

Maria is soon engaged to Mr. Rushworth, an incredibly wealthy but also incredibly stupid young man with a large estate nearby. Sir Thomas sends his consent from abroad, and everyone is quite content. Shortly after Fanny's eighteenth birthday, Mansfield Park receives two newcomers—the brother and sister of Mrs. Grant, the parish priest's wife. Mary Crawford is beautiful and charming, while her brother Henry, though not handsome, is heir to a large estate and shares his sister's charisma. Mary Crawford immediately sets her sights on Tom Bertram and his large estate, although she finds him dull. Mrs. Grant decides to play matchmaker for Henry and Julia Bertram, despite Henry's aversion to marriage.

The Bertrams and the Crawfords are immediate friends, and Henry seems attracted to Maria despite her engagement. He explains to his sister that, engaged or married, women are "safe" and therefore more fun. Fanny is a puzzle to the Crawfords, who are unsure of her status in the family; after a somewhat convoluted explanation, Mary decides that Fanny is simply not "out" yet (that is, she has not been formally debuted in society).

Despite her best efforts, Mary has made no progress with Tom, and she is disappointed when he leaves Mansfield to carouse with friends. She expects dullness under Edmund. Mr. Rushworth's visits have become more frequent; in the course of one of those visits, he begins to talk of the remodeling and landscaping he wants to do at his estate, Sotherton. The whole party becomes involved in a discussion of estates and style, and they resolve to visit the place. Meanwhile, Mary and Edmund are becoming acquainted, and she finds herself attracted to him. She complains of the difficulty she has had in getting her harp delivered—it is harvest time, and the farmers are not willing to use their carts for hauling.

Despite her vanity and her obviously corrupted sense of the world, Edmund is fascinated by her, and speaks to Fanny of her the next day. They agree on her improprieties, but Fanny does not find her as charming as Edmund does. The conversation troubles Fanny, who cannot admit to herself that she is jealous of Mary as a rival for Edmund's affections. Soon Edmund and Mary are spending a great deal of time together, and eventually Mary is using Fanny's horse almost every day to ride out with Edmund and his sisters. Fanny is neglected and left almost entirely to her two aunts, who abuse her and force her to do their errands. Finally, Edmund discovers Fanny ill after a long day with the two women. He berates them, and himself, and the horse is restored to Fanny.

Plans are finalized for visiting Sotherton. Seats in the carriages are limited, and it is decided that Fanny must stay home with Lady Bertram, although Edmund intervenes on her behalf. Finally, Edmund declares that he will stay home so that Fanny can go. In the end, Mrs. Grant volunteers to stay with Lady Bertram, and all the young people are free to go. The carriage ride to Sotherton is tempestuous. Maria and Julia are now competing more or less openly for Henry Crawford's affections, despite Maria's engagement to Mr. Rushworth. Mrs. Grant instructs Henry to allow Julia to ride on the carriage's open seat for a driving lesson with him, and Maria is furious. Fanny is simply pleased with the view from the carriage. Maria takes solace in bragging of Rushworth's holdings, and is in a much better mood when they arrive at Sotherton.

Analysis

While the last few chapters have focused on social change on an individual level, these chapters focus on broader social changes. The introduction of the Crawfords brings the city to Mansfield Park. Neither Crawford is aware of the conventions of rural estate life, as Mary's fuss about the transport of her harp shows. She remarks that, in London, anything, even transport during harvest season, can be had for the right price. Her comment startles the inhabitants of Mansfield Park, particularly the logical and sensitive Edmund. Clearly she represents a challenge to the old order. Henry Crawford also chooses to be away from his estate much of the time; he knows little of the old-fashioned duty to the land and the local farmers that Edmund feels so strongly.

The two Crawfords' superficiality in matters of everyday life foreshadows their emotional superficiality. While Rushworth seems to be more sympathetic to Edmund's point of view, he too espouses modernity, talking of improvements to his estate and of the latest vogues in landscaping. His comments provoke raised eyebrows and some quoting of poetry between Fanny and Edmund, who are both sensitive to nature and tradition. Julia, Maria, and the others, however, are eager to suggest even more changes. Country estates are quickly shifting from being benevolent, if authoritarian, centers of agrarian society to serving merely as showy hunting parks for the wealthy. As the Bertrams and the Crawfords explore Sotherton in the next chapters, these issues will be explored in more detail.

The romantic entanglements of the novel see their genesis in these chapters as well. Maria is engaged to a man whom she is marrying for money, and the disaster her brother Edmund foresees has just arrived in the form of Henry Crawford, who has absolutely no interest in forming a sincere attachment with anyone. Edmund himself, though, has fallen under Mary's spell, to the extent of inadvertently hurting Fanny in his rush of attentiveness to Mary. When Fanny falls ill, Edmund is partially shocked back to his senses. The feelings of Fanny herself are even more complicated. At this point, she is clearly beginning to feel a romantic interest in Edmund, although she cannot admit this to anyone, even herself. This suggests that Mrs. Norris's plans for her proper upbringing have failed.

In these chapters, Fanny has become increasingly self-effacing and, to the modern reader, annoying in her deference to one and all. While Fanny can be grating, she also proves a masterpiece of psychology on Austen's part. Abused by all and pulled in every direction, she must try to please everyone at once, leaving her in a position where she cannot be herself, save perhaps at odd moments with the understanding Edmund. Very likely, Fanny annoys herself as much as she can annoy us, and when we step back and look at her overall situation, she emerges as a very realistic and sympathetic character. With Sir Thomas absent, nearly everyone at Mansfield Park is engaging in play-acting. While Fanny does it to survive, the others do it for amusement or to "practice" being adults. Edmund plays at being family patriarch, and does a fair job of it, despite his occasional neglect of Fanny. Maria, despite her engagement, plays at being a coquette. Mrs. Grant plays at matchmaker, and Mrs. Norris, of course, plays at being both mother and father to the Bertram children. Play-acting can be seen as both a beneficial exercise—something these young people must do to learn to be adults—and as a morally questionable act—something that can cause trouble, as Maria shows. When the group undertakes "real" acting in the next chapters, issues of sincerity and morality become even more prominent.

Chapters 9-11

Summary

The party arrives at Sotherton and is immediately given a tour of the house by Mr. Rushworth's mother, a garrulous old woman as dull as her son. Fanny is disappointed by the chapel, which is a mere room. She conveys her feeling to Edmund and Mary Crawford, who disagree with her and with each other. Mary finds the idea of going to chapel disagreeable and, unaware that Edmund is to become a priest, makes a snide comment about clergymen. Neither Edmund nor Fanny inform her of her gaffe, but a chance comment of Julia's leaves her mortified at her mistake. Julia's comment, that if Edmund had taken his orders he could marry Maria and Mr. Rushworth in the chapel that day, is an attempt to embarrass her sister and warn her away from Henry Crawford, with whom she has been flirting more and more obviously.

The party leaves the house to view the grounds. Maria, Henry, and Rushworth form a threesome, as do Fanny, Edmund, and Mary. To her anger, Julia has to stay with Mrs. Norris and Rushworth's mother. Mary teases Edmund about his decision to become a clergyman. Fanny is mostly left out of their flirtatious conversation, but she continues to accompany them about the grounds. Fanny becomes tired, and the threesome sits. Mary is restless and prevails on Edmund to accompany her further while Fanny rests. Fanny is left behind. Some time later, Maria and her two suitors arrive. They wish to pass through a nearby gate to the rest of the park, but the gate is locked. Rushworth returns to the house to get the key, but Maria and Henry slip through the side of the spiked gate and go off alone together, to Fanny's dismay. A few minutes later, an annoyed Julia arrives and follows after Maria and Henry. Finally, Rushworth arrives with the key and is clearly disappointed. He asks Fanny what she thinks of Henry; he is clearly aware of Maria's flirtations. Fanny evades his question. Finally, the rest of the party returns for Fanny, and they depart for the house, where they dine quickly and then leave for home. Julia again shares a seat with Henry, and the women in the coach are crowded by the plants, cheeses, and eggs Mrs. Norris is bringing back as gifts.

Soon after the trip to Sotherton, a letter arrives, informing the family that Sir Thomas will return in November, thirteen weeks from the present. Maria is anxious, because her father's return will mean her marriage; the rest are concerned that his return will mean an end to their gaiety. For Edmund, his father's return will also mean his taking orders, and, at a party one evening, Mary takes the opportunity to tease him again. In her teasing she includes some insults to Dr. Grant, which offends Fanny. Fanny and Edmund escape Mary and go out to look at the stars. Edmund again speaks of Mary to Fanny, trying to justify her bad habits and her cruelty by pointing to her precarious upbringing. Fanny changes the subject to point out constellations. Edmund soon rejoins the party, to Fanny's dismay.

Analysis

The various features of the Sotherton grounds reflect both actual vogues in landscape and a metaphorical commentary on the action of the novel. Aesthetic considerations are one of the few things that can provoke Fanny to speak her mind, as the conversation in the chapel shows. The chapel highlights the differences among Fanny, who is romantic and conservative yet sensitive, Edmund, who is practical above all but still retains his aesthetic sense, and Mary, who is wholly modern and more interested, as Fanny notes, in people and politics than in beauty. Edmund represents a sort of golden mean, as he is neither stuck in the past nor forward-looking to the detriment of all else. The park at Sotherton represents the attempts of man to control nature over the centuries. It even includes an artificial "wilderness," an area that is supposed to look wild and natural but is in reality carefully groomed. The action that takes place in the park is heavily reliant on the setting.

The park is not a house, so it can seem like a place where normal social rules do not apply. Maria's flirtations with Henry are an indication of this. However, this is no Eden; it is a place made by human hands (hands which represent a source of exploited labor, no less). Therefore, rules do apply. The passage of Maria and Henry around the locked gate reveals this. They violate the park together, a transgressive act. Their act is a penetration of a previously locked-off space, which is clearly meant to suggest a sexual act. The spikes on the gate and the threat to Maria's gown hint at the violence that Maria could possibly do herself by undertaking such actions with Henry.

Edmund's skirmishes with Mary over his future as a clergyman are also telling. Edmund views clergymen as a powerful moral example for their parishioners; he feels that by knowing those to whom he preaches he can do good in their lives. Mary feels that the job is outdated and filled by those who harangue to a congregation of strangers and then don't live up to their own precepts. While her brother-in-law Dr. Grant may not be perfect, he is nevertheless far better than Mary makes him out to be. That Edmund is still attracted to her despite her flawed reasoning and her generally disturbing outlook is proof that passionate love is not a positive thing in this society. Edmund is blinded by his attraction to her. His relationship with Fanny, on the other hand, is based on companionable, if not brotherly, love and mutual interests. A mark of the depth of his relationship with Fanny is his willingness to discuss romantic interests with her. While this is, in its way, transgressive—it is not really proper conversational material for a brother and sister—it also speaks to the depth of their attachment and the essential un-brotherliness of his feelings for her. She is his closest friend in a world where friendship between the genders is normally superficial; it is also possible that Edmund is unconsciously trying to make her jealous.

The two threesomes that form to tour Sotherton foreshadow the two love triangles that are developing. In the park at Sotherton, the characters have a chance to compare alternatives and try out potential couplings just as they try out possible rehabilitation plans for the estate. Both are serious business, yet both are treated as proper holiday fun. While the triangle involving Maria, Rushworth, and Henry seems more serious—Maria and Henry are always on the verge of actual involvement—they represent more of a comic situation. It is Fanny, Edmund, and Mary who grapple more directly with social issues and sincerity, who provide the serious commentary on choosing a proper mate. Although our sympathies are obviously meant to be with Fanny, and we are meant to distrust Mary, at this point she is ahead in the quest for Edmund's affections. The passive Fanny, not sure whether to view Edmund as a brother or as a lover, cannot counter Mary's aggressive style. Mary's quasi-sexual assertiveness will increasingly become an issue, first for Fanny and then for Edmund

Chapters 12-15

Summary

In anticipation of Sir Thomas's return, Tom returns to Mansfield Park. Mary Crawford is now repelled by him and definitely interested in Edmund. Henry Crawford returns to his own estate to take care of some business, and Maria and Julia are pained by his absence. Upon Tom's return, a small ball is held at Mansfield; it is Fanny's first ball.

Tom has brought his friend Yates to Mansfield with him. Yates is dull, constantly telling the story about the amateur theatricals in which he had been taking part at the estate he visited before Mansfield. Unfortunately, the host's grandmother had died and prevented the performance. Inspired by Yates's story, Tom proposes that the group put on a play at Mansfield Park. Everyone is enthusiastic, save Edmund and Fanny. Edmund is opposed to private theatricals and points out that the production could jeopardize Maria's engagement. His objections are ignored, however, and a grand plan is laid out for the construction of a theater in Sir Thomas's room and the billiard-room. Fanny soothes Edmund by pointing out that the plan may be abandoned due to the fickleness of the group and the difficulty of finding a play to suit everyone's tastes. Indeed, the selection of a piece turns out to be difficult; half the group wants a comedy, the other half a tragedy, and a piece is needed which has enough good roles for everyone. Finally, they settle on *Lovers' Vows,* the piece Yates was to have performed in the prior theatricals. The play is scandalous, as it features illegitimate children and bold declarations of love, and the casting will create some awkward on-stage couples. Passed over in favor of Maria and Mary Crawford for the good parts, Julia refuses to participate in the play.

The rest of the play is then cast. Rushworth is given a small role, and his involvement in the play gives Austen a chance to engage in some comedy; he is an idiot and a fop. Edmund, hearing which play is to be performed, is aghast, but again he is ignored. Mrs. Norris is as excited about the play as anyone, bustling around making preparations for the stage. One part is still uncast, that of Anhalt, the clergyman who ends up married to Mary Crawford's rather sexually aggressive character. Tom tries to get Edmund to take the part; when he refuses, Tom decides to ask a neighbor to participate. He then attempts to get Fanny to take the last uncast female role; when she refuses, she is attacked by both Tom and Mrs. Norris, who call her ungrateful and try to remind her of her place. Mary Crawford comes to her rescue, but Fanny distrusts her friendliness.

Analysis

While the young people have been engaging in acting all along, Yates's suggestion that they put on the play literalizes some of what's been going on. The play is highly inappropriate, because it is so close to the truth: Maria and Henry will be playing mother and son, and will be forced to play some rather intimate scenes. Acting casts doubt on sincerity and destabilizes the relationships between these individuals; in their behavior towards each other, what is "acting" and what isn't?

That the house is physically turned into a theater confirms the powerful influence of acting on the lives of these people. Particularly since we already know that some of these characters are acting on hidden motives (Maria is marrying Rushworth for his money, while trying to get Crawford to declare his love at the same time, for example), anything that calls their sincerity into question is a threat. Acting is also inappropriate for the professional connotations it bears. Edmund speaks of having seen plays performed by professional companies and notes that their performances are perfectly appropriate. For his sisters and his brother, though, to undertake a task that is normally the job of middle-class individuals who learn it as a craft and are then paid for it would be highly inappropriate. Turning the house into a theater is almost like turning it into a commercial establishment, even though no audience will be brought in.

Most importantly, though, this play gives the women a chance to behave in a sexually aggressive manner. Given that this is Maria's and Mary's tendency already, the play is dangerous to a nineteenth-century world. Although they would purportedly be playing a role and not behaving as themselves, the danger and the inappropriateness are still there, and even to pretend that women could behave in such a way is a threat to society.

Fanny and Edmund set themselves apart by refusing to participate. While Edmund has some knowledge of the play and is opposed to the idea of acting in general, Fanny reinforces her opinion with research. She actually reads the play. As she goes through the script, the correlation between intimacies on stage and desired intimacies in real life is immediately apparent to her. In its way, the play is more "real" than the "real" lives of these characters right now; at least the affections displayed on stage will be consistent with the emotions felt in her friends' hearts. Thus, although the production of the play represents a form of public behavior—"acting"—that is inappropriate, it also serves to cast light on the great deal of "acting" going on in the everyday lives of these people.

Tom and Mrs. Norris's attack on Fanny demonstrates the blurring of the boundaries between acting and reality. While she has always been aware of her precarious position in the family, Fanny has never been subjected to aggression like this before. Mrs. Norris states Fanny's situation without any of the niceties that normally accompany it. In other words, disoriented by the goings-on onstage, she has stopped acting. Clearly, the play is dangerous in many ways, and Edmund's opposition to the production is logical, even though it can seem priggish. In some ways, though, Edmund is indeed a prig. Facing the prospect of little or no inheritance as the younger son, he constantly seeks to distinguish himself from his dissolute older brother through his moral behavior. On the one hand, this allows Austen to criticize the rigid English system of inheritance. Protected by convention and to some extent by law, Tom is allowed to behave as badly as he pleases, knowing that he is guaranteed to become master of Mansfield Park at his father's death. Edmund is the better person, but he must take up a profession. Edmund's priggishness also shows his humanity, though. He is not perfect, and despite his role as teacher to Fanny, he is still in need of some education himself. Only when he has learned as he is supposed to will Edmund be able to achieve happiness. Until then, he relies on a stilted moral code to guide the family.

Chapters 16-18

Summary

Fanny, still distressed by Tom and Mrs. Norris's attack on her, retreats to the old nursery where she keeps her books and other possessions. Edmund comes to ask for her advice. Having found out that Tom intends to ask a neighbor to take the remaining part in the play, he has resolved to take the part himself rather than allowing an outsider to take part in and witness the production. He is also aware that Mary Crawford is unhappy about having to play opposite a stranger. Fanny is unable to give her full consent to Edmund's plan, but she reluctantly agrees that his idea is probably for the best. Inwardly, she is in turmoil; she cannot believe that Edmund has agreed to act, and she blames Mary for leading him astray.

Rehearsals continue. To Fanny's relief, Mrs. Grant takes the part Tom tried to push on Fanny; Mary has saved Fanny once again. It has become increasingly obvious to all, particularly to Mary and Mrs. Grant, that Maria and Henry are interested in one another, despite her engagement to Rushworth. Mary criticizes Maria for trifling with a man with such riches; he might "escape a profession" and simply live as a gentleman, Mary notes. Both Mary and Mrs. Grant agree that Sir Thomas's return will help immensely, by bringing back some much-needed common sense and authority.

Fanny becomes the confidant of all involved in the play and hears all the gossip and complaints. She is also valuable as a rehearsal partner and acting coach, although she is unwilling. Henry and Maria both prove to be fine actors, and Fanny cannot help but admire their talent. Rushworth is an inept actor and an annoyance to all, and Fanny must tolerate the others' complaints about him as well as his constant requests for a rehearsal partner. The time soon comes for Edmund and Mary to rehearse a scene together in which their characters make declarations of love for one another. Fanny is dreading its performance. As she hides in the former nursery, Mary seeks her out and asks her to rehearse the scene with her. Just as she reluctantly agrees, Edmund arrives, to ask the very same favor of Fanny. Edmund and Mary happily decide to rehearse together, with Fanny as audience. The emotional strain is nearly too much for Fanny.

Finally, the time comes for a dress rehearsal. Mrs. Grant must stay at the parsonage to care for her sick husband, and the group pressures Fanny to read her part. Even Edmund urges her to cooperate. She is forced to yield, and is about to begin the reading when Julia, who is still not participating in the play, rushes in with news that Sir Thomas has just arrived at the house.

Analysis

Everyone's alarm at the return of Sir Thomas is a signal that they know they are doing wrong in performing the play. That even Fanny has been forced to take a part suggests the potential destruction involved in the performance; it has slowly corrupted every part of the household, even Fanny and Edmund. Sir Thomas represents wisdom, authority, and an older, tried-and-true standard of behavior; as has already been noted, his return means Maria's marriage and Edmund's taking orders. While Edmund has done his best to protect the family from themselves, he is not the patriarch, and does not have his power or his authority. Edmund's consultation with Fanny over his part in the play is both an attempt to seek legitimacy and a test of Fanny. Although Edmund knows that his reasoning is meager and will only include him in the common ruin, he is hoping to gain Fanny's approval. At the same time, he is also testing her reaction, curious to see how she will react to the news that he is to play opposite Mary and hoping that she will not agree with him just to appease him. This, of course, only increases Fanny's turmoil. Seeing Maria come so dangerously close to displaying her true emotions has been bad enough for Fanny; seeing Edmund do so nearly destroys her.

Even so, Fanny is fascinated by the rehearsals and performances. Despite her aversion, she knows nearly all the parts by heart, and she admits that she gets an "innocent" enjoyment out of the proceedings. Fanny's enjoyment is not wholly innocent, though, for she is involved in most of the political intrigues among the cast. Again this shows how far-reaching the corruption of the "acting bug" is, but it also shows to what an extent "real life" is similar to a play acted on stage. The return of Sir Thomas brings an end to the danger and a return of stability to the family. Whether Fanny will be any worse off, or any better off, for his return remains to be seen. His dramatic return signifies the end of the first volume of the novel.

Summary and Analysis of Chapters 19-24

Fanny waits in the drawing-room with the Crawfords and Mr. Yates while Sir Thomas is reunited with his immediate family. The Crawfords quietly return to the parsonage, but Mr. Yates stays behind. In great trepidation, Fanny goes to see her uncle, and is stunned by his kind manner towards her: "his kindness was such as to made her reproach herself for loving him so little." Sir Thomas meets Mr. Rushmore for the first time, and everything seems comfortable. Tom glosses over the whole acting business until Sir Thomas goes to see his room and finds both it and the billiard room converted into a stage. Here, he makes Mr. Yates's acquaintance. He holds his temper as he hears from him the whole history of the endeavor, and looks askance at Edmund: "On your judgment, Edmund, I depended." Edmund explains to his father that everyone was to blame for the theatrical fiasco except Fanny, who consistently opposed the play for her uncle's sake. Mrs. Norris attempts to remove any blame from herself by pointing out to Sir Thomas her role in making the match between Maria and Rushmore, which Sir Thomas is beginning to find a matter of some concern. He orders the removal of anything having to do with the play, and Mr. Yates leaves soon afterwards. Maria wants more than anything for Henry Crawford to declare his love for her, but he leaves Mansfield for Bath, at which point Maria decides she will follow through with her decision to wed Rushworth. Mansfield seems "an altered place" in the absence of the Crawfords.

Sir Thomas makes it clear that he wants, for a while at least, only the company of his immediate family. He does, however, include Rushworth in this circle. Maria and Rushworth marry quickly and honeymoon in Brighton: no longer a rival, Julia accompanies her sister. Fanny, now the only young woman at Mansfield, moves toward center stage. Sir Thomas pays particular attention to her and comments on her improved good looks. Edmund goes to great lengths to complement Fanny-she has grown into a pretty young woman—and to explain to her the depth of his father's approval of her. Fanny becomes indispensable to Lady Bertram and, without any other distractions to occupy her time, Mary Crawford seeks out her company, as well. One day, in a shower of rain, Dr. Grant rescues her with an umbrella, and the young women spend time together. During this conversation, Mary discusses her feelings for Edmund but criticizes his social position, and Fanny remains quiet.

Soon afterwards, Fanny-to her great delight-receives an invitation to dine at the parsonage. It is her first social invitation ever. In fact, with the exception of Sotherton, Fanny has only ever dined at Mansfield. After a great deal of fussing between Lady Bertram and Mrs. Norris about whether Fanny should accept the invitation, it is finally agreed that she should.

She wears the dress she wore to the wedding, and feels extremely nervous. Mrs. Norris attempts to put Fanny in her place by declaring that she should walk, but Sir Thomas orders the carriage to take her to the parsonage.

Edmund accompanies her, and when they arrive they are surprised to find that Henry Crawford has returned from Bath, a popular resort. Fanny is happy Henry has returned, because his presence makes her less likely to be forced to talk at the dinner table. She finds herself annoyed by his comments about Maria and Julia, but remains quiet. She is unable to remain silent, however, when Henry criticizes Sir Thomas for putting an end to the play: Fanny tells him off, saying that it was a good thing Sir Thomas returned, and that things had gone far enough. Henry, at this point, becomes much more interested in Fanny Price. Meanwhile, Mary finds out that Edmund still plans on taking orders, and is much put out that he hasn't more interest in bettering himself socially and financially.

The next day, Henry tells Mary that he plans to stay on at Mansfield because he plans on making Fanny Price fall in love with him. Mary tells him that he only finds her attractive because he doesn't have anyone to compare her with since the two Bertram girls are missing. However, Henry, who is used to having women pay great attention to him, tells Mary that Fanny presents a challenge for him. Meanwhile, Fanny receives a letter from her brother William, a navy midshipman, informing her that he will be coming for a visit to Mansfield at Sir Thomas's invitation. The siblings haven't seen each other for seven years, and are overjoyed at the prospect of their imminent reunion. Henry realizes he can find the way to Fanny's heart by paying attention to her brother, whom he does come to greatly admire, and offers William the use of a horse during his visit.

Analysis

Everyone's response to Sir Thomas's return reveals that they all felt that they were doing something wrong, yet proceeded with their plans nonetheless. They were, in fact, acting like children while the parents were away. The engaged

Maria forgot her social position and reputation by flirting with another man and causing gossip to spread about her. Tom Bertram, who is supposed to be in charge, set up a totally inappropriate form of entertainment and revealed himself as willing to cast a bad light on his family name by making it public. Here, Austen criticizes the deeply-embedded social practice of primogeniture, which dictates that the first, or oldest (and not necessarily the best) son is the one who inherits the estate. While Lady Bertram and Mrs. Norris are present, the women remain entirely clueless as to the inappropriateness of the young people's behavior. Although putting on a play is a practice that we might dismiss laughingly today as innocent, we must keep in mind the strict mode of conduct expected during this era.

Mansfield Park, Austen seems to be saying, is much in need of a strong, masculine hand. The absence of Sir Thomas resulted in chaos, but upon his return, things are set right.

In the absence of her cousins, the Bertram daughters, Fanny moves into a far more central role at Mansfield. She is favored by Sir Thomas: she finds his accounts of Antigua fascinating and wants to hear more about slavery, a practice which, although outlawed in England, remains legal in the Caribbean. Although Austen merely remarks on its existence in passing, the practice of slavery was a point of great contention in Britain at this time. The author could have been gently alluding to Fanny's social position, which casts her into a sort of no man's land. She is provided for by the family, but is expected to be at their beck and call without being given any wages. Furthermore, her future lies entirely in their hands.

The corrupting influence of Henry and Mary Crawford, who hail from London, come fully to light in these chapters. They are both manipulators intent on changing the country traditions of Mansfield. Mary is intent on disregarding Edmund's traditional second son status by urging him to aim higher. She cannot stand that he is the second son, and cannot view herself as the wife of a parson. Mary dismisses Henry's attempts to make Fanny fall in love with him, and seems impervious to the pain this might cause her friend. Simply put, the modern customs of the town (in the form of the Crawfords and Mr. Yates) are invading the peace, propriety, and traditions of the country. Edmund has made every attempt to maintain the proper high standards, but he is not the heir, and he too has become contaminated by his desire for the dazzling Mary Crawford. Even Fanny, at the last moment, almost fails under their spell. The patriarch's return, however, soon sets everything right.

Lord and Lady Bertram's marriage, here, is viewed in a very positive light. Although their engagement was initially of some concern because of the discrepancy in their social ranks, they married for love and remain in love-unlike their daughter, Maria, who has married for money and social position. Austen stresses the importance of companionate marriage, a popular nineteenth-century social construct, which declared that mutual feelings of love should be the primary criteria in selecting a mate. Although most people in the Western world consider it the individual right of every person to select the one with whom they desire to spend their life, it should be remembered that this idea is relatively new in the course of human history. Indeed, in many parts of the world arranged marriages are still carried out in the name of tradition. During Austen's time, the idea of companionate marriage was just coming into style. Clearly, Austen herself was a proponent of such marriages, and all of her novels champion this cause

Chapters 24-28

Summary

The day after the dinner, Henry announces to his sister Mary that he will be staying in Mansfield for a while. His entertainment, he tells her to her amusement, will be to make Fanny fall in love with him. Mary tells him that, while Fanny is pretty, she only appears so attractive because Maria and Julia are not around; the challenge, Henry tells her, is in Fanny's lack of interest in him. Henry hardly has a chance to begin wooing Fanny when a letter arrives telling her that her brother

William, who is in the navy, will soon be in England. Sir Thomas has invited him to spend the holidays at Mansfield with Fanny. Henry notes Fanny's intense devotion to her brother and decides to use it to his own advantage. William has become a fine young man and impresses all who meet him with his carriage and his tales of adventure on the sea. The obvious delight Fanny takes in her brother and their sincere familial love move Henry, and he decides that he is genuinely in love with her. Sir Thomas notices his attentions to Fanny and resolves to support the match. At a dinner party at the Grants', Henry begins to woo Fanny in earnest, sitting next to her to teach her a card game.

Edmund and Mary's courtship takes yet another turn at the dinner party. Henry begins to suggest improvements to Edmund's parsonage-to-be at Thornton Lacey; Edmund resists, citing practicality and expense and claiming that he likes the place as it is. Mary is obviously disappointed, especially when Edmund states that he plans to occupy the parsonage himself and will not rent it to Henry. Fanny is disappointed too, since she will no longer see Edmund every day. William and Fanny speak of William's imminent departure for his ship. He tells her of his disappointment at not yet being made lieutenant and then talks of how much he will miss her. He says he wishes he could dance with her, and he asks Sir Thomas if Fanny is a good dancer. Sir Thomas does not know, and Henry steps in to try to flatter her. The comment gives Sir Thomas an idea, however; he will have a ball for William and Fanny.

Preparations are quickly made, much to the dismay of Mrs. Norris, who hates to see Fanny benefit. Edmund is planning too: he will be ordained shortly, and then he wishes to ask Mary to marry him, despite his reservations about her. Mary is leaving to visit friends soon; he must act quickly. Fanny is preparing her dress for the ball. William has given her a small amber cross that she wishes to wear, but she has no chain for it. Mary offers to give her one of her own, and, after much reluctance, Fanny chooses one. Once she has chosen, Mary reveals that the chain was a gift from Henry.

Fanny tries to return it, uncomfortable with Henry's recent attentions to her, but Mary insists that she keep it. Returning home with the chain, she finds Edmund in her room, leaving her a gift: a much more pleasing chain that he has gotten her for the cross. She tells him about the chain from Mary, and he counsels her to use Mary's chain, so as not to be rude. His praise of Mary nearly breaks Fanny's heart. Edmund then visits the Parsonage to request Mary as a partner for the first two dances at the ball. She accepts the offer but again attacks his career choice, and he decides not to propose to her, a fact which he shares with Fanny. Again Fanny and Edmund discuss Mary's upbringing and her "evil" qualities.

Fanny dresses for the ball. To her delight, the chain from Mary does not fit through the cross, and she must use Edmund's. She decides to wear Mary's chain as well, out of politeness. Lady Bertram, in an act of kindness, sends her own maid to help Fanny dress. The woman arrives too late, but Fanny is touched by the gesture.

The ball is a success. Fanny is given the honor of leading the dancers, and the honor is especially great, for this is the first ball that has been given at Mansfield, despite her cousins' pleas. They are, of course, away from home and will miss it. Fanny at last feels that she is being treated like her cousins. William is to leave the next day, and Henry is to accompany him, taking William to meet with his uncle the Admiral. Mary teases Fanny about Henry. The men are to leave early, and Fanny is tired, so the ball is broken up. Sir Thomas is certain of Henry's affections for Fanny and believes he means to approach him about a marriage.

Analysis

The incident with the amber cross and the two chains is somewhat similar to the incident with the locked gate at Sotherton that Maria and Henry slither past. The cross and chain, like the gate, convey a great deal of symbolism. Here, though, the focus is on the second of the two love triangles that first came together at Sotherton. The idea of a chain suggests that Fanny will be fettered by choosing a partner. The fact that only one chain fits implies that only one of these men—Edmund—is an appropriate "fit" for Fanny. Behind all this, too, is a certain level of sexual suggestiveness, with the chain being passed through the loop on the cross. The incident brings together the three men in Fanny's life—William, who gave her the cross, and Edmund and Henry, who give her (indirectly, in Henry's case) the two chains. The situation is facilitated by Mary, who has her own interests in mind. The love triangle from Sotherton has become a love quadrangle, with Henry now drawn in to the drama between Mary, Edmund, and Fanny.

The presence of William reinforces the suitability of Edmund as a partner for Fanny. While Henry represents a base, physical kind of love, William represents the ultimate in spiritual, Platonic love. Edmund is a happy medium between the two, brotherly yet still available as a sexual partner for Fanny. Mary seeks to draw him over into the base side of love, and she nearly succeeds. Only her greed in wishing to secure a better income for him before she commits destroys her plan. Her brother's motives are closely aligned with hers, although it is not money he is after. His pursuit of Fanny will lead the plot into some morally ambiguous territory; the very same qualities that make wooing Fanny a challenge are the qualities that make her a worthy partner, and to many, Sir Thomas and Edmund included, Henry seems to be displaying his good taste and moral excellence, not his love of sport, in courting Fanny. She also promises to be a good influence on him; perhaps their marriage would be beneficial overall for its effects on his character, despite the damage to Fanny's happiness.

William, Edmund, and Henry are compared in another way, too: their choice of occupations. William's career at sea has made him a glamorous figure; he is brave, committed, and hard-working, but he has not yet been rewarded with a promotion. Edmund is also committed and will probably be hard-working as a parson; he, however, has the luxury of a wealthy family to ensure that he does not need to worry about money. His decision to take orders is as much a philosophical position as it is a career move; he doesn't need to live at Thornton Lacey and give the sermons himself, but he will. This highlights his essential incompatibility with Mary and angers her most. Henry, of course, has no career; he is a wealthy young heir. His daily "work" involves entertaining himself, and does not contribute to character formation in the way that Edmund's and William's livelihoods do/will. The choice of a career for the male characters in this novel parallels the choice of a husband for the female characters, as financial pressures often come into conflict with more noble considerations, and the proper choice is not always simple or obvious.

Chapters 29-31

Summary

William and Henry leave, followed a few days later by Edmund, who is to take orders. Those remaining at Mansfield Park are melancholy, particularly since Julia is delaying her return home to go to London with Maria and Rushworth. Sir Thomas and Lady Bertram begin to appreciate Fanny more than ever. Mary Crawford, in the meantime, is beside herself with anxiety. Stuck in the Parsonage by bad weather, she misses Edmund and regrets her behavior. Finally, she braves the rain to visit Fanny, hoping to learn something about Edmund. She finds out that he is staying with a friend who has two attractive sisters, and this distresses her. Her feelings for Edmund become clear to Fanny, who is again conflicted.

That night, Henry returns from London. He visits Fanny, then returns to the Parsonage to tell Mary that he has decided to marry Fanny. Mary, seeing that the marriage would only help her chances with Edmund, is delighted, but wonders what Maria and Julia will say. Henry seems glad that they will be disappointed. Both Henry and Mary are sure that Fanny will accept the proposal.

The next morning, Henry goes to Mansfield Park. He has news for Fanny: William has been made a lieutenant through the influence of Henry's uncle the Admiral. Fanny is overjoyed and grateful to Henry for his involvement. Henry then makes his own proposal. Fanny is embarrassed and disappointed that he would mix a good deed—William's promotion—with an evil one—his lovemaking. Henry also brings a letter from his sister, which congratulates her on the match. Fanny writes her a brief note refuting her intentions; she also unequivocally rejects Henry's proposal.

Analysis

Henry's proposal is the climactic event of Volume II, just as Sir Thomas's return was the climax of Volume I. In both situations, we find Fanny resisting the entreaties of her friends; in the first case, to act in the play, here to marry. Austen puts her reader in a rather curious position. Privy to the conversations between Henry and Mary, we are fully aware of the justice of Fanny's position. Because she is forming her conclusions without as much information as the reader has, we can see what an excellent judge of character she is. The additional information makes Edmund's misguided love for Mary all the more vexing to the reader. Austen typically does not allow her reader this kind of access; in her other novels, the "truth" about characters other than the female protagonist is kept hidden until the end. Here the additional information lets us see the education of the characters, particularly Edmund, taking place.

Once again, Fanny is in jeopardy thanks to her position within the Bertram family. Sir Thomas is pleased with Henry's attentions to Fanny, and she will have a difficult time opposing his wishes. The criteria by which the family evaluates Fanny's suitor will be quite different from the criteria used to evaluate Maria's suitor, and these differences will speak to the possibilities for social mobility and for women's autonomy within this society. For now, Fanny thinks that Henry is her only adversary; this will soon change. Henry's attentions to William are a reminder that Fanny and her siblings owe their success to other people, who may at any time demand repayment. The state of Edmund and Mary's relationship is also in flux. Edmund's absence increases Mary's feelings for him, but instead of leading to sincerity and resignation to being a clergyman's wife, it only provokes Mary into assisting Henry in his dubious pursuit of Fanny. Henry's marriage to Fanny would have a double purpose: it would eliminate an undeclared rival, and the additional family connection would throw Edmund and Mary together frequently. Both Mary and Henry are wise in their choice of mates; it is in their romantic strategies that they display their essential immorality

Chapters 32-36

Summary

Fanny hopes that she has discouraged Henry Crawford permanently. To her dismay, though, he comes to see her uncle, Sir Thomas, to plead his case. Fanny is upstairs in the nursery when her uncle comes to talk to her. He is startled that she has no fire in the cold upstairs room (Mrs. Norris had previously forbidden it) and tells her that she will have one from now on. He also asks her to come downstairs with him to talk to Henry, who is waiting.

Fanny cannot believe Henry has had the nerve to repeat his proposals after her denial the night before. Sir Thomas does not understand why Fanny is rejecting such a charming and wealthy young man, and she does not want to tell him about Henry's dalliances with Maria and Julia. He is a bit worried that her affections are directed elsewhere—towards Edmund—but she tells him she loves no other. Sir Thomas accuses her of ingratitude, and her tears and pleading convince him she may be softened towards Henry.

He tells her that she will meet with Henry the following day to explain herself. Henry does indeed show up the next day to try once again. His expressions of sincerity make an impression on Sir Thomas. Again he reminds Fanny of his role in William's promotion, and Fanny is hard-pressed to deny him given this fact. But deny him she does. Sir Thomas tells her that he will respect her wishes, but that he will inform Mrs. Norris and Lady Bertram of the proposal; he also tells her that she will receive Henry for as long as he stays in the neighborhood of Mansfield Park. Mrs. Norris is enraged and barely speaks to Fanny; Lady Bertram tells her she ought to have accepted the proposal. Lady Bertram's vanity is flattered by the proposal, though, and she compliments herself both on sending her own maid to dress Fanny the night of the ball (which is surely when Henry must have fallen in love with her) and on having such a good-looking family.

Edmund returns to Mansfield after his ordination. He is disconcerted to see Mary Crawford still at the Parsonage; he had stayed away longer in hopes that she would leave before he returned. Sir Thomas informs Edmund of Henry's proposal to Fanny; Edmund is gentle with her but, as a friend of Henry's, encourages her to accept the proposal.

The night after Edmund's return, Henry comes to Mansfield Park for dinner. After dinner, he reads from Shakespeare for the entertainment of Lady Bertram. Although he claims that Shakespeare is not one of his favorites, he reads exquisitely, and the group is impressed with his dramatic skills. Fanny is reminded of the play that was to be put on in Sir Thomas's absence. Edmund and Henry have a conversation about delivering sermons, and Henry lavishes Fanny with unwanted attention. Edmund hopes Fanny will be able to get rid of him, but he does nothing to help her.

The Crawfords are to leave Mansfield, and Sir Thomas is eager for Fanny to change her mind. He asks Edmund to intervene. Edmund reluctantly agrees. Fanny's emotions are turbulent as she talks to Edmund about the situation. He tells her that he agrees with her conduct, but he urges her to reconsider. She becomes quite passionate, clearly moved by her feelings for Edmund himself, in her refusals even to think of Henry Crawford. She reminds Edmund of Henry's attention to Maria; he brushes her concerns off.

So, of course, on the subject turns to Mary Crawford. Edmund is pleased that Mary seems so eager to see her brother marry Fanny. Fanny is moved to make a declaration of near-feminist principles: "I think it ought not to be set down as certain, that a man must be acceptable to every woman he may happen to like himself." Unfortunately, Edmund misinterprets Fanny's words and tells her that he has told Mary and Mrs.

Grant that Henry simply needs to be persistent in his addresses to earn her love.

Mary comes to see Fanny before she leaves Mansfield. She jestingly scolds Fanny for rejecting Henry's proposals, but cannot keep from talking about Edmund. She reminisces about the scene from the play that she and Edmund rehearsed with Fanny's help, and she tells Fanny that she does not want to leave Mansfield. She gives Fanny a brief account of the friends she is going to visit; they seem to be a corrupted, overly sophisticated lot—all unhappily married, and all at one time or another conveniently in love with Henry Crawford. She then gives Fanny a piece of shocking news: the necklace she gave to Fanny was intended as a gift from Henry; Fanny was duped into taking it. Again Mary attests to Henry's sincerity, and again Fanny is reminded of Henry's aid to William's career. That night, the Crawfords take leave of Mansfield. Henry seems miserable, and Fanny softens toward him for a moment, but not enough to consider accepting him. The next morning, the Crawfords leave.

Analysis

Henry's little game has quickly become serious business. Fanny's natural reticence and her reluctance to disobey Sir Thomas directly get her into trouble. Fanny is contrasted implicitly with Maria, the first woman to marry in the novel. While Maria is secure in her position in the family and therefore has a right to consult her feelings in deciding whom she will marry, Fanny is a guest; never has this been so obvious as it is now. Sir Thomas accuses her first of having designs on Edmund (which, of course, she does, although they are innocent and she can't even admit them to herself), then of ingratitude.

Mrs. Norris's constant comments on the money needed to support the Price children are a reminder that Fanny is literally indebted to her uncle. In essence, she has been enslaved in exchange for her upbringing. She must either wait on Lady Bertram or else marry—for money—as her uncle sees fit. Again we see Fanny trapped: she cannot speak the truth.

Were she to expose Maria and Julia's behavior during Sir Thomas's absence, she would most likely not be believed, and would probably be kicked out of Mansfield. Fanny is good-hearted, too, and realizes that it would not be ethical to sacrifice her cousins to relieve her own discomfort.

Analysis

It is more obvious than ever that Henry is not the man Fanny should marry. These chapters are constantly interrupted by references to the play that was to be put on at Mansfield. That the play was a bad thing has been well-established by Sir Thomas's reaction to it. The constant reminders of the play are meant to remind the reader, and Fanny, of Henry's essential amorality. While it is more difficult to attack him for his interference in William's career, since it has done William good, Henry is still clearly culpable for his behavior toward Maria and Julia at the time of the play.

The play is also what drew Edmund and Mary together. Edmund, aware of this, makes excuses for the play and tries to clear everyone involved of blame. The fact that it was the setting for his initial contact with Mary reminds us that theirs, too, would be a bad match. Most of all, though, the references to *Lovers' Vows* suggest that most of the people in this world are "acting," that sincerity is not necessarily a given. Henry's reading of Shakespeare is a dramatic reminder of this; he can mimic every character perfectly, although Shakespeare has no intellectual or aesthetic attraction for him.

While the rest of the group sees this as a reflection of Henry's tastes and talents, Fanny sees it as a sign of his essential insincerity and emotional dishonesty. It seems that Edmund and Fanny have both been saved by the Crawfords' departure. Fanny has triumphed through persistence and gentle reasoning; Edmund has gotten away through luck and a battle for self-control. Each benefits from the other's counsel, although neither is honest in their feelings for the other (which do not yet seem to be openly romantic on Edmund's part). Yet forces seem still to be aligned against them, in the form of Sir Thomas and the plotting Crawfords.

Chapters 37-42

Summary

Sir Thomas hopes that Fanny will begin to miss Henry in his absence. Particularly, he thinks she will miss the attention of being at the center of such a situation. Edmund is more realistic about Henry's chances, but he is surprised that Fanny does not seem to miss Mary, who has been her closest companion recently. In reality, Fanny is distraught that Mary and Edmund seem closer to marriage than ever before. William, on leave again, comes to Mansfield Park. He is not allowed to wear his new lieutenant's uniform off-duty, so everyone decides Fanny should accompany him back to Portsmouth to see the uniform while it is still new.

She can visit her family as well. Sir Thomas, and to some extent Edmund, feel that being reminded of her "real" family's circumstances may induce her to accept Henry, in order to maintain her lifestyle and her standing at Mansfield Park. Fanny has not seen her family since she came to Mansfield as a child of ten, and she is happy to go. She also feels the separation from Edmund will do her good in preparation for his marriage. William warns Fanny that her father's home will seem rough in comparison to Mansfield, and that her parents and siblings are crude in their manners. Aware that Fanny's absence will be a hardship to his parents, Edmund delays his trip to London, the trip on which he is to propose to Mary. He tells Fanny of his plan to propose. Thus, her journey sees her both happy and distraught.

William and Fanny have an enjoyable journey to Portsmouth. She is worried still about Henry's addresses, since he has been writing to her via his sister, and William, aware of Henry's role in his promotion, wishes she would accept the man. Mary has been writing often. Fanny's mother is overjoyed to see her, but she is too busy to spend quality time with her daughter. The household is a mess: the children are dirty and ill-behaved, and Fanny's father drinks excessively. Fanny is well-aware of the niceties of behavior and environment to which her uncle's patronage have accustomed her. William has to leave almost immediately, as his ship has sailed early. Fanny's only consolation is her sister Susan, now fourteen, who is brash and lacking in manners but well-meaning, only needing guidance. Most of her other siblings are unruly beyond Fanny's capacity to influence them. Fanny reflects that the political doings of Mansfield are far less unpleasant than this chaos. Fanny receives another letter from Mary which describes the London social whirl; Mary has been visiting with Maria and Julia. Fanny settles a quarrel between Susan and another of her sisters, which cements her relationship with Susan, who now looks up to her for guidance. Edmund has not written, which disappoints Fanny. One day, Henry Crawford shows up at Fanny's home in Portsmouth. He is introduced to the family as William's benefactor.

He tells Fanny that Edmund has just arrived in London, where Mary is staying. Fanny is sure that Edmund has proposed by now. Henry insists on going for a walk with Fanny and Susan. On their way out, they encounter Fanny's father. Fanny has a moment of terror, sure that her father will behave crudely, but he is instead gentlemanly and offers to show Henry the Portsmouth shipyard. Henry manages to spend a little time alone with Fanny, who continues to resist his attentions. She is relieved that Henry cannot accept the dinner invitation her mother tenders him; she does not want him to see her vulgar, dirty family.

Henry appears the next day to go to church with the family, and they walk afterwards. He offers to take Fanny back to Mansfield, but she refuses. Henry tells her that he must leave to take care of business, and tells her a story about a poor tenant whose rights he seeks to protect. Clearly, he is trying to impress her. Fanny is in fact impressed and hopes that the "improvement" she sees in him means that he will cease his unwanted attentions to her soon. She is relieved that he is leaving Portsmouth.

Analysis

Fanny's trip to Portsmouth is implicit punishment for her disobedience of Sir Thomas. It is a direct reminder that he has "made" her and that she can be returned to misery if she chooses to disobey him. Fanny's family shows all the effects of unfortunate circumstances, as Fanny's analysis of her mother shows: having a temperament similar to Lady Bertram's, Mrs. Price would have done well as a wealthy woman, but she has a difficult time managing a household for her drunk husband. Fanny's siblings are a reminder of the nineteenth century's interest in children and the nature vs. nurture question, which is directly relevant to the plot of this novel. Susan has a good nature and a level head, but she is trapped by her miserable family life. Only through the guidance of someone like Fanny can her essential goodness be realized. The other children, though, seem beyond Fanny's assistance. Fanny's siblings are meant to reflect on Mary and Henry, who have also suffered from bad guardianship as children. Although Edmund constantly excuses Mary's behavior on the basis of her upbringing, it is apparent that she is no Susan, that no amount of proper guidance could have molded Mary into someone like Fanny.

On the other hand, left in her natural milieu, Fanny would have ended up much more like her siblings: undignified and crude (or perhaps she would not have lived at all, as her physical delicacy suggests). In the confusing, demeaning world of the Bertrams, she has grown up by necessity withdrawn and demure. Both one's essential nature and one's environment matter. At the same time, there are no absolutes in terms of environment, as Sir Thomas's coldness in exiling Fanny and Fanny's father's surprisingly gracious behavior toward Henry show; neither Mansfield nor Portsmouth is perfect. Fanny clearly sees Mansfield as her true family, though. Henry's continued "improvement" seems more sincere when Mary is not around to expose his motives. That Fanny is almost swayed by his new attitude speaks to the quality of his dissembling. It also indicates just how vulnerable high moral principles like Fanny's are in a modern social world; under pressure for so long and faced with such a virtuoso performance, she is beginning to crumble. All forces seem to be aligned against her.

Analysis

The flurry of letters that passes between characters in these and the following chapters reflect the power of the written word for persuasion and influence. In most of Austen's novels, letters figure prominently as means of justifying oneself or communicating important information. Letters differ significantly from face-to-face conversation in that instant reply cannot be made; the writer must judge his reader and shape his message accordingly.

Thus, letters are miniature rhetorical performances; they must accomplish their work without aid from a persuasive speaker, impassioned looks, or profound gestures. Because writing is work, too, letters are indications of fidelity and commitment on the part of their writer; in some way, a letter means what it says more than verbal communication can. Letters will play a crucial role in the climax of the plot. For now, Mary's infrequent letters can be read as a sign of her inconstant allegiances, while her brother's pretty speeches, delivered in person, can still be seen as insincere productions requiring little effort

Chapters 43-45

Summary

Fanny receives a letter from Mary, teasing her about Henry's visit. Mary also mentions Edmund's presence in London in terms that make Fanny sure an engagement is imminent. No more letters arrive, and Fanny is nervous about Edmund. She sets aside her fears, though, and undertakes to improve Susan's education. Susan is a ready pupil, and Fanny is concerned that she will have to leave her behind when she returns to Mansfield Park.

Finally, a letter from Edmund arrives. He has returned to Mansfield, discouraged by Mary's behavior. Her London friends are clearly bad influences. Edmund tells Fanny that he is too much in love with Mary to think of marrying anyone else, and in his comments he mentions that he is certain Fanny will end up marrying Henry, which will make his situation even more difficult. He tells Fanny that he has seen Henry in London, and that Henry shows no signs of wavering in his devotion to her. His sisters Maria and Julia, on the other hand, are enjoying London and have no plans to return to Mansfield. Everyone misses Fanny desperately, he tells her, but Sir Thomas will not be free to come get her until after Easter. He also informs her that the Grants are going to Bath.

Lady Bertram is disappointed that Edmund has told Fanny of the Grants' trip; an inveterate letter writer, she wanted to convey the news herself. She soon has occasion to write Fanny, however. Tom Bertram, worn down by a bout of drinking, is desperately ill, and Edmund has gone to care for him. Tom's illness grows worse and worse. Finally, he improves a bit and is brought home to Mansfield. Unfortunately, the move makes him sicker, and it is feared that he will die. Easter comes and goes, and no plans are made for Fanny's return to Mansfield Park. She is disappointed that she will not be in the country to see the beauties of spring, and she is also sad not to be there to help the family.

Another letter arrives from Mary. She states quite directly that Tom's death would be a boon to her, since it would leave Edmund the heir. In her letter, she also mentions that Henry has been staying near Maria, although she claims that Fanny has no reason to be jealous. Fanny is sickened by her letter and distraught at Edmund's probable fate as the husband of such a woman, who "had only learnt to think nothing of consequence but money."

Analysis

Now Edmund is the one in jeopardy. Clearly, his education has not prepared him for a woman like Mary. Sure that she has won Edmund's heart and only wanting to make certain that she gains it on her own terms, she does not hide her plottings from Fanny. In the family's time of crisis, though, and in her absence, the Bertrams have come to value Fanny's moderation and good sense. Her mentoring of Susan demonstrates her essential worth as a role model. Edmund has become a slave to his passions; rather than seeking a loving companion, he has been charmed by coquetry and flirtation. Mary and Fanny actually have something in common: their precarious upbringings have left them in situations where a good marriage would be quite helpful. Fanny, however, does not think enough of money to sacrifice her morals for it. Mary is quite willing to do so, even going so far as to wish for Tom Bertram's death to improve her situation with Edmund. Emotions, save those of friendship and familial love, are dangerous in Austen's world, for they lead otherwise good people astray. Only Fanny, who has managed to control her feeling for Edmund and instead operate on the basis of reason, is still in the right.

Again the reader is privy to hints of trouble: Henry has seen Maria again, and Mary is up to her usual tricks. At this stage in the novel, the main goal to be accomplished is the education of Edmund and his parents; that will also prove the vindication of Fanny and should provide both her and Edmund with a proper mate. Tom's illness is a signal to the family that their corrupt ways will only bring disaster, and that a change is necessary. Unsure of where else to turn, the family begins to look to Fanny, the only one among them who offers something different. This is the critical point of the novel: will Fanny prevail? Or will Mary win Edmund's heart and determine the family's direction? Mary's rather direct comments suggest that she is confident of a victory

Chapters 46-48

Summary

Fanny receives a second letter from Mary Crawford. The letter is vague and mysterious, warning Fanny not to believe any stories that might reach her concerning Henry and Maria. Fanny is surprised by the letter; Mary would never have mentioned anything unless a major scandal were brewing. Fanny had been almost convinced that Henry really was sincere in his feelings for her. That afternoon, Fanny is sitting in the front room with her father, who is reading a newspaper. The newspaper contains mention of a scandal in the

Rushworth household; it claims that "Mrs. R" has run off with a "Mr. C." Fanny is shocked; this is an even worse scenario than Mary's letter had suggested.A letter soon arrives from Edmund.

Fanny is wanted at Mansfield immediately. Edmund will be coming to fetch her, and she is invited to bring Susan with her. Edmund has one more piece of news: in the aftermath of the scandal, Julia has eloped with Yates.

Despite Sir Thomas's best efforts, no one has been able to find Maria and Henry. Edmund arrives the next day to pick up Fanny and her sister. He is clearly distraught, although he will not open up to Fanny in Susan's presence. Upon their arrival at Mansfield, Lady Bertram rushes to greet Fanny, warm in her greetings to her adopted daughter. Fanny is delighted to be back home, despite the unfortunate circumstances. She finds Mrs. Norris in quite a state; having arranged Maria's marriage and often bragged about her role in it, she feels foolish at its sudden collapse. Mrs. Norris blames the entire situation on Fanny's rejection of Henry. Lady Bertram gives Fanny a fuller account of the situation: Sir Thomas had been informed of Maria's flirtations by an old friend and had been about to go to London to intervene when Maria and Henry disappeared. Servants had been involved in the elopement and now are threatening to make events public. The shock of all of this has caused Tom Bertram to relapse into illness.

The possibility of a match between Edmund and Mary has now disappeared, to Sir Thomas's dismay. Fanny must wait a few days before she has a chance to talk to Edmund about Mary. When she does, she finds out that Edmund went to see Mary immediately after Maria and Henry's disappearance, under the pretense of saying goodbye. He was horrified when Mary justified the runaways' conduct and began making plans for their societal rehabilitation. Mary, like Mrs. Norris, blames Fanny for rejecting Henry and causing the situation. In the course of the conversation, Edmund at last revealed to Mary his feelings for her, then told her in no uncertain terms what he thought of her character. Fanny is relieved that Mary has lost her hold over Edmund, and she finally gives her own opinion of Mary. She also tells Edmund that Mary wished for his brother's death for her own benefit. Edmund declares that he will never love another woman, and he tells Fanny that her friendship is all he has left.

The book concludes quickly. Mansfield Park slowly returns to normal. Sir Thomas is hard on himself for having allowed Maria to marry Rushworth. Julia asks for forgiveness, and she and Yates, who have married, are accepted into the family and seem eager to reform. Tom recovers his health and, changed by his experience, becomes a quiet, dependable young man. Edmund slowly regains his spirits, thanks to Fanny's company. Sir Thomas thinks over his errors in raising his children.

Maria and Henry continue to live together, she hoping that they will marry. Eventually, they begin to quarrel; they separate. Rushworth has already divorced her. Mrs. Norris advocates allowing Maria back at Mansfield; when this is denied, Mrs. Norris and Maria leave for continental Europe, where they set up a quarrelsome little household. Sir Thomas is glad to have Mrs. Norris gone. The Grants, ashamed by the behavior of Henry (who is Mrs. Grant's brother), also leave Mansfield, as Dr. Grant has just gotten a position at Westminster.

Mary goes to live with them, and has a hard time getting over Edmund. Finally, Edmund begins to realize that he is in love with Fanny, and the two marry. The narrator is vague as to how long after Maria's elopement this takes place; presumably the turnaround has been fairly quick. Sir Thomas, chastened by recent experiences, is delighted at the match. Susan takes Fanny's place at Lady Bertram's side. William, too, continues to do well, and Sir Thomas is pleased at how well his "investment" in his nieces and nephew has paid off.

Edmund and Fanny move into the Mansfield Park parsonage after Dr. Grant's death (although he had gone to London, he had continued to hold the living), and they live happily ever after.

Analysis

Fanny is thoroughly vindicated in this rapid succession

of events. Henry and Mary are both proven to be immoral creatures, and the education of both Edmund and Sir Thomas is completed. Even the incorrigible Tom is chastened. Virtue has its reward, and vice is either reformed or punished. Why, then, does *Mansfield Park* end so quickly, without dwelling on the "happily-ever-after" aspects of its resolution? For one thing, the happy ending of this novel is in part a product of luck—Maria and Henry just happened to cross paths, thus enabling the eventual marriage of Edmund and Fanny.

There is no sense of inevitability here, and the rest of society has definitely not been put right. Rushworth will again marry some beautiful woman who is only interested in his money; hopefully things will turn out a little better this time, and his new wife will only engage in "standing flirtations," as Mary puts it, using a bit of a Freudian pun. Maria and Mrs. Norris are not reformed, but instead kicked out of the family circle and even out of England. Mary Crawford seems to be merely resting, and will continue her conniving ways when the time is right. Most of Fanny's biological family, too, remains in squalor back in Portsmouth. Although the good have been rewarded and the bad punished, these fates seem only temporary in many cases. No real education or reform has taken place, except in the mind of the now fairly old and isolated Sir Thomas. He will most likely continue to help Fanny's siblings, but overall the world has not been set right.

The main thing that was to be accomplished in this novel was the assignation of Fanny to a place in the social order. This has indeed happened: she is now a daughter to the Bertrams, both by marriage and by adoption. The way in which Austen ends novels by not really ending them—we don't see anything of Fanny and Edmund's married life—suggests that fixing one's social position is not the end of the story, despite the nineteenth-century belief that social position was the most important thing about a person. Do they, in fact, live happily? Do they have lots of children? Is Edmund a good minister? Does Tom Bertram die young and leave Edmund the heir to Mansfield Park? We don't know, and this lack of resolution is deliberate. The fact that Maria is ruined while Henry and

Rushworth both may yet marry and are still valued members of society suggests the arbitrariness of the social order, which says little about a person's inner worth. The lack of closure is also a brilliant artistic stroke on Austen's part; the reader is left wondering about Fanny's future life, and this active involvement with them makes the characters stick in our minds longer than they might have otherwise.

The marriage of Fanny and Edmund celebrates the ideal form of love: a companionate relationship based on family. That their relationship skirts dangerously close to incest—they were, after all, raised as brother and sister—is an issue that is avoided here. *Mansfield Park* is not the only novel to feature such a relationship; *Wuthering Heights* is a more prominent example. Perhaps the close kinship of Fanny and Edmund is meant to reflect their essential similarity to one another as people. We are constantly reminded that Edmund has formed Fanny's mind; in this way, he has been a father to her as well as a brother. While again, to modern sensibilities, this seems both incestuous and dangerously paternalistic in the imbalance of power between man and woman, it also suggests an ideal for intellectual and emotional companionship. Fanny and Edmund are, almost literally, everything to one another

Analysis

Mansfield Park is an enormously complicated novel, even by the standards of Jane Austen, who creates characters and situations of unusual complexity in all her novels. Like other Austen novels, this one is concerned with a young woman trying to find her place in the social order. Fanny comes from a poor family but is being raised by her rich aunt and uncle. She prefigures the orphans of later Victorian novels in her separation from her parents, who will not be the primary determinants of her eventual status. Like other Austen heroines, Fanny will, in part, determine her status by marrying. Since women could not enter the professions, marriage was the only way, in the nineteenth century, to ascend or descend the social ladder. Fanny's mother has fallen downwards quite a bit through her own marriage to a sailor who turns out to be a drunk; her aunt Lady Bertram and her cousin Maria, on the other hand, do fairly well by marrying. While the marriages of others have been formulated based on beauty and family connections, Fanny is to "earn" a marriage partner based on her character.

Virtue is definitely rewarded in this world, and it is the primary determinant of an individual's eventual fate.*Mansfield Park* is interested in far more than just the settling of social status, though. In part, it takes up the age-old debate over whether "nature"—one's innate qualities—or "nurture"—the environment in which one is raised—is the primary determinant of character. Fanny and her siblings, and Mary and Henry Crawford, are ambiguous figures in this regard; all of them are shuttled between different households growing up, and it is never clear whether it is their underlying personalities or their situations that have made them what they are. This makes for much interesting debate in the novel, particularly as Edmund struggles with his feelings for Mary and tries to justify her behavior.

The idea of education is a part of this debate: can people change? Clearly, by the end of the novel, both Sir Thomas and Edmund have learned something, and the role Edmund has played in forming Fanny's mind (and, to a lesser extent, the influence Fanny has exerted over her sister Susan) speaks to the capacity of some individuals to change for the better. Others, like Maria and Henry, never seem to learn. Urban and rural settings are used as backdrops for this debate, with the suggestion being made that city life promotes vice and inhibits one's moral development, while growing up in a country house exposes a child to all that is good. The Bertram daughters and their oldest brother complicate this, though.

This may be because country life is not free from corruption. This is Jane Austen's most socially-aware novel. Sir Thomas is absent for nearly a third of the novel, tending to his business interests in the Caribbean. He is a slaveholder, and this fact is directly addressed when Fanny asks him about the slave trade. It is while he is gone that the family goes astray, and while this suggests the need for paternal authority, it also implies that his affairs—trafficking in humans—are a moral liability. In general, Austen is very aware of the world around her in this novel.

She depicts urban poverty in her portrait of Fanny's parents' home, and she uses the gossip sheets and other forms of then-modern media to further her plot. This is also Austen's most sexually-aware novel—notice the dramatic, nearly Freudian symbolism of the scene where Maria squeezes around the gate at Sotherton and the scene where Fanny puts the amber cross pendant her brother has given her on a chain. Mrs. Price's excessive child-bearing and Maria's dalliances also suggest sexuality rather directly for a novel written in the 1810s. Sexuality is newly crucial in this modern world of feigned emotions and performances.

Sexuality itself can even be acted out on stage, as the play that the group tries to put on shows. The idea of "acting" is central to the moral calculus of this novel. In a world of mobility, where people move from Bath to London to the country every few months, it is impossible to know anyone's character with any certainty; large periods of their lives have taken place out of your view. Thus, sincerity becomes a crucial quantity. The possibility that someone might be acting—feigning an emotion or even faking their entire character to gain something—is truly threatening when one is making decisions about a marriage partner.

Fanny's self-denial and withdrawn nature are not only proper for a young lady, but also an excellent defense. The new pressures of the modern world and the uncertainty they bring lead Fanny and Edmund, the novel's two most vulnerable characters, to adopt a sort of melancholy pose; they seem weary of the world. Melancholy was to become an important concept to the Victorians. Reason, too, assumes critical importance. Being guided by emotions can lead to dreadful mistakes; reason, on the other hand, which often counsels caution or withdrawal, is safe. Fanny, with her keen perceptions and her faith in her ability to reason out how she should behave, is an ideal, if odd, heroine.

Finally, in its resistance to closure—the novel ends with a

marriage, but we don't see anything of married life afterwards—*Mansfield Park* hints at the essential ambiguity of knowledge. Austen cannot give a complete account of Edmund and Fanny's entire life together, so she leaves things hanging. On the other hand, Fanny's marriage has fixed her social position, and she is no longer a single, unpartnered woman, so *Mansfield Park* has achieved the two major goals of a nineteenth-century novel. In its ambiguity about nearly everything else, however, Austen's novel is revolutionary.

Chapter 7

Major Themes

Social Mobility

Scholars suggest that social mobility is the primary theme in all of Austen's novels; this idea seems especially apparent in *Mansfield Park*. The opening chapter, in which the three Ward sisters marry men of very different social categories (high, middle and low), fixes this construct as the novel's primary theme. Maria Ward moves above her designated social station by marrying the baronet, Sir Thomas Bertram of Mansfield Park; the middle sister, Mrs. Norris, marries at a more socially appropriate (middle) station; the youngest sister marries a common sailor, Mr. Price, who will in time become an unemployed drunkard. Austen utilizes this triad to illustrate that high morals do not necessarily come with high social standing, and that people born into lower social ranks should be given the opportunity to move up through their moral behavior.

Lady Bertram has four children with the baronet, but her oldest son, Tom Bertram, moves to London, where he finds himself corrupted by city life. A gambler, he drinks to excess and causes his father so much financial hardship that he is forced to go to Antigua to oversee his financial investments in the island's plantations. Lady Bertram's daughters are spoiled, selfish, and act immorally, the married Maria going so far as to run away with Henry Crawford. Her youngest son Edmund, although a minister, is so distracted by his sexual desire for Mary Crawford that he forgets his upbringing and his own moral imperative of impeccable social behavior. Thankfully,

Mrs. Norris has no children, but she is implicated in the fate of the Bertram children because she had great influence over them when they were young.

It is Fanny Price, one of the nine children fathered by the drunken sailor, who proves to be the character in the novel with the highest moral standards. From early on in the novel, Fanny is portrayed as shy, retiring, and helpful to all. Patient to a fault, she never complains, has the ability to see through people, and possesses an innate capability to determine right from wrong. In time, everyone comes to admire her. No one objects to her marrying her social superior, Henry Crawford, but Fanny refuses although she knows her life would be far easier if she agreed. In keeping with Austen's theme of social mobility for the deserving, it is hardly surprising that Fanny winds up the daughter-in-law of a baronet who could, in time, even come to replace Lady Bertram as the mistress of Mansfield Park.

The Evils of Primogeniture

The British aristocratic social system embraces the concept of primogeniture, the right of the first-born child (usually the eldest son) to inherit the parents' entire estate. In her novels, Austen examines and criticizes this aristocratic class system. Since the privileged oldest son inherited the entire estate under primogeniture, the younger sons were forced to "do something" for themselves, and usually enlisted in the army or the navy, or sought careers in the law or the clergy.

Girls were viewed as financial assets when they "married to advantage," and as heiresses only when they had no brothers. As the oldest Bertram, the profligate Tom Bertram, who drinks and gambles too much in London, will become the next Sir Thomas, while his younger brother Edmund is slated for the clergy. No one ever considers the possibility that Tom might not inherit the estate, despite the fact that his unconscionable behavior causes the family great financial hardship and necessitates his father's trip to Antigua to oversee his financial investments in the Island's plantations. Clearly, Edmund would make a better baronet and lord of the manor, but there is nothing he can do but wish for his brother's death-something the upright Edmund would never dream of doing, although the highly doubtful Mary Crawford wishes this later on in the novel. Daughters are expected to marry within (or, ideally, above) their own social strata, and Maria Bertram scores high social points in this regard for marrying the insipid and boring Mr. Rushworth, one of the richest men in the county.

Austen uses the character of Tom Bertram to bring the inherent problems of the primogeniture system to light. Sir Thomas's forced departure to manage his investments leaves his children without any real supervision and ultimately results in grievous events that deeply affect his daughters' lives. Also, as a result of Tom's profligacy, Sir Thomas cannot afford to hold the parsonage position for Edmund, who is not yet an ordained minister. Instead, he is forced out of financial necessity to let the position go to Dr. Grant, an action which allows for the introduction of Mrs. Grant's younger siblings, the highly immoral Mary Crawford and Henry Crawford, who in time come to "infect" Mansfield. Edmund must remove himself from Mansfield to take a lesser job at a poorer parsonage. Clearly, the wrong brother has the power, while the more deserving Edmund is helpless to do anything about it. Edmund's only other options are to join the Navy as an officer or to enter the legal or medical profession-jobs that Edmund would hardly find suitable or rewarding.

Town and Country

Although everything changes at the bucolic Mansfield Park after Henry and Mary Crawford arrive from London, the meeting between the Country Bertrams and the Town Crawfords is far more than a plot device intended to intensify the novel's action. Indeed, the introduction of the new arrivals demonstrates the ongoing tension between modernity and traditional values. For example, Mary demonstrates how out of touch she is with the rural need of the farmers to harvest the hay by selfishly insisting upon obtaining a wagon merely to transport her harp. Time is of the essence, and all vehicles are necessary for this vital project. She believes that given enough money she can have her way, but fails to realize that if the hay isn't brought in while the weather is right, people might not eat for the entire winter. Edmund, like Fanny, is put off by her selfish attitude, but his better judgment is cast aside by his sexual attraction to the lovely lady.

Furthermore, although Mary's brother Henry is heir to a country estate, he is continually absent. Henry would have been abhorred by early nineteenth-century readers as an absentee landlord who spends the proceeds from his farm estates to live the high life of fun and frolic while his tenants and property are neglected. Henry is thus also ignorant of the needs of rural life.

Rags to Riches:

In *Mansfield Park,* Fanny Price is transformed from a poor, bedraggled nine-year-old to the "daughter" of Mansfield Park and the wife of the Mansfield "prince," Edmund Bertram. Simply put, *Mansfield Park* is the classic Cinderella tale revisited. Fanny arrives at Mansfield as a disheveled, impoverished relation, and is made to feel unwelcome by her cousins (with the exception of Edmund). Although she doesn't have to literally clean out the ashes from the fireplace as the fairy-tale Cinderella did, Fanny nevertheless must be at the beck and call of her relatives and provide constant care for Lady Bertram. With the exception of the trip to the Sotherton estate, Fanny is never allowed to leave, and thus could be viewed as a prisoner at Mansfield: after all, Lady Bertram "cannot do without Fanny." Since Mrs. Norris is responsible for the day-to-day running of Mansfield, she takes on the evil stepmother role, treats Fanny as a servant, and generally makes the young girl's life miserable. The Bertram girls, who represent the fairy-tale evil stepsisters, denigrate young Fanny because she doesn't have fashionable clothes and are favored by the evil Mrs. Norris due to their higher social rank.

Unlike Cinderella, Fanny doesn't seem to have a fairy godmother. She must develop her own skills to find her way in the world, and soon becomes an idealized daughter figure to Lady Bertram and Sir Thomas, whose own two daughters fail to make sensible decisions-especially concerning men. After Maria and Julia leave for London, Fanny attends her first ball, an affair thrown in her honor by Sir Thomas. When she leads the dance, all eyes are cast upon her, because everyone realizes that over time Fanny has come to look more and more like a beautiful princess. Fanny is so captivating that a prince with a fortune and an estate, Henry Crawford, falls in love with her and asks her to wed. Fanny sees through him, unlike Sir Thomas, who locks her up in Portsmouth until she "comes to her senses" and accepts Henry's offer of marriage. Over time, the true prince Edmund comes to rescue Fanny and takes her away from Portsmouth in a carriage. She returns to Mansfield with her lady-in-waiting, Susan, and is happily received by Sir Thomas and Lady Bertram, who have come to view Fanny as a loyal daughter of Mansfield. By the end of the novel, Fanny has married the young "prince", Edmund, while the evil Maria and Julia have been cast out into the dark world. Aunt Norris leaves as well, and all left at Mansfield Park live happily every after.

Chapter 8

Study Questions

Q. Discuss Jane Austen's Historical Background.

Or

Q. Give an Introduction to Jane Austen's Time.

Introduction to the Times

During Austen's career, Romanticism reached its zenith of acceptance and influence, but she rejected the tenets of that movement. The romantics extolled the power of feeling, whereas Austen upheld the supremacy of the rational faculty. Romanticism advocated the abandonment of restraint; Austen was a staunch exponent of the neo-classical belief in order and discipline. The romantics saw in nature a transcendental power to stimulate men to better the existing order of things, which they saw as essentially tragic in its existing state. Austen supported traditional values and the established norms, and viewed the human condition in the comic spirit. The romantics exuberantly celebrated natural beauty, but Austen's dramatic technique decreed sparse description of setting. The beauties of nature are seldom detailed in her work.

Just as Austen's works display little evidence of the Romantic Movement, they also reveal no awareness of the international upheavals and consequent turmoil in England that took place during her lifetime. Keep in mind, however, that such forces were remote from the restricted world that she depicts. Tumultuous affairs, such as the Napoleonic wars, in her day did not significantly affect the daily lives of middle-class provincial families. The ranks of the military were recruited from the lower orders of the populace, leaving gentlemen to purchase a commission, the way Wickham does in the novel, and thereby become officers. Additionally, the advancement of technology had not yet disrupted the stately eighteenth-century patterns of rural life. The effects of the industrial revolution, with its economic and social repercussions, were still most sharply felt by the underprivileged laboring classes. Unrest was widespread, but the great reforms that would launch a new era of English political life did not come until later. Consequently, newer technology that existed in England at the time of *Pride and Prejudice*'s publication does not appear in the work.

Jane Austen's England

Jane Austin's major novels, including *Pride and Prejudice,* were all composed within a short period of about twenty years. Those twenty years (1795-1815) also mark a period in history when England was at the height of its power. England stood as the bulwark against French revolutionary extremism and against Napoleonic imperialism. The dates Austen was writing almost exactly coincide with the great English military victories over Napoleon and the French: the Battle of the Nile, in which Admiral Nelson crippled the French Mediterranean fleet, and the battle of Waterloo, in which Lord Wellington and his German allies defeated Napoleon decisively and sent him into exile. However, so secure in their righteousness were the English middle and upper classes — the "landed gentry" featured in Austen's works — that these historical events impact *Pride and Prejudice* very little.

The French Revolution and Napoleonic Wars

The period from 1789 to 1799 marks the time of the French Revolution, while the period from 1799 to 1815 marks the ascendancy of Napoleon — periods of almost constant social change and upheaval. In England, the same periods were times of conservative reaction, in which society changed very little. The British government, led by Prime Minister William Pitt, maintained a strict control over any ideas or opinions that seemed to support the revolution in France. Pitt's government suspended the right of *habeas corpus,* giving them the power to imprison people for an indefinite time without trial. It also passed laws against public criticism of government policies, and suppressed working-class trade unions. At the same time, the Industrial Revolution permanently changed the British economy. It provided the money Pitt's government needed to oppose Napoleon. At the same time, it also created a large wealthy class and an even larger middle class. These are the people that Jane Austen depicts in *Pride and Prejudice,* the "landed gentry" who have eamed their property, not by inheriting it from their aristocratic ancestors, but by purchasing it with their new wealth. They have few of the manners and graces of the aristocracy and, like the Collins's in *Pride and Prejudice,* are primarily conceded with their own futures in their own little worlds. Unlike other Romantic-era writers, such as William Wordsworth and Samuel Taylor Coleridge, Austen's works are very little impacted by the French Revolution and revolutionary rhetoric. Members of Austen's own family served in the war against Bonaparte and the French; two of her brothers became admirals in the Royal Navy. The only hint of war and military behavior in *Pride and Prejudice,* however, lies in the continued presence of the British soldiers in Meryton, near the Bennet estate at Longbourn. The soldiers include George Wickham, who later elopes with Lydia Bennet, disgracing the family. In the world of *Pride and Prejudice,* the soldiers are present only to give the younger Bennet daughters men in uniforms to chase after. Their world is limited to their own home, those of their friends and neighbors, a few major resort towns, and, far off, the city of London. There is no hint of the revolutionary affairs going on just across the English Channel in France.

English Regency Society

On the other hand, contemporary English society is a preoccupation of *Pride and Prejudice.* At the time the novel was published, King George III had been struck down by the periodic madness (now suspected to be caused by the metabolic disease porphyria) that plagued his final years. The powers he was no longer capable of using were placed in the hands of his son the Prince Regent, later George IV. The Prince Regent was widely known as a man of dissolute morals, and his example was followed by many of society's leading figures. Young men regularly went to universities not to learn, but to see and be seen, to drink, gamble, race horses, and spend money. Perhaps the greatest example of this type in *Pride and Prejudice* is the unprincipled George Wickham, who seduces sixteen-year-old Lydia Bennet. Lydia for her part also participates willingly in Regency culture; her thoughts are not for her family's disgrace, but about the handsomeness of her husband and the jealousy of her sisters.

Most "respectable" middle- and upper-class figures, such as Elizabeth Bennet and Fitzwilliam Darcy, strongly disapproved of the immorality of Regency culture. But they did participate in the fashions of the time, influenced by French styles (even though France was at war with England). During the period of the Directory and the Consulate in France (from 1794-1804), styles were influenced by the costumes of the Roman Republic. The elaborate hairstyles and dresses that had characterized the French aristocracy before the Revolution were discarded for simpler costumes. Women, including Elizabeth Bennet, would have worn a simple dress that resembled a modern nightgown. Loose and flowing, it was secured by a ribbon tied just below the breasts. Darcy for his part would have worn a civilian costume of tight breeches, a ruffled shirt with a carefully folded neck cloth, and a high-collared jacket. Even though these costumes were in part a reaction to the excesses of early eighteenth-century dress, they became themselves quite elaborate as the century progressed, sparked by the Prince Regent himself and his friend, the impeccable dresser Beau Brummel. Brummel's mystique, known as "dandyism," expressed in clothing the same idleness and effortless command of a situation that characterizes many of Austen's heroes and heroines

Q. Discuss the importance of home In Jane Austen's Mansfield Park

Or

Q. Discuss the definition of home as according to Fanny price

Jane Austen's Mansfield Park is a novel obsessed with home and family. It begins a story of óne family, three sisters, and quickly expands to a story of three families, the Bertrams, the Prices, and the Norrises. Family upon family is added, each one growing, expanding, and moving until the novel is crowded with characters and estates. An obsession with movement creates an overall feeling of displacement and confusion. Fanny Price is moved from Portsmouth to Mansfield and then back to Portsmouth and back to Mansfield. She occupies several houses, Mansfield, Thornton Lacey, the parsonage, and almost Mrs. Norris' house. Julia and Maria Bertram, the Crawfords, the Grants, Susan Price, even Mrs. Norris experience a move. The only constant is Mansfield Park itself with its immovable Lady Bertram and pug. More positively, Mansfield becomes a visual representation of family. The novel's title, more an abstraction than a reference to place, attempts to define "home," an idea in the novel not contained by place.

In Mansfield Park, what defines home becomes the essential question for Fanny Price. The estate as a reflection of self is a prominent theme in the novel. Henry Crawford's suggestions for improving Thornton Lacey would raise it "above a mere Parsonage House" by "giv[ing] it a higher character[.]... From being the mere gentleman's residence, it becomes... the residence of a man of education, taste, modern manners, good connections". Crawford's improvements would give the house "such an air as to make its owner be set down as the great land-holder of the parish". Edmund refuses to let his identity be consumed, asserting that Henry's plan will not be "put in practice". A "gentleman's residence" is "comfortable" and fitting. For the homeless Fanny, self is not defined. With no home, she has no self. She must, therefore, grow into Mansfield Park before asserting selfhood. As Fanny defines and redefines "home," she is able to define herself and ultimately fit into Mansfield Park and the family it represents.

At her arrival, Mansfield Park is clearly no home to Fanny.

Displaced from her home in Portsmouth, Fanny is almost a not-Fanny. The initial description of her is marked by negation. There is "not... much in her first appearance" though "nothing to disgust". She has "no glow of complexion, nor any other striking beauty". She is "awkward" but "not vulgar". The negatives (not, nothing, no, nor) reduce Fanny to nothingness. The modifiers, too, are diminutive. Though Fanny is not much younger than Julia and Maria, she is described as "just ten years old" and "small of her age". She is "timid," "shy," "shrinking from notice", all words that reflect deficiency. The Miss Bertrams feed off of this diminishment, "increasing from their cousin's shyness". Fanny's self threatens to dissolve altogether. After meeting the Bertrams and seeing the display of a "remarkably fine family," who were "all at home", Fanny finds herself "longing for the home she had left". Fanny's "longing" contrasts with the Bertrams being "at home", in a double sense. This juxtaposition emphasizes the home-family-self completeness of the Bertrams while revealing its absence in Fanny, who has no home, family, or self at this point.

The largeness of the house contrasted with the smallness of Fanny reinforces the idea of displacement and, therefore, insignificance. Fanny finds the house overwhelming; its grandeur... astonished, but could not console her. The rooms were too large for her to move in with ease; whatever she touched she expected to injure, and she crept about in constant terror of something or other; often retreating towards her own chamber to cry. The words "injure," "crept," "constant terror," "retreat," and "cry" set up a minimal existence for Fanny, a completely unassertive victimized self. This minimal self is often unnamed, being described as "little girl" and "my dear little cousin". Edmund, however, does refer to her affectionately as "my dear little Fanny" but still includes a reference to her smallness with the adjective "little". Her cousins often reflect "on her size", and diminutive words are continually attributed to her: "shyness," "ignorance," "despondence," and "sunk". Fanny's discomfort at Mansfield reflects her diminished self.

However, as Mansfield increases in attachment to Fanny,

her selfhood increases, though the change occurs slowly. With the threat of being removed to Mrs. Norris' White house, Fanny begins to recognize Mansfield as home, though not exactly home. Fanny is merely "fixed at Mansfield Park" but is "learning to transfer in its favour much of her attachment to her former home". She grows up there "not unhappily"-a more positive negative. Fanny clings to Mansfield saying, "I love this house and everything in it" but still considers herself not "important". Her identity is only loosely defined, but she begins to grow. She now thinks and speaks though willing to believe Edmund right "rather than [her]self". She considers the self-home dilemma even if it confuses her: "Here, I know I am of [no consequence], and yet I love the place so well". She understands and communicates a relationship between home and self though her language signifies importance and place. Edmund rightly tells Fanny it is "the place" she "will not quit". She focuses on the place, the house, the things in it, on the material instead of the abstraction. Melissa Edmundson finds Fanny's ability to "connect materialistically" precursor to an emotional connection. These connections establish Fanny's identity.

Through her family relationships, Fanny adapts to Mansfield. She recalls her early fear of horseback riding and describes it in her former victim-like terms. She "used to dread riding": It gave her "terrors;" she "trembled" whenever her uncle mentioned it. But she moves beyond this victimized language to a more rational language when she recalls Edmund's pains "to reason and persuade" her out of fear. As Fanny adapts to life at Mansfield, she literally fills more space by moving into the East room. The East room reinforces self. She contemplates there what she "ought to do," whether she were "right". As self increases, her significance in the family increases. Edmund asks her "advice and opinion" As Edmunson explains, Fanny's occupation of the room shows she "occupies more space" in the Bertram family.

The family evaluates and reinforces her identity. On his return Sir Thomas notices her maturity. He still calls her "little Fanny" but then moves beyond this diminutive, calling her "his dear Fanny,... observing with decided pleasure how much she was grown!". Sir Thomas approves her growth, thinking her "very pretty" and is quite pleased with her "transplantation to Mansfield". Fanny, in turn, starts to lose her former dread of Sir Thomas and begins to understand him, explaining, "The repose of his own family-circle is all he wants". As a result of approval, Fanny's worth to the family "increase[s]": "it was impossible for her not to be looked at, more thought of and attended to, than she had ever been before; and 'where is Fanny?' became no uncommon question, even without her being wanted for anyone's convenience". Fanny gains selfhood by understanding her relationship to others. This new self or identity Fanny has discovered is contested by the family after Henry's proposal. The family now becomes her antagonist. Leroy W. Smith explains, "The patriarchal system. .. works to stifle the potential selfhood of Fanny Price". She reverts to her gothic victim identity and is once again frightened by her uncle. She hears "a heavy step, an unusual step in that part of the house; it was her uncle's;... she had trembled at it as often, and began to tremble again, at the idea of his coming up to speak to her".

Sir Thomas questions her self-knowledge: "I am half inclined to think, Fanny, that you do not quite know your own feelings". His rejection-"You do not owe me the duty of a child"-excludes her from the family, making clear that she is not his daughter. Even Edmund's-"This is not like yourself, your rational self"-questions her identity. Thomas R. Edwards Jr. argues a theme of manipulating existences and notes an extreme example in Mrs. Norris' "attempt virtually to become Fanny". Mrs. Norris threatens to consume her altogether, admonishing Fanny through negation: "Depend upon it, it is not you that are wanted; depend upon it it is me;... I am sure; Sir Thomas wants me". These verbal affronts attempt to strip Fanny of her identity.

For Fanny, the uprooting to Portsmouth becomes a crucial evaluation of home and self. Her arrival there parallels her earlier arrival at Mansfield when she had no home or self. As Kenneth L. Moler relates, placing Fanny in Portsmouth reinforces her "growth". Extending Moler's argument, Fanny has literally outgrown Portsmouth. Unlike the largeness of Mansfield, Portsmouth is characterized by its smallness. Fanny immediately remarks the "narrow entrance-passage of the house" and the "small" parlor. She notices the "smallness of the house", "the thinness of the walls", and every thing being "so close to her". She believes herself "at home. But alas! it was not such a home, she had not such a welcome". Being initially ignored at Mansfield, Fanny is here "undistinguished" and "unthought of". She rejects Portsmouth as home, noting its "deficiencies". Fanny's mother uses the word "little" constantly, saying in one paragraph "Poor little Betsey," "little thought it would be," "Poor little soul," "Poor little dear," and "little people". Portsmouth is a world of children. Though once small and insignificant at Mansfield, Fanny is now older, and the smallness of Portsmouth is not attributed to her.

At Portsmouth home and self are realized. In "exile" Fanny "yearn[s]" for Mansfield with "intense desire": When she had been coming to Portsmouth, she had loved to call it home, had been fond of saying that she was going home; the word had been very dear to her; and so it still was, but it must be applied to Mansfield. That was now the home. Portsmouth was Portsmouth; Mansfield was home. This realization is not only an understanding of Mansfield, but also of self. She comes to understand Mansfield by understanding her place in it. What she essentially finds is her role, a way of fitting into the family that does not diminish her. She truly desires to be "of service to every creature in the house". She likes that she has "been of use to all," taking pride in "supporting the spirits" of her aunt, "keeping her from the evil of solitude" and from "restlessness". When Fanny returns to Mansfield and fills her former place beside Lady Bertram, she is changed. She is "devoted to her aunt," and though she returns "to every former office," she does so "with more than former zeal". She realizes that she fits into Mansfield Park, not as a servant, but as a daughter. Marriage to Edmund only reinforces her legitimacy. Sir Thomas finds Fanny "indeed the daughter that he wanted". A coming together of families at the end resolves the chaotic expansion of the novel, which rests its last sentence "within the view and patronage of Mansfield Park" Julia and Maria, the Grants, the Crawfords, even Mrs. Norris have all left Mansfield. Only the Prices remain: William, Susan, and Fanny, who becomes a Bertram by name at last. Though the Prices have in some ways supplanted the Bertrams, Fanny's oxymoronic title, Fanny Bertram, works to dissolve any differences. What we are left with is simply one family very much at home in Mansfield Park.

Q. Discuss the Character of Mrs. Norris in Mansfield Park

Or

Q. Do you think that Mrs Norris is the shallowest character

For any character there are three main ways of learning about them. Firstly, how the character themselves thinks and behaves. Secondly, how other characters respond to the character. Lastly, how the author discusses the character is very revealing. Each of these views of Mrs. Norris is provided by the author. Mrs Norris is only related to Mansfield Park through her sister, Lady Bertram. While she may not have managed to make the affluent marriage that her sister did, there is no doubting her love of money.

Sir Thomas Bertram provides an income for Mrs Norris' husband, a member of the clergy. This enables them to live in comfort and in close proximity to the house at Mansfield Park. Mrs Norris is possibly the shallowest character in the community of Mansfield Park. She has no qualms about marrying for security, not love. Outward appearance is everything to her, especially how others perceive her. However, this leads her to make decisions for the wrong reasons: "[She] found herself obliged to be attached to the Rev. Mr Norris". When Rev. Mr Norris dies, Austen hints at the perhaps loveless marriage that Mrs Norris was a part of: "[She] consoled herself by considering that she could do very well without him". Carrying on without her husband gives Mrs Norris another very welcome burden to bear. It is Mrs Norris who makes the initial break from her youngest sister, Mrs Price, after she marries against her family's wishes. Yet, once she sees a way of making herself seem charitable and generous, Mrs Norris is keen to establish contact with Mrs Price once more. Her wish to be involved in every aspect of her familyís life conflicts with her standing on her sister's marriage to a Lieutenant of the Marines, but this does not seem to bother her.

The language that Mrs Norris uses is very persuasive and there are few ways of overriding what she says. Even those who are close to her are shown not to expend much effort arguing with her. In her attempts to persuade Sir Thomas to take Fanny Price, she declares: "[I] would rather deny myself the necessaries of life, than do an ungenerous thing". She is indifferent to others' protests and has an answer to everything. Mrs Norris is presented as the sort of person who believes herself to be liked by all, but is actually hated by most.

Mrs Norris has no qualms about favouring her niece, Maria, and also no worries about stirring relations between all three of her nieces at Mansfield Park. Rather than admonishing her niece's prejudices against their less fortunate cousin, she explains that Fanny is to be pitied and once more wastes no time in praising her nieces' accomplishments: "You must not expect everybody to be as forward and quick at learning as yourself". The superficiality of the praise perpetually being given to the Bertrams on the upbringing of their children is somewhat undermined by Lady Bertram's own admission that she has only recently persuaded Julia to leave her dog alone.

While there is pity for Fanny being treated like a parcel after Rev. Mr Norris' death, there is surprise when Mrs Norris refuses to take her niece under her wing. Her attitude of being unable to care for Fanny contrasts strongly with the image of the doting aunt she gave when persuading to take her in in the first place. When Rev. Mr Norris was alive, it was his presence that proved the stumbling block when it came to Fanny living with them at the Parsonage. Now he is deceased, it is Mrs Norris' lack of husband that becomes her reason for not accepting Fanny into her household to live. Any far fetched reason will do for Mrs Norris as she tries to reason with her sister. Her need for money and the rank of a noblewoman is put down to honouring the memory of her late husband. The impression already given by Austen opposes this; the reader knows perfectly well that Mrs Norris only cares about herself.

Mrs Norris exclaims about the moral impossibility of Fanny falling in love with one of her male cousins, yet her hypocrisy is evident as it was obviously perfectly acceptable for her to marry for convenience and public status.

Other characters appear to be worn down by Mrs. Norris' indifference to outside opinions. While Sir and Lady Bertram are surprised at Mrs. Norris' refusal to take responsibility for Fanny, they do little in the way of arguing back. They simply resign themselves to the fact that they will care for their niece, despite it having been Mrs. Norris' idea at the start. When Edmund mentions his aunt's "love of money" to Fanny, it is the first time that someone other than Jane Austen has acknowledged a fault of the domineering aunt.

The way in which Austen has written Mrs Norris is comical, but none of the arrogant selfishness of her character is lost through being able to laugh at how she behaves. Austen writes of Mrs Norris having a "spirit of activity". It was this busybodying that severed the link between the Ward sisters in the first place. However, once she sees a way of doing good, Mrs Norris gives herself a key role in writing to Mrs Price: "Mrs Norris wrote the letters". This sums up how, while she may not be in complete control, she must play an important part. In contrast to the part she played in causing the rift, it is almost worthless.

Mrs Norris' self-importance is never more evident than when she meets Fanny at Northampton: "[Mrs Norris] regaled in the credit of being foremost to welcome her". From then on however, Fanny is bullied and dominated by her Aunt Norris. On the journey to Mansfield Park, the frightened girl is constantly reminded of how grateful she should be. The idea of Fanny being homesick is quite beyond Mrs Norris' grasp and she sees her as rude. Mrs Norris obviously has no direct experience with children and Austen explains that Fanny never received kindness from her aunt. Jane Austen is always influencing our view of Mrs. Norris, whether directly or indirectly. Mrs Norris own actions show what an opinionated, bossy woman she is. While the relative indifference of those around may more suggestive of their own characters, it shows how oppressive she is. Finally, Austen herself directly affects what we think of Mrs. Norris with her own commentary in the the text. There are moments of authorial voice that simply give frank insights into the character of Mrs. Norris. The summation of these three points is how the reader comes to an understanding of Mrs. Norris.

Q. Critically comment on Mansfield Park

Or

Q. Write a short note on the reader's view(nineteenth century) on Mansfield Park

This novel, originally published in 1814, is the first of Jane Austen's novels not to be a revised version of one of her pre-1800 writings. Mansfield Park has sometimes been considered atypical of Jane Austen, as being solemn and moralistic, especially when contrasted with the immediately preceding Pride and Prejudice and the immediately following Emma. Poor Fanny Price is brought up at Mansfield Park with her rich uncle and aunt, where only her cousin Edmund helps her with the difficulties she suffers from the rest of the family, and from her own fearfulness and timidity. When the sophisticated Crawfords (Henry and Mary), visit the Mansfield neighbourhood, the moral sense of each marriageable member of the Mansfield family is tested in various ways, but Fanny emerges more or less unscathed. The well-ordered (if somewhat vacuous) house at Mansfield Park, and its country setting, play an important role in the novel, and are contrasted with the squalour of Fanny's own birth family's home at Portsmouth, and with the decadence of London.

Readers have a wide variety of reactions to Mansfield Park-most of which already appear in the Opinions of Mansfield Park collected by Jane Austen herself soon after the novel's publication. Some dislike the character of Fanny as "priggish" (however, it is Edmund who sets the moral tone here), or have no sympathy for her forced inaction (doubtless, those are people who have never lacked confidence, or been without a date on Friday night!). Mansfield Park has also been used to draw connections between the "genteel" rural English society that Jane Austen describes and the outside world, since Fanny's uncle is a slave-owner (with an estate in Antigua in the Caribbean; slavery was not abolished in the British empire until 1833). Like a number of other topics, Jane Austen only chose to allude glancingly to the slave trade and slavery in her novels, though she was aware of contemporary debates on the subject. Mansfield Park was one of only two of Jane Austen's novels to be revised by her after its first publication, when a second edition came out in 1816 (this second edition was a failure in terms of sales).

Q. What is the Importance of the Country Estate in Pride and Prejudice and Mansfield Park

Or

Q. Is it right to say Austen uses the country estate to give the reader an insight into the personalities of her characters, and as a way of discussing political, religious and aesthetic ideas of the period.

The world of Jane Austen's novels is a world of the country estate. Her central characters are members of the parish or landed gentry and their lives and adventures often circle around the local estate and the people who live there. One of Austen's main literary principles was to write only about the things she knew about in her own life, and the world of the landed gentry was one to which she had access. However the country estate in her novels serves a greater purpose than that of a mere background to the lives of her characters. Austen uses the country estate to give the reader an insight into the personalities of her characters, and as a way of discussing political, religious and aesthetic ideas of the period.

One of the most obvious functions of the country estate in both Prideand Prejudice and Mansfield Park is that of mirroring the character of its owners and Inhabitants and thus of providing a symbolic representation of their values and traits of personality. When Elizabeth Bennet visits Pemberley, she is impressed by what she sees: It was a large, handsome stone building, standing well on rising ground, and backed by a ridge of high woody hills;-and in front, a stream of some natural importance was swelled into greater, but without any artificial appearance. Its banks were neither formal, nor falsely adorned. Elizabeth was delighted. She had never seen a place for which nature had done more, or where natural beauty had been so little counteracted by an awkward taste.

This description occurs at a point when Elizabeth is being forced to reconsider her opinions of Darcy. She has already read his reply to Wickham's slurs on his character, but still believes Darcy to be a man of excessive pride, a belief which is overturned during her visit to Pemberley, and this view of the estate is the first stage of her transformation of opinion. The information which the author gives us enables us to start challenging our assumptions about Darcy, and follow the process which is occurring within the mind of Elizabeth. This description of the estate gives us information about many aspects of Darcy's character. The beauty of the house and grounds make us feel that perhaps he has justification for any pride he displays. Pemberley shows many signs of the healthy estate.

It has a good position, on a hill surrounded by the vital natural resources of water and timber. However, it is the aesthetic taste of the estate's owner that Elizabeth finds most impressive. Both the stream and the rest of the estate are modifications of nature, improvements of the original countryside, and therefore have the potential to cause controversy. But Elizabeth is pleased with the aesthetic choices made during the course of the estate's development, mostly for the reason that they show great moderation. In the description of the flaws avoided by the landscape, Austen uses the phrases 'formal' and 'awkward'. These are both flaws which Elizabeth had previously ascribed to Darcy. The flaws which Elizabeth perceives in Darcy are the very flaws which are absent from his estate. This tells both Elizabeth and the reader that perhaps we have judged Darcy too hastily as his taste seems to contradict our belief in his excessive pride, but it is also possible to read this description of Pemberley as a symbolic description of Darcy's character and thus as a moment of illumination for Elizabeth. She has previously accused him of excessive pride but in this passage it is implied that any pride Darcy might have is justified by his station in life. The house has literally a high position, 'standing well on rising ground' and the stream is 'of some natural importance'. However, the overall impression of the estate is that it is 'without any artificial appearance' This impression is strengthened as Elizabeth enters Pemberley House to find the housekeeper 'less fine, and more civil' than expected and the furniture 'with less of splendour' than that of Rosings. These symbolic revelations of Darcy's character are parallelled by the housekeeper's praise of her master and prepare us for the moment when Elizabeth meets Darcy once more and finds him more than content to socialize with the despised Mr Gardiner.

However, the information about character which we can glean from Austen's descriptions of country estates is not restricted to the owners and residents of the estate; Austen also reveals vital information through her characters' reaction to their surroundings.

It is generally considered a positive personality trait to be fond of the countryside, the political implications of which I shall examine in more detail later on and in Mansfield Park we certainly learn a lot about the Crawfords from their reactions to the countryside. We are told that Mary 'had been mostly used to London' and that her although her brother owned a large estate in Norfolk he disliked a 'permanence of abode'. Mary's true feelings about the countryside are revealed when she amuses the Bertrams with the following anecdote:

> To want a horse and cart in the country seemed impossible, so I told my maid to speak for one directly; and as I cannot look out of my dressing-closet without seeing one farm-yard, nor walk in the shrubbery without passing another, I thought it would be only ask and have.

She has so little understanding of the country way of life that she does not realise that farming gets priority over luxury use during the busy harvest- time. When Edmund explains the situation, she still does not grasp that she is the one at fault, making a joke about 'country customs'. On the trip to Sotherton in Mansfield Park Maria Bertram gives a description of the view of the road to Mr Rushworth's estate:

The rest of the way is such as it ought to be. Mr Rushworth has made it since he succeeded to the estate. Here begins the village. Those cottages are really a disgrace. The church spire is reckoned remarkably handsome. I am glad the church is not so close to the great house as so often happens in old places. The annoyance of the bells must be terrible. There is the parsonage; a tidy looking house and I understand the clergyman and his wife are very decent people. Those are the alms-houses, built by some of the family...the situation of the house is dreadful. We go down hill to it for half-a-mile, and it is a pity, for it would not be an ill-looking place if it had a better approach.'

Q. Shelley's Frankenstein and Austen's Mansfield Park as Vehicles for Social.Comment

Or

Q. How can you say Shelley's Frankenstein and Austen's Mansfield Park are clever repositories for social commentary and judgment.

It has been often noted that the Romantic writers of English literature were rebelling against the established positions and views of society. Most of the Romantic artists were indigenes of the well-established middle class and they were swiftly tiring of the self-serving political depredation perpetrated by the hands of the upper class. The Romantics were flouting convention, thumbing their noses and calling for radical and widespread reform not only in governmental politics, but within the politics of their own trade—creativity and art. Their myriad of works are clear evidence of this. Contumely against established society was found mostly in the poetical works of the day. However, much social commentary found its way into seemingly unlikely novels. Two such novels are Mary Shelly's Frankenstein and Jane Austen's Mansfield Park. Both of these novels are clever repositories for social commentary and judgment. The overwhelming social judgment by Austen and Shelly was an intolerance for class distinction. Though they were hardly deluded enough to posses Utopian ideals, they nevertheless felt that a society with very little class distinction and especially without class-specific opportunity and quality of life was indeed attainable. Given that Karl Marx formulated many of his socialist ideals as a result of his exposure to the conditions of working class Englishmen, one might venture to say that the Romantic artists were forerunners of the socialist ideal, though perhaps this is a stretch. However, neither Austen nor Shelly saw socialism as an antidote to class distinction, or if they did, it did not find its way into their novels. They were quick to show, though, that a class blending could occur that was acceptable to all. In fact, such a theme is clearly prevalent in many sections of both Mansfield Park and Frankenstein.

For example, in Frankenstein, Shelly describes the acceptance of a lower class individual into an upper class family. Justine is a lower class servant who is taken into the Frankenstein family to alleviate the dire straits into which she has fallen. However, the Frankenstein's do not view her as a servant in the typical, expected sense. Rather, in a letter to the maniacal, creature-creating Victor Frankenstein, Elizabeth (adopted sister-come-wife of Victor) notes about Justine's situation: "the republican institutions of our country have produced simpler and happier manners than those which prevail in the great monarchies that surround it. Hence there is less distinction between the several classes of its inhabitants...the lower orders being neither so poor nor so despised," and Elizabeth further notes that Justine, accepted into the family even if as a servant, was fortunate to "[learn] the duties of a servant; a condition which, in our fortunate country, does not include the idea of ignorance, and a sacrifice of the dignity of a human being". Here Shelly has a difficult time portraying a lower class individual as equal to that of an upper-classman, likely because Shelly herself is not Swiss, but rather is British, and the centuries-old belief in separation of the classes is well entrenched in her, if unwelcome. However she still is clearly, tersely and forcefully presenting a character who is heartily accepted by those from a class above her, a radical notion in her time. More importantly, Shelly presents this servant as a woman of dignity and sagacity (well, except for that sorry moment when she confesses to the murder), qualities long deemed impossible for one of the lower class. In this respect, Shelly embodies the Romantic ideal of a less distinct social order, and an ability for man to relate to one another on a human rather than class scale.

Much like Shelly, Jane Austen also puts forth subtle social assertions in Mansfield Park. In this case, however, the ideal comes across more generally than Shelly's specifics. The idea of class blending is an overall theme of Austen's novel, rather than a specific episode (or episodes). The principal character is Fanny Price, a young girl whose mother left her relatively high class family to marry a lower class seaman. When Fanny's mother encounters dire straits, she asks for assistance from her wealthier relations, which is granted in the form of Fanny being adopted by the Bertrams (another curious theme throughout both novels: charity of the upper classes towards the lower). In the beginning of the novel, Fanny is regarded as lower class, the fortunate recipient of generous philanthropy who should never question her established position.

However, in many extremely subtle ways, Fanny does continually and persistently question that position and by the end of the novel she has triumphantly risen to the social level of her benefactors. Austen is apparently less confident in making overt references to a more unified class ideal. As a result, she finds that she must rely on a conventional story to express an unconventional point. It was, perhaps, more socially acceptable for one to rise out of one's class through marriage, especially for women, and it is unfortunate that Austen has her character follow this convention. Yet, literature often shows characters rising beyond their expected fortunes by creatively employing the limited resources available to them; such is what tends to define the strong character, especially women characters, in literature. And what saves Austen's novel from pedantic uselessness is that Fanny manages to affect many people along her arduous ascent. Lord Bertram, for one, had originally refused to accept Fanny as anyone of consequence, and certainly no one even approaching the level of his own children. Yet, by the end of the novel, Lord Bertram has come to regard Fanny as more dear than his own children, and certainly more worthy of her new position than his offspring. Thus Austen has been most successful by employing a perfectly traditional role (a staunch, conservative, old-order noble) as a facilitator and commentator of a new social order. And so, Austen as well shines out as an example of the Romantic ideal.

The use of the novel as an avenue for social commentary was a clever route for the loosely organized Romantics. While the novel had played host to political commentary since its creation in the Restoration era, by the Romantic era, it had sunk to a more popular, less serious form. Percy Shelly undoubtedly had much influence on inclusion of social commentary in her otherwise straightforward horror novel, but she penned it regardless. And Austen can likely be fully credited for her commentary. As such, both of these authors are commendable as Romantic visionaries, and can be admired for choosing a more obscure art form as the vehicle for their political expressions.

Q. Discuss the Theater in Jane Austen's Time

Or

Q. Discuss the theatre of nineteenth century

All the best plays were run over in vain. Neither Hamlet, nor Macbeth, nor Othello, not Douglas, not the Gamester, presented any thing that could satisfy even the tragedians; and the Rivals, the School for Scandal, Wheel of Fortune, Heir at Law, and a long etcetera, were successively dismissed with yet warmer objections. No piece could be proposed that did not supply somebody with a difficulty, and on one side or the other it was a continual repetition of, 'Oh! no, that will never do!'. As seen here, Jane Austen was more than familiar with the plays that were being produced and read during her lifetime. It is safe to assume that Jane Austen, an educated and talented writer would not include in her list of theatrical critique a play with which she was unfamiliar. More probable than not, the plays above listed were one's she understood quite well. With that assumption in mind, it is also probable that the characters for certain reasons rejected the plays. Perhaps the subject matter was a bit too close to home. In this light, I have undertook to find out about the playwrights that wrote the plays and the story lines each play followed.

Edward Moore was the son of a minister. He began his career as a simple linendraper. However, that soon became to dull for such an active mind, and Moore began to write. His first attempt was a collection of Fables for the Female Sex. The nominal success was soon followed by his first play The Foundling, which is still rather well known in theatrical circles. The play of his the Jane Austen mentioned was The Gamester. It follows the story of a gamester's downfall through and infatuation with gambling. Basically, he had a gambling addiction. The story also included the elements of murder, suicide, and men who wanted other men's wives, a bit too close to the lives of Tom Bertram and Henry Crawford for their liking. John Home was the son of a town clerk. He attended the University of Edinburgh where he followed the curriculum of a minister in the Church of Scotland. He was licensed to preach, however his enlistment in the loyalist ranks made his taking order difficult. Eventually, after a complicated military history of imprisonment and escape, he took orders.

Home had always been deeply interested in Greek and Roman culture. Somewhere along the line he began to write plays. Jane Austen mentioned his play Douglas. This is the story of secret marriages, lost sons, and defending family honor. I can see where Henry would exclaim "no!" to this one (British Drama). Richard Cumberland, son to a rector who later became an Irish bishop, was educated at Westminster and Trinity. Both schools were well known for their education of clergy. Cumberland was secretary to the Earl of Halifax. In his spare time, he would write plays including Wheel of Fortune. It was this play that Jane Austen made note of. As the theme of the story was revenge and repentance, it is sure that someone among the Mansfield "back stabbing" party would have a strong objection (English Drama).

Son of George Colman the Elder, George Colman the Younger was born to a family already entrenched in theatrical life. Colman the Elder was educated at Westminster School and Christ Church, Oxford. It is with Colman the Younger that we conclude the interesting trend of Jane Austen's reading playwrights who had strong ties to the clergy. Not surprising for the daughter of a minister. Colman's play mentioned by Jane Austen was Heir at Law. Born to a family with a theater history, Richard Brinsly Sheridan was not a man with strong connections to the clergy. He eloped with a woman after fighting two duels for her.

He later married her but not until he had spent a number of years living with her out of wedlock. His education was conducted in Bath and London. In essence, the streets of the city educated him. Jane Austen mentioned two of his plays, The Rivals and School for Scandal. The Rivals is the story of disguised suitors, wagging and exaggerating tongues (it was probably Mrs. Norton who objected to this play), and woman who refuse men they love on the basis on the excess of money. The play School for Scandal relates forbidden love, deceit, cheating spouses, and beautifully charming villains. The way this play captures the language of its time period has been compared to the way Shakespeare captured the Elizabethan language. The play finally decided upon by the Mansfield party was Lover's Vows. Elizabeth Inchbald, and actress, playwright, novelist and editor wrote this play. Her life was steeping in the theater, as she married an actor in conjunction with all she did with the stage.

The theatrical culture of Jane Austen's time was as diverse as the literary culture. Many of the same trends were being repeated. Since Jane Austen lived in the breach between the 18th and 19th centuries, trends in theater were moving from the old to the new.

The two main centers for the production of plays were Drury Lane and Covent Garden in London. These two theater houses were the only legitimate theaters, the only two supported by the monarchy. Many little theater houses sprung up allover the city and the country, however they continued the trends set by the two larger ones. They created no trends of their own.

In Jane Austen's time, the propriety of attending theater was in an upheaval. Though the upper classes were still attending plays by disconnecting themselves from the common crowd by sitting above them in the boxes, the theater became a place of wildness hedonism. Audiences actively engaged in the show by booing, clapping, or hissing at appropriate and not-so-appropriate moments. The middle classes sat in the pit below the stage, and the working classes sat on the edges, in the galleries. The theater reached its heights of hedonism at this time when it became popular to pick up prostitutes here instead of the streets.

A wide variety of trends were seen in the types of plays audiences viewed. Between 1800 and 1830, gothic tragedy or gothic thriller dominated main stage. As we see in the trends of art and fashion a pseudo classicistic style was emerging in other areas of theater. Operas began to flourish at the same time as a means of escape from the high melodramas and dark Gothicism. Similarly, pantomimes began to be staged in between acts of such plays in order to give the audiences a moment of relief from the emotional intensity of the plays (Nineteenth C. Drama). Highly decorous comic operas, comedies of manners and sincere poetic dramas were tends also seen during Jane Austen's life (English Drama). Another common trend was the publication of poet dramas that were published for the single purpose of being read. These plays were never produced. The authors of these plays believed that this type of play enable the audience to get into and understand the psychology of the character more so than stage production would allow. To them, Hamlet was the perfect example of a play meant to be read, not watched ("Mental Theater").

Among these smaller movements, a large movement emerged that greatly changed the face of theater. The idea of sentimentalism was given birth to as it related to thought, idea, and conception. With sentimental theater came a surge of true and false sentimentalism. False being that of mushy, weak, pitiable theater. True sentimentalism focused on thought and reflection as well as humanitarianism, recognition of social problems, and the expression of ideas, opinions, and stands on issues. It was the first time that theater was used as a vehicle to promote social change (English Drama).

Q. Write a short note on Fanny's Character in Jane Austen's Mansfield Park

Or

Q. Is Fanny Price a colorfully insubstantial character

Jane Austen's *Mansfield Park* is a colorful novel of character, a study of the development of individuals as figures in a complex of emotional, social, and political tapestry. In her attempt to portray characters as figures, Austen fails to animate these characters with the life and passion that makes a character stand out in a work of literary art. Fanny Price of *Mansfield Park* is the ultimate example of Austen's rare capacity to create colorfully insubstantial character, full of quirks but lacking inner depth. Fanny Price not only lacks passion, but has no comprehension of passion, either objectively or subjectively. The novel's apparent lack of passion results from the alliance of the narrator to the perspective of Fanny.

One of the most common criticisms of Fanny's character involves her lack of assertion or initiative in the determination of her own fate. Feminist criticisms fail when the blame the structure of her society for its limitations of her freedom because the source of her problem lies in Austen's formulation of her character. Indeed, Fanny agrees that "I could not act any thing if you were to give me the world. No, indeed, I cannot act". The acting of the play provides an opportunity for the reader to compare Fanny's character in the novel with those of others. Each of the actors, even Edmund, eagerly participates in the production of the play, quite contrary to the known feelings of Sir Bertram on the subject. Fanny alone maintains her objection to the play, not on moral grounds for she is too timid to have any developed sense of morality, but because she lacks any sense of her own character. Whatever trace of life she has Fanny draws from those around her: "Her eyes brightened at the sight of Edmund". Fanny looks to

Edmund for moral direction, looking to his profile "to see" if she "could catch any of his counsel".

Fanny's lack of passion is counter-defined by Mary Crawford ebullience of passion. Indeed, Mary has "the same energy of character" as her brother, the immature and impetuous Henry. In contrast, Fanny's idea of a good time includes sitting "in the shade on a fine day, and [looking] upon verdure".

If there is any hint of passionate response in the novel, such response does not come from Fanny. As shallow and insubstantial a character as he is, Henry Crawford at least is familiar with human emotion. With adolescent fervor, he passionately seeks to capture Fanny's heart. His plan is "to make Fanny Price in love with me". Sir Thomas names Fanny's deficiency: "I am half inclined to think, Fanny, that you do not quite know your own feelings".

Indeed, Fanny is so much an emotional and moral void, she feels threatened when the order of her world is shifted, as when she moves from Mansfield Park back to her family at Portsmouth. She laments the loss of "consideration of times and seasons, [the] regulation of subject, [the] propriety, [the] attention towards everybody which there was not" in her parents' house. Indeed, Fanny is defined by the novel by her relationships with other character, while other characters are people unto themselves. Edmund, as her tutor, has "taught [Fanny] to think and feel". She disguises her lack of self as being "too humble" and fails to consider herself a part of the family with whom she has grown up and experienced life. So void of the feeling and thought that makes a character real, she is "all surprise and embarrassment" when any attention turns towards her, especially after the ball. She can not be the center of attention because she has no "center" to which one can be attentive. Near the end of the novel, when she should have grown and matured, "Fanny's friendship was all that [Edmund] had to sling to", implying that Fanny's personal void of personality is infectious. As readers, we are inclined to lament the inevitable descent into ennui that married life with Fanny must certainly predict.

Charlotte Brontë is correct her assertion that "Passions were perfectly unknown" to Jane Austen. *Mansfield Park* fails to generate passionate within its cast of characters, but, inadvertently generates that passion in its readers. Since its publication, the novel has angered, bored, and challenged readers to look for something more in the text. The unique brilliance of this particular novel is the radical way in which the book teases and taunts the reader's expectations of character. The novel leads the reader on, seduces him or her, until he or she simple fumes that there is nothing more to be read. The novel elicits passion because the novel is void of passion: a unique symbiotic relationship masterfully contrived by Austen.

Chapter 9

Critical Essays

"The Charm is Broken": Sexual Desire and Transgression in Jane Austen's Mansfield Park

In a letter to her brother dated 1814, Jane Austen boasted about a compliment she had received from a friend on her most recent work, Mansfield Park: "It's the most sensible novel he's ever read". Austen prided herself on creating literature that depicted realistic characters and honest situations, but perhaps more importantly, she strove to create fiction that was moral and instructional as well as entertaining. So what does sensible say about the sexual? In Mansfield Park, the answer appears blaringly before us, as we repeatedly witness sexuality and desire represented in the darkest of terms, and often resulting in the most sinister of outcomes.

Those who emit a sexual persona or awareness are to be seen as dangerous, and those whom possess sexual desire are inevitably the ones in danger, and are often punished for their untamed emotions and erratic behavior. The Bertrams and Fanny Price reside at Mansfield Park peacefully enough until their quiet, domestic world is turned upside down by outsiders, all of who, in their own ways, threaten to upset the lives of the inhabitants with a passion, desire, and sexuality that is new to them. In this essay, I would like to examine the relationships that arise from connections with these outsiders, what role sexuality and desire play in them, and what Austen's treatment of them says about sexual transgression and desire in a larger sense as well.

It seems only natural to begin with the two most

prominent intruders in Mansfield Park, Henry and Mary Crawford. As jaded individuals accustomed to the fast-paced (and amoral) life of the city, Mary and Henry view Mansfield Park and its residents with a sort of novelty interest, regarding them almost as if they're playthings set out for their amusement. Mary is "remarkably pretty" and wins the Bertrams over with "her lively dark eye, clear brown complexion, and general prettiness" and her brother, after just a few visits, is declared, "most agreeable young man the sisters had ever known". Henry (who I will discuss in greater length momentarily) sees Maria and Julia as conquests, women to be won over just for the sake of doing so. Mary, however, is sincere in her emotions toward Edmund (at least, as sincere as Mary Crawford could ever be), but the combination of Edmund's desire for her and her own seductive nature makes her a precarious character.

Perhaps Mary's biggest problem is that she is too knowledgeable for her own good. Her skepticism and cynical attitude often seem out of place at the naïve and sheltered Mansfield Park, particularly when compared to the ideological views of Edmund. Unlike Edmund, who is strikingly ignorant about the matter, Mary becomes preoccupied with understanding Fanny's position in society, and subsequent availability, inquiring, "pray, is she out, or is she not?". Later, she remarks to Edmund, unaware that he is soon to be ordained, upon the apathy she feels (and blindly assumes others feel, as well) about attending church:

"Cannot you imagine with what unwilling feelings the former belles of the house of Rushworth did many a time repair to this chapel? The young Mrs. Eleanors and Mrs. Bridgets‹starched up into seeming piety, but with heads full of something very different‹especially if the poor chaplain were not worth looking at‹and, in those days, I fancy parsons were very inferior even to what they are now"

These instances, both tinged with sexual overtones, demonstrate that Mary's worldliness and sophistication are dangerous attributes, because they are not representative of good manners or refinement, but a thin veneer that, when peeled away, reveals narcissism, superficiality, and a lack of morals. Although never told in so many words, we have a tacit understanding that Mary's knowledge extends past the limits of what a proper young woman out to know about‹including, of course, sex and desire. It is this combination of awareness and corruption that makes Mary Crawford so ominous, and consequently, means danger for Edmund.

Edmund's reckless longing for Mary, while it does reveal a weakness on his part, also seems to serve as a reiteration of her menacing nature. Repeatedly we, along with Fanny, must suffer through Edmund's oblivious veneration of Mary, which quite clearly has sexual implications. After all, his attraction to her is initially, and primarily, a physical one: "it is her countenance that is so attractive". Later, at the end of a conversation with her, Edmund watches Mary walk away, in "ecstasy of admiration of all her many virtues". This passion clearly has negative connotations and consequences. Because of Mary's charm, or more accurately, because of Edmund's "bewitched" state, he frequently forgets himself, his family, and his duty. Edmund's lack of composure is most apparent in the strain that it puts on his relationship with Fanny. In Jane Austen and the War of Ideas, Marilyn Butler states, "Edmund, who has always been considerate of Fanny, is now seduced by his physical delight in Mary in forgetting her". Once Edmund realizes Mary's callous and manipulative disposition, he alludes to his awareness as if he had has been released from a siren's spell: "the charm is broken. My eyes are opened".

While Mary Crawford is both tempting and threatening to Edmund, Henry Crawford is equally, perhaps even more so, a danger to Julia, Maria, and later to Fanny. We quickly learn from Mary that Henry's favorite hobby is wooing women he has no sincere interest in: "he is the most horrible flirt that can be imagined. If your Miss Bertrams do not like to have their hearts broke, let them avoid Henry". Tragically enough, however, both Julia and Maria are soon taken in by his charismatic persona and sex appeal, and, for the first time in their lives, the sisters find themselves at odds with one another.

From the beginning of the novel, we are informed of Julia

and Maria's vanity and weakness of character, which inevitably foreshadow the disastrous events to come. Maria, "so surrounded by admirers, must be difficult in her choice" accepts a marriage proposal from the foolish but wealthy Mr. Rushworth who endures humiliation and disgrace because he allows his eyes instead of his brain to guide him in his decision: "he was from the first struck with the beauty of Miss Bertram". This act alone makes us skeptical of Maria, but Austen pushes us to become even more incredulous as we see her shamelessly unable to restrain herself from returning Henry Crawford's flirtations, despite her engagement and her sister's obvious interest in him. Maria lacks sexual self-discipline because Henry is irresistible, but also because she is used to and enjoys being flattered and admired.

In one of Austen's more symbolic moments, we see a grim prediction of Maria's transgressive nature and inevitable ruin. During an outing at Rushworth's estate, a fraction of the party find themselves trapped in a garden that has a locked gate, and are instructed to wait while Rushworth goes to fetch the key. Maria, however, lacks the patience for this, and attempts to squeeze through the gate in order to go off alone with Henry. When Fanny begs her to wait until the gate is properly unlocked, Maria says, "Prohibited! Nonsense!" I certainly can get out that way, and I will!". This attitude seems to encapsulate Maria's life philosophy: she has little, if any, conscious of right or wrong, and does not seem to feel that it is any concern to her.

This selfishness and immorality inevitably lead Maria to public a sexual scandal and public dishonor. When she tires of her husband, whom she married for money and not love, she is easily won over again by Henry's advances. Lionel Trilling duly notes in "Mansfield Park" that it is this relationship with Maria in which Henry's sexual charisma catches up with him: "he becomesŠthe prey to his own charm, and in his cold flirtation with Maria Bertram he is trapped by his impersonation of passion‹his role requires that he carry Maria off from a dull marriage to a life of boring concupiscence.". Both are weak characters, and allow their depravity to take whatever forms it might‹in this case, their downfall is desire that goes so unchecked that it unavoidably turns into acting outside of social norms. Maria's lust for Henry, and Henry's disingenuous return of her affections lead to elopement, a shocked and hurt family, and a divorce for Maria. Julia's constant attempts to catch up to (and outdo) Maria (she quickly scrambles over the fence when she discovers that Maria and Henry have gone off alone together) are often ignored by Henry and thwarted by the somber realization that her sister is the preferred one.

Although Julia ends up eloping with Yates (who appears, like Rushworth, to be a rather simple and ridiculous man), and this exploit is obviously deemed sexually transgressive by society, it doesn't seem that Julia's act was the result of anything related to sex or desire, but rather, the reaction of a girl who has been overlooked and craves attention. We cannot help feeling a certain sympathy for Julia when we are told that her family has an easier time forgiving her than her sister: "Julia escaped better than MariaŠto a favorable difference of disposition of circumstanceŠher beauty and requirements had held but a second place. She had always used to think of herself a little inferior to Maria".

No one but Fanny seems to notice Henry's indiscretions towards Julia and Maria (Edmund might, but his impression of Henry is quite obviously influenced by Mary). Consequently, when he turns his interest toward her, she resists wholeheartedly, and unlike her cousins, who were quickly charmed into thinking him attractive, "still continued to think Mr. Crawford very plain". Henry, unused to such reluctance, only becomes more intrigued by and passionate about Fanny. He declares to his sister that, "it would be something to be loved by such a girl, to excite the first ardors of her young, unsophisticated mind!" Fanny's inexperience is alluring (and most likely, fascinating from Henry's jaded viewpoint) because it means that she is untainted‹virginal in every conceivable way. Naturally, Henry appears to be a shady figure because of his indiscretions with Maria and Julia, but his corruption seems to soar to a new level altogether as he actively pursues the disinclined Fanny. Although the climax of his pursuit would most obviously be the marriage proposal, the pinnacle of his flirtations toward her are revealed during the necklace incident. Fanny unwittingly accepts a necklace from Mary to wear to the ball, without having any idea that it was a gift from Henry. Once Fanny becomes aware of who truly gave her the necklace, she feels awkward and violated, having let a piece of jewelry from an unwanted admirer sit around her neck all evening without having any idea of the more scheming and sexual intentions for which it stood.

The production of the play, Lovers' Vows, is perhaps the sole episode in the book that is most abundant with sexual desire and transgression. While their father is away, Tom, Maria, Julia, at the suggestion of Yates and the delighted approval of the Crawfords, decide to put on a play to pass the time. They begin with elaborate plans for a building a stage, which turn out to be excessive in both cost and production, and then proceed to disrupt the house, both literally by rearranging the furniture and taking over the billiards room, and also figuratively by engaging in an activity of which they know Sir Thomas would not approve. The play accentuates the sexual tensions and desires that have surfaced earlier in the novel by allowing, as Butler says: "a license for what would normally be entirely improper. Their scenes together permit physical contact between the sexes (as when Henry holds Maria's hand) and a bold freedom of speech altogether outside the constraint imposed by social norms."

Although Edmund protests against the play in the beginning, his resistance gradually fades in order to take place alongside Mary in the production. Fanny bitterly cites Edmund's lapse of good judgment as "all Miss Crawford's doing. She had seen her influence in every speech, and it was miserable". Austen again peaks our suspicion about Mary Crawford when we hear of her intention "to rehearse it (the scene) with Edmund‹by ourselves‹against the evening". The notion of the rather worldly and aggressive Mary Crawford rehearsing a romantic scene alone with her love interest seems far from innocent. Other characters reveal their sexually charged agendas during the rehearsals as well. Henry Crawford snubs Julia, and consequently, strengthens his flirtation with her sister, by proposing the part she wanted to play go to Maria.

Maria, instead of declining to participate on account of her engagement, sees nothing wrong with accepting the part offered to her. Julia, hurt and perhaps, desperate to be noticed and flattered, flirts with Yates. Fanny, the sole member of their party who staunchly refuses to condone the play or participate in it, notices that, during rehearsal, Maria acts "too well", implying that the emotions that directed toward Henry's character are most likely more than just acting. Fanny also notes that "Mr. Crawford was considerably the best actor of all", allowing Austen to suggest that Henry too effortlessly takes on whatever role is required of him for us to have faith in the possibility that he may evolve into something more than the glib showman he appears to be.

Thus, the play is dangerous because it allows sexuality to be acted out, desire to be demonstrated, in a public arena. Furthermore, it brings out the more conniving attitudes and selfish natures of the individuals involved. We are to be wary of those who are so oblivious that they regard the play as nothing more than a harmless pastime (such as Yates and the Crawfords), and feel concern for those (such as Edmund) who are persuaded to take part in it against their better judgment.

It is only Fanny who realizes that the play is inappropriate, and remains firmly against for the duration of the rehearsals. This emphasizes Fanny's level-headedness, her self-righteousness, modesty, and perhaps even prudishness. But does Fanny's condemnation of the play seem to be a condemnation of sexuality and passion? Although we are aware of her unwavering desire for Edmund throughout the novel (most commonly expressed through modest blushes and an intense jealousy toward Mary), it would never occur to anyone reading Mansfield Park to suspect Fanny Price of possessing sexual desire or impure thoughts. Butler compares her feelings to Edmund to her emotions toward William, saying that they have a "childish quality". Given Fanny's naivety and the nature of her earnest yet unassuming devotion, this description seems quite accurate.

Nina Auerbach is even more daring in her speculation of Edmund and Fanny's relationship, likening Fanny (perhaps, a bit brutally) to Frankenstein's monster, and calling her "a charmless heroine who was not made to be loved". In "Jane Austen's Dangerous Charm" Auerbach contends that Fanny does not aim as high as love or romance, but her goal is merely for equal companionship. This notion does seem to be supported by the text: Fanny does not appear to be concerned with love or desire, but sameness: she dislikes Mary because she threatens to create the "danger of dissimiliarity" between Edmund and herself, and later rejects Henry on the grounds that "we are so totally unlike".

Incest has been a much-debated topic in critical discourse concerning Fanny and Edmund's relationship. This notion of a brother/sister marriage is not entirely shocking in the context of other relationships in Austen's novels: Emma, after all, marries her "brother", Mr. Knightley, who is twenty years her senior and has watched her grow up right in front of his eyes. Mansfield Park, however, is the only novel of Austen's novels that directly and consciously addresses this social taboo. When Sir Thomas expresses hesitation toward Fanny's presence at Mansfield Park because he fears the possibility of one of his sons falling in love with her, Mrs. Norris argues, "Šdo you not know that of all things upon earth that is the least likely to happen; brought up, as they would be, always together like brothers and sisters: It is morally impossible."

Not only is the union possible, but by the end of Mansfield Park, it seems the only plausible solution. After the tumultuous experience Edmund has with Mary, a quiet marriage with Fanny naturally sounds attractive. Furthermore, there is no one left for Edmund but Fanny: immediately before we are told of their marriage in the last chapter, the previous one ends by stating, "Fanny's friendship was all that he (Edmund) had to cling to". In Jane Austen and the Fiction of Culture, Richard Handler and Daniel Segal accurately note that, "neither the social rules defining a desirable marriage nor even the most uniformly held social rules defining a possible marriage control human interactions."

Although both Edmund and Fanny end up getting what they want (Edmund a wife, and Fanny, Edmund), and we can envision a happy marriage for them, it is not one of passion or sex or anything that would require more than a PG rating. In Mansfield Park, sexual desire often results in the loss of control, impaired judgment, and thoughts and actions that are guided by emotions rather than logic or rationality. We are told what is immoral and what not to do (play sexual games, flirt insincerely, lose oneself in passion or lust, etc.) but we are not given proper examples of how to conduct ourselves. Instead, Austen leaves us, rather uneasily, stranded between the platonic relationship of Fanny and Edmund, and the debauched affairs of the other characters, wishing for some sort of happy medium.

Analysis

AnalysisEpistolarity in Mansfield Park: Mary's and Edmund's letters to Fanny

I have been wanting to respond to Helen Battersby's perceptive posting tracing the changes in tone and attitude we find in Mary's letters from London to Fanny. Helen showed us that Mary ever so gradually falls away from the depth of individual feeling and imaginative musings we find her expressing in her last interview with Fanny in Fanny's attic as Fanny's attic awakens her memories of childhood and the whole of her time at Mansfield to the strained coquetry and pragmatic arguments of her last interview with Edmund The points I'd like to add are that Mary's letters are interlaced with Edmund's and both sets of letters also tell the story of the gradual involvement of Henry with Maria in London and their elopement.

I'll deal with the second element in Mary's letters first. There are 4 letters not three, and each is carefully situated in the context of a series of events going on London and alert us to what's happening (even if Mary is unconscious of how

Henry is heading into danger, and Fanny too fails to read between the lines); and finally from the very beginning to the very end there are the touches of both cold disdainful mockery and genuine imaginative sympathy Mary is occasionally capable of.

The letters are as follows:

- Letter from Mary, London, to Fanny, Portsmouth, telling of her first meeting with Mrs Rushworth and Julia, in which Mary says she hopes Maria's access to splendor will satisfy her, mocks Yates as a sad catch for Julia ("if his rents were but equal to his rants"), and says she misses Edmund, Fanny, and so does Henry ("write me a pretty one in reply to gladden Henry's eye");
- Letter from Mary, in London arrives 2 days after day Henry left, to Fanny, Portsmouth, in which Mary writes of Henry's pleasure in his visit to Fanny in his place, but in which she also tells of that coming party wherein Henry will meet Maria; she is more supercilious in tone, and there is an insouciance in her description of how she "welcomed" Edmund to London;
- Letter from Mary Crawford, London, to Fanny, Portsmouth, inquiring after Tom's possibly dying: Mary's infamous salivating at the idea of Edmund's becoming the older son has been done to death on this list, while we have not been noticing what is equally central to the letter: Mary is concerned to assure Fanny that "Henry cares for nobody but you," because, as we see (and Fanny doesn't) the projected visit by Henry to Richmond where Maria is tells of a story we cannot see in which Henry is getting more and more deeply involved with Maria; and
- Letter from Mary, London, to Fanny, Portsmouth, in haste, with reference to elopement; here to Helen's comment on Mary's "chameleon-like" adaptation to the hollow people she's among, we can now add the climax to the story which unbeknowst to herself and

Fanny Mary has been telling us: the dangerous liaison of Henry and Maria has culminated in an elopement.

We are nowadays very alive to the debt modern novels which present a strongly persuasive psychologized consciousness as the central passages of the text owe to epistolary narrative. It has been shown more than once that Jane Austen learned to use narrative for clear revelation of a character's inmost self from the epistolary narratives that were so popular in her period, and that heavily influenced gothic novels, both of which she consumed We forget that epistolary narrative also tell stories, plots, and that by doing so in a disguised single- voice perspective they provide the novel with both suspense (the character who reads the letter doesn't get what's coming any more than the character who writes it) and dramatic irony (the reader is supposed to get it).

Austen is using letters to tell her story, to fit into *Mansfield Park* a subnovel or novel at a distance which we may glimpse the first time (in the way we catch on to a few of the clues in *Emma*), but which on the second reading we get much more of (in the way we read *Emma* so differently on the second reading).

The other element I want to add to Helen's posting is that we are expected to read Mary's letters alongside Edmund's, for the two sets gain meaning in terms of one another. Edmund writes two. Now his perspective on how Mary "welcomed" him is quite different from Mary's. Here we have the usual revelation of character and differing points of view modern readers are alerted to. but we should also note that as well as providing a counterpoint to Mary's letters, a backdrop (so to speak) in which we find Edmund gradually finding himself an alien in Mary's inner & outer worlds, Edmund too, obtuse as he is, tells us a little more about this story of Henry and Maria that is going on in London. The final letter written by him in which he too gives us the climax of Henry and Maria's story (as well as his and Mary's) is also meant to contrast to Mary's: it is deliberate & anguished. It also compares, for, like Mary, he is utterly self-involved and cannot see any point of view about the interview but his own; both are brief. The author however expects us to distance ourselves and judge impartially based on high standards of integrity and kindness Austen assumed her readers shared with her.

For those who would like to look at Edmund's letters and see how they are psychologically counterpointed to Mary's while filling in an objective story we are supposed to pick up from both their letters, here are pages:

- Letter from Edmund, Mansfield, Park, to Fanny in Portsmouth in which Edmund actually details scenes from London including something of what happened on the important night of Mrs Frazer's party; and in which his real love for Fanny comes out because while he says Mary is "the only woman in the world whom I could ever think of for a wife" the woman he misses, longs for, cannot bear not to have at "home" with him is Fanny; and
- Letter from Edmund, London, to Fanny, Portsmouth, telling he is coming to bring her home, the events of the failed search, Sir Thomas's awakened need of Fanny—and interestingly Sir Thomas's invitation to Susan to come.

We might note that Sir Thomas is the only one in all this mess who can get out of himself, who has apparently read through and into Fanny's letters to garner how much Susan has come to mean to Fanny, and the lifestyle Susan will have to endure much more bitterly once she has had Fanny with her for a bit. Susan is of course ecstatic, and I am reminded of Auden's poem about how dogs go on with their complacent doggie life in the midst of great calamities all the people around them seem to be experiencing. Susan at least gets something out of it. The narrator says "Fanny's last meal in her father's house was in character with her first; she was dismissed from it as hospitably as she had been welcomed", and we have the quiet comedy of Susan trying to hide her happiness, and Edmund's ridiculous remark feeling sorry for *Fanny* because forsooth, "How a man who had once loved, could desert *you*!" Love is blind. And then ever the egoist: "'But *your's*—your regard was new compared with— Fanny, think of *me*!'" Always our novelist is unsentimental in her approach to even a favored character; in Volume III she tells us very complicated truths about life through her remarkable uses of epistolary narrative.

Epistolarity in *Mansfield Park*: Mary's & Edmund's letters to Fanny (II)

This is written in answer to Brooke Church Kolosna's commentary on part of Mary's second letter to Fanny, which can be dated as Wednesday, March 8th: Fanny receives a letter from Mary two days after Henry left Portsmouth, which letter Henry has insisted upon her writing the day after he arrived; we are told Henry spent the Saturday and Sunday in Portsmouth which occurred just before the 4th week of Fanny's stay whose anniversary is Tuesday, March 7th. I bring the dates up partly because it's easier to refer to them this way, and because the time lapses and the implied events that occurred between the letters are important.

Brooke writes:

"As you state, Mary writes with concern to Fanny about Henry's resumed relationship with Maria—she appears to not want this to occur. Why, then, does she encourage Henry to stay in London and attend a party where Mary knows he will see the Rushworths? Henry needs to go to Norfolk to attend to business, he knows that he should go, and yet his sister encourages, even demands, that he stay in London for this party. The passage I'm speaking of is in the postscript of a letter from Mary to Fanny:

"Henry I find has some idea of going into Norfolk again upon some business that you approve, but this cannot possibly be permitted before the middle of next week, that is, he cannot anyhow be spared till after the 14th, for we have a party that evening. The value of a man like Henry on such an occasion, is what you can have no conception of; so you must take it upon my word, to be inestimable. He will see the Rushworths, which I own I am not sorry for—having a little curiousity—and so I think has he, though he will not acknowledge it."

Brooke thinks the above shows Mary at her worst, but I

would counter that to interpret the passage that way is to use hindsight. Remember we as readers are supposedto see far more than Mary—or Fanny; that's what the technique of dramatic irony depends upon. If, however, you are like me, you didn't get it the first time through, but we do have a second chance—as in the first time through I had no idea Frank Churchill was actually engaged to Jane Fairfax, on the second reading I saw how much I had missed. Mary doesn't not get this second chance. The basic idea behind epistolary narrative, as in his preface to *Clarissa* Samuel Richardson wrote, is to show minds which are engaged in what is happening in the here and now and do not know what is to come:

"Much more affecting and lively... must be the style of those who write in the height of a present distress... the events then hidden in the womb of fate) than the dry, narrative, unanimated style of of a person relating difficulties and dangers surmounted, can be"

We might say, should not Mary have foreseen what would be the results of such an encounter? Notice that at this point that although because Fanny is less blinded by her ego and able to distance herself from her own appetites, Fanny feels apprehensive that the meeting between Henry and Maria will be very uncomfortable for Maria and degrade him if he is driven there by curiosity or seeks some triumph, and for a moment foresees possible trouble for everyone involves, it is only for the moment; and it does not occur to Fanny that Henry will again try to conquer and subdue Mari. After Portsmouth, Fanny begins really to believe in his love for her, Fanny; Mary's fourth letter to her is at first incomprehensible. She never imagines that Maria left Rushworth for Crawford and it is Crawford with whom Maria has fled. She is genuinely startled and a bit hurt too when she hears he was making love to Maria while he held himself publicly to be an man engaged to her. Why does she only dwell momentarily on why she is apprehensive, why she would not have inveigled Henry to stay, why she would have urged him to go to Evringham? Well partly she doesn't love Henry; she loves Edmund, and as she reads the letters she dwells on what Mary says about her and

Edmund far more than she dwells upon what Mary says about Henry. One very long paragraph and then another following Fanny's fleeting thought about the coming party at Mrs Frazer's are all about Edmund and Mary; her mind reverts to Henry but for these three sentences:

"Those parts of the letter whichrelated only to Mr. Crawford and herself, touched her,in comparison, slightly. Whether Mr. Crawford wentinto Norfolk before or after the 14th was certainlyno concern of hers, though, everything considered,she thought he *would* go without delay. That MissCrawford should endeavour to secure a meeting between himand Mrs. Rushworth, was all in her worst line of conduct,and grossly unkind and ill-judged; but she hoped hewould not be actuated by any such degrading curiosity. He acknowledged no such inducement, and his sisterought to have given him credit for better feelings thanher own"

It is in Mary's third letter that we find her covering up; it is written between April 24th and 28th, which is six weeks after after Mrs Frazer's party of Tuesday, March 14th (by my and Chapman's dating). If we look at Edmund's letter we see that Edmund saw nothing. When I spoke of Mary's concern to "assure Fanny that 'Henry cares for nobody but you,'" I was referring to this third letter six weeks later, and written after Mary has had news of Tom's illness in order to gain information about that illness. We are told it is after Easter (April 16th if we follow A. Walton Litz's construction), and, as the narrator tells us more than 3 months after Fanny came to Portsmouth which takes us into the 4 day span of April 24th to 28th. Mary has been content to have no communication with Edmund since March 18th; she has cold-shouldered him, and now suddenly she begins to think again maybe she was precipitate. If we look at that third letter, we find the first thing we are told is Mary has been silent for the kind of long time that requires an apology: "Forgive me, my dear Fanny, as soon as you can for my long silence, and behave as if you could forgive me me directly. This is my modest request and expectation" (ever Mary, no?). We also notice that most unlike her previous two letters, she does not breath a word of Henry until a postscript, which is only written because Henry has come upon her before she could seal her letter and only because *he* insists and as she finds herself telling Fanny about the proposed trip to Richmond, she is suddenly wary or frightened (wrongly of course, Mary ever sees the world as if it centered on her and as if others had all the information she has) lest Fanny hear Henry is gone to Richmond *after Maria*, lest Fanny hear of the tryst to come or that has been had.

The postscript is of interest because there is an urgency in the last few sentences whose real import Fanny doesn't get. Fanny too lives within the compass of her mind—and which of us doesn't? Fanny sees Mary's offer to come and get her in terms of what she has seen of Henry in Portsmouth (more on this in a separate post) and sincerely believes Mary's offer is a product of Henry's desire to come and get her; period. She sees in it also their characters, as rich people, their casual assumption of the power to do as they wish. Faced with Henry's sudden entrance into the room and his response to the idea of Fanny as he watches her pen her letter, Mary sees that Henry does still yearn for Fanny, and if Fanny were to tell them to come, this would put off his visit to Richmond. Thus (according to Mary) all would be well. If Fanny does not so write, and Henry goes to Richmond, things might get let us call it inconvenient. There is also a sudden impulse in Mary to return to Mansfield and to Edmund partly motivated or inspired by Henry's presence and his renewed memories of Fanny (from his visit to Portsmouth) and his as yet strong passion to make Fanny his.

But on the second reading, we are supposed to see in Mary's urgency her knowledge of what happened at that fateful Tuesday party, of what has been happening over these long weeks, over why Maria is going—apparently alone—to Richmond and Henry is to follow her. Here are the relevant lines:

"I had actually begun folding my letter when Henry walked in,but he brings no intelligence to prevent my sending it. Mrs. R. knows a decline is apprehended; he saw her this morning: she returns to Wimpole Street to-day; the old lady is come. Now do not make yourself uneasy with any queer fanciesbecause he has been spending a few days at Richmond. He does it every spring. Be assured he cares for nobodybut you. At this very moment he is wild to see you,and occupied only in contriving the means for doing so,and for making his pleasure conduce to yours. In proof,he repeats, and more eagerly, what he said at Portsmouthabout our conveying you home, and I join him in it with allmy soul. Dear Fanny, write directly, and tell us to come. It will do us all good. He and I can go to the Parsonage,you know, and be no trouble to our friends at Mansfield Park...

As I believe Dorothy Gannon and Elaine Bander (among others) have pointed out repeatedly, again and again throughout the novel, Mary shows herself to have a shallow appreciation of people's emotions and little real understanding of her own. She is a "chameleon." I think Helen's word is perfect. Stuart Tave says of both Henry and Mary Crawford that their emotions and behavior are pleasant in an initial encounter, but do not run very deep. Mary is willing to throw over what could apparently have given her deep joy (she does love Edmund insofar as she is capable and she loves him for the intensity and strength and sincerity of his loyalty, integrity, and love for her) in order to gain a partner whom *Mrs Frazer* could respect. She is willing to guide her choice by the level of Mrs Frazer's mind. She actually seems puzzled over Mrs Frazer's unhappiness; after all the woman obeyed her friends, thought about it for three whole days, and the guy had money:

"Poor Janet has been sadly taken in, and yet there wasnothing improper on her side: she did not run into thematch inconsiderately; there was no want of foresight. She took three days to consider of his proposals,and during those three days asked the advice of everybodyconnected with her whose opinion was worth having,and especially applied to my late dear aunt, whoseknowledge of the world made her judgment very generallyand deservedly looked up to by all the young peopleof her acquaintance, and she was decidedly in favourof Mr. Fraser. This seems as if nothing were a securityfor matrimonial comfort"

The woman who could make the above speech is the same woman who cannot foresee what troubled waters she is stirring up by selfishly wanting another handsome debonair witty man about. I like Brooke's analogy with "someone I knew once who told me that she always makes sure to invite enemies to her parties, just to see what will happen" and agree this is a ugly motive.

But it's that Mary thinks human emotions are a kind of game. She again and again remained untouched and inattentive to depths in Edmund or Fanny or Henry except when it is a question of Edmund's love for her or his what shall we call it solidity.

Some instinct not thought out tells her that this man will stick to her and do all he can to make her happy; she sees he's smart, tender, loving—especially (and this is ironic) to Fanny. He's also handsome. But it's not enough.

So I agree with Brooke's basic assessment of the situation, but qualify it by saying given Mary's nature she could not foresee what would happen. I also think the set up of the letters, the dating, the time-frame, and all the implicit half-hidden but half-revealed (through the letters) events partly exculpate Mary because it is a rare person could have controlled events and shaped them in another direction.

A final note: as we interpret the letters we are also supposed to read and take into consideration the recipient's response to them. In my posting I neglected this. I talked only of the interlace of Edmund and Mary and how these are to be read in terms of the immediate events they recount as well as their psychologies.

As all epistolary narrators do, Austen also expects us to consider the response of the reader. Fanny doesn't get it; she is apprehensive and intuits some danger here, but she is too involved with her love for Edmund to think much about it. We might remember how Austen develops this aspect of epistolary narrative in Emma: again and again in that novel the focus is squarely on the interpreter of the letter (e.g., Miss Bates retelling of Jane's letter about the happenings at Weymouth; Emma and Knightley responding to Frank

Churchill's last missive) in such a way as to get a continual multiperspective meaning into her novel.

Ellen Moody

Henry VIII: Fanny as Shakespearean and Maria as 18th Century Fallen Heroine

The following postings were prompted by comments made by members of both Litalk and Austen-L. First I was struck by the use of *Henry VIII* in the one scene where Henry Crawford succeeds in wooing Fanny. He is irresistible when he reads from this text, and I see in it a significant analogue for Fanny Price.

Thus I wrote in response to Tony Prince who objected to my sympathetic portrayal of Fanny as an Antigone, that Fanny's literary and archetypal analogue is precisely the kind of strong heroine who renounces as a form of rebellion but yet keeps her values and humanity intact. And I think this may be demonstrated by an allusion in Austen's text to Katherine of Aragon in Shakespeare's *Henry VIII*. In sum, in *MP* Austen says that Edmund was the comfort of Fanny's existence more than once; she uses the word "comfort" in a way that calls attention to the word and Fanny's desolation at the loss of the one person who gave joy (this word is used too) to her life.

In Shakespeare's *Winter's Tale* Hermione says in her great trial and ordeal that she cares nothing for life nor threats nor any worldly losses for she has lost all comforts of her existence and any joy it gave her when she lost her children and husband. The words "comfort and joy" are repeated in the speech. There is an exactly similar scene in *Henry VIII* where Katherine of Aragon's words closely recall Hermione's, where she talks of Henry as the comfort of her existence which she has lost, but in which again the lady which alas I is not frightened from her moral stand or dignity, and she remains a cynosure of gentleness and courtesy while she refuses to budge. Henry Crawford (I wouldn't make too much of the name Henry here because of Austen's brother and use of the name elsewhere, still there it is) reads the speech of Wolseley in which the same idea is repeated. Wolsley has lost all worldly goods, and he has now lost his master's favor; had he been as loyal to his God as he has been to his master, his God would not have left him to mourn alone.

All these analogues are part of the literary background in which we are to understand Fanny Price as heroine. The ultimate or most extreme of them is Antigone as the ultimate or most extreme of the self-immolating type before an ideal of self-sacrifice and meaning in the universe is St Teresa. Then on Austen-L in response to Eugene McDonnell I wrote:

This is really a continuation of my posting addressed partly to Eugene McDonnell in which I said Antigone, Clarissa, but not St Teresa are part of the literary background in which we are to understand Fanny Price as heroine. I want here to be more specific and attach Fanny to Antigone figures I think Austen means us to attach her and to suggest the very different kind of figure which lies behind Maria Bertram.

As I suggested I think Austen expects us to see in Fanny that type of strong heroine who renounces as a form of rebellion but yet keeps her values and humanity intact, and who was familiar to 18th century readers in the form of Clarissa and her daughters (meaning all the many many heroines in the novels of the period based on Clarissa's struggle against her mercenary status-seeking family and then against the rake who would make her his toy).

But there is another specific allusion to the type in MPthrough Austen's use of *Henry VIII* in the scene where Henry so mesmerizes Fanny with his ability to comprehend Wolsey and Katherine of Aragon who are given the magnificent speeches of the play. Very briefly, in *MP* Austen says that Edmund was the comfort of Fanny's existence more than once; she uses the word "comfort" in a way that calls attention to the word and Fanny's desolation at the loss of the one person who gave joy (this word is used too) to her life. First in Shakespeare's *Winter's Tale* Hermione (a similarly virtuous stubborn figure who turns the other cheek) says in her great trial and ordeal that she cares nothing for life nor threats nor any worldly losses for she has lost all comforts of her existence and any joy it gave her when she lost her children and husband. The words "comfort and joy" are repeated in the speech. There is an exactly similar scene in *Henry VIII*; again the idea is Katherine of Aragon is not frightened, and she remains a cynosure of dignity and courtesy while she refuses to budge. Henry Crawford reads the speech of Wolsey in which the same idea is repeated. Wolsey has lost all worldly goods, and he has now lost his master's favor; had he been as loyal to his God as he has been to his master, his God would not have left him to mourn alone.

Behind Maria is an utterly different type. Agatha Friburg is neither the gay witty heroine nor the serious sober one which dominated the stage in the 18th century. Instead what we have is a fallen heroine, a woman who is one step from prostitution. This type became prevalent not only on the stage but in fiction. An epistolary novel which some people think Austen modelled *S&S* on, Edgeworth's *Julia and Caroline* has a Marianne figure who, Eliza Williams-like, runs off with her beloved only to end deserted, abandoned, starving, and finally dead, cut off from her children, family, all the "comforts" of her existence (this idea if not the word is brought up in Edgeworth's novella—it's very short).

After all the opposition people are always talking about—Mary Crawford versus Fanny Price—is not the only one of *MP*. We have two other rivals, two other women who are opposed to one another—Fanny Price and Maria Bertram. It is between them that Henry Crawford is to choose. Maria Bertram may be the most interesting character of the novel if we insist on looking into the novel for intimations of what was to come. It is she who demands passion in the end; she who defies everything, and loses everything. The moral is conservative, and she is anything but noble. She does however *know* precisely who her Aunt Norris is.

I think what needs to be done to understand *MP* is to read the very different kind of plays which emerged on the stage at the close of the 18th century, not witty ones at all. Several are mentioned as our characters look for a play that suits them. Also more ought to be made of the Shakespearean analogies—as someone said Richard III is mentioned too in connection with Henry Crawford. Now for the 18th century reader and today's too one of the most powerful scenes in that play is when Richard III seduces the wife of the man he has just murdered—in the recent movie we see him do it as he and the wife, Anne (played by Kirstin Thomas—she gets around) stand over the dead husband's body. The sexual angle is very strong whenever one starts to look at analogues for either Henry Crawford or Maria Bertram.

Fanny Becomes a Renter and Chuser of Books: Rejoicing with Fanny Using Eva Sedgwick

I have always been touched by Fanny's reaching out to Susan during her time at Portsmouth. Just yesterday I read for the first time the famous (or maybe infamous) article by Eva Sedgwick, "Jane Austen and the Masturbating Girl." While I disagree with most of her assertions, and most of all with her "methodology," I do like her distaste for reading Austen as if we were perpetually being taught things. She makes fun of what she describes as typical Austen criticism from the left or right as follows:

"Austen criticism is notable mostly not just for its timidity and banality but for its unreasing exaction of the spectacle of a Girl BeingTaught a Lesson...Thus Tony Tanner, the ultimate normal and normalizing reader of Austen, structures sentence after sentence: "Emma.... *has to be tutored*... into correct vision and responsible speech. Anne Elliot *has to move*, painfully, from an excessive prudence.' Some Jane Austen heroines have to learntheir true 'duties.' They all *have to find* their proper homes' Catherine 'quite literally is in danger of perverting reality, and one of the things she *has to learn* is to break out of quotations'; she has to be disabusedof her naive and foolish 'Gothic' expectations. Elziabeth and Darcy '*Have to learn to see* that their novel is more properly called'.... A lot of Jane Austen criticism sounds hilariously like the leering school-prspectuses or governess-manifestoes brandished like so many birch rods...".

I know I often fall into this kind of talk: so-and-so learns this lesson or that, and Sedgwick is right to say it's inane and has little to do with why we feel pleasure when we read

Austen. Thus today I would like to say I don't give a damn whether Fanny is more or less active at Portsmouth; don't care whether we can say she takes more things on herself there than she did in Mansfield Park—I rather think she does, but only because for the first time in her life she is given an opportunity to act for herself for the good of others; she has power at Portsmouth because her mother creates a vaccuum of do-nothingness into which she Fanny may step. Aunt Norris, let us give her this, left little for others to do.

What I simply enjoy is her stretching out to someone like herself—Susan—who is like her in need of some companionship and respectful attention. I find congenial her way of solving the quarrel between the spoilt favored child, Betsy, and Susan, the child who has become overemotional over a small thing because she is not loved, or cared about, or even appreciated for the efforts she makes by those she is surrounded by in the least bit. Fanny simply buys another knife. I have done this in quarrels between my daughters—simply gone out and bought another object that has become the pretext for a quarrel about far deeper things that are finally often impossible to resolve.

The story of the circulating library also brings home to us how the vulnerable and powerless, the fringe person in the later 18th century and throughout the 19th could get her hands on a good book. You needed but a few shillings—of course many did not have that to spare, but Fanny is lucky enough to be attached to those who do. And I rejoice with Fanny to see her overcoming her paralysis at first, to see her find those places or channels in her society which will give her pleasure and which are available to her, and to see her take advantage of them for herself and her new friend, Susan.

I also think Austen as narrator means us to take pleasure in Fanny, to feel happy for her in this carving out of a space for herself and Susan in their minds and in the even tinier room than Fanny had in Mansfield Park. I believe Austen herself made do in this way. Austen herself read enormous numbers of books, and they were available to her through the circulating library. I always find myself wondering when I read this section when Austen herself took her first trip to the library, became a subscriber; there is a little piece in one of her letters where she frets over the fact that the circulating library in the town she and her family have stopped at have so little to offer. Why? Because her male servant has read the first volume of *Robinson Crusoe* already, and will be bored.

Here is the passage which I do not enjoy because I am having a lesson or want to imitate Fanny or take her for a model. I agree with Sedgwick that is not what I read any novel for. I read Austen's because I find them congenial to my heart and ways of thinking:

The intimacy thus begun between them was a material advantage to each. By sitting together upstairs, they avoided a great deal of the disturbance of the house; Fanny had peace, and Susan learned to think it no misfortune to be quietly employed. They sat without a fire; but that was a privation familiar even to Fanny, and she suffered the less because reminded by it of the East room. It was the only point of resemblance. In space, light, furniture, and prospect, there was nothing alike in the two apartments; and she often heaved a sigh at the remembrance of all her books and boxes, and various comforts there.

By degrees the girls came to spend the chief of the morning upstairs, at first only in working and talking, but after a few days, the remembrance of the said books grew so potent and stimulative that Fanny found it impossible not to try for books again. There were none in her father's house; but wealth is luxurious and daring, and some of hers found its way to a circulating library. She became a subscriber; amazed at being anything *in propria persona,* amazed at her own doings in every way, to be a renter, a chuser of books! And to be having any one's improvement in view in her choice! But so it was. Susan had read nothing, and Fanny longed to give her a share in her own first pleasures, and inspire a taste for the biography and poetry which she delighted in herself".

And what is most congenial here? While Fanny worked hard at Mansfield Park, it was always work which was forced upon her, and when the effort was made, she was either not thanked or asked to do more or denigrated by Mrs Norris for not doing more or mocked (as in Fanny cannot do two things at once—Mrs Norris says this during the sequence when the play is being rehearsed and Fanny is in fact doing 10 things at once, at least). When she takes it upon herself to get Sam's things ready, she has chosen to do this; when she finds it important to her to make friends with Susan, she has gotten outside of herself to see the world from Susan's eyes—something Edmund never shows any ability to do.

And then when she realized that Susan is just not going to value books in the way she, Fanny, does, it doesn't matter. I was going to say Fanny learns the truth that a love of books and reading is a habit which must be formed early or not at all. But Sedgwick has stopped me, so I will say rather Fanny observes this truth, and we are left to understand that memories must be tied up, woven into our beings from life and into books for us really to love them. Fanny's deepest happiness has been in books, and it is too late for Susan to be formed in this way.

Little truths of all sorts come home to the Fanny as she makes a place for herself in the house at Portsmouth. I find her to have enormous strength in this section, the strength Elinor Dashwood exhibits, the strength to be, to carry on as yourself firmly. Not a small thing. But I agree there's no lesson here. I won't after reading this section behave like Fanny. I simply like her—and the author who wrote this way.

Ellen Moody

Here was that elasticity of mind, that disposition to be comforted, that power of turning readily from evil to good, and of finding employment which carried her out of herself, which was from Nature herself. It was the choicest gift of Heaven...—Jane Austen, Persuasion. To this Brooke Church Kolosna replied:

Ellen,

That was a wonderful post about Fanny. As I read the passage you quoted, I was struck by the language that Austen uses, and the transition of mood that this language conveys as the passage continues. I'll snip some..."The intimacy... a material advantage... Fanny had peace... They sat without a fire; but that was a privation familiar even to Fanny, and she suffered the less because reminded by it of the East room.... she often heaved a sigh at the remembrance of all her books and boxes, and various comforts there.

By degrees the girls came to spend the chief of the morning upstairs, at first only in working and talking, but after a few days, the remembrance of the said books grew so potent and stimulative...wealth is luxurious and daring, and some of hers found its way to a circulating library. She became a subscriber; amazed at being anything *in propria persona*, amazed at her own doings in every way, to be a renter, a chuser of books!...Fanny longed to give [Susan] a share in her own first pleasures, and inspire a taste for the biography and poetry which she delighted in herself"

In one passage, Austen gives us three distinct insights into Fanny's moods. At the beginning of the passage, Austen uses language to create a sense of peace and respite. She quickly moves to a somber mood, though, in comparing the comfort of MP with the privations of her family's house. Then, the mood shifts again, and Austen uses language that introduces an air of real excitement and pleasure, as Fanny begins to make use of her little bit of "luxurious and daring" wealth to increase her own comfort, and introduce a real pleasure to her sister.

I can't describe my impressions of this passage as well as I would like. In the above passages Austen's language leads us into a kind of dance, where we join with the characters in MP in all their human complexity...

Brooke

Epistolarity in *Mansfield Park*: Lady Bertram's Letters to Fanny

We ought not to neglect Fanny's other correspondent, and a much more faithful one than either Mary Crawford or Edmund Bertram. I don't know whether everyone has taken note of how much the post office must have profited from Fanny's time away from her aunt in Portsmouth. We may remember the comment of Austen's narrator at the close of

Lady Susan and laugh that the state had a loss on the day Fanny returned home and Lady Bertram "came with no indolent step," the "one of the suffering party" who expects Fanny with "such impatience as she had never known before" to throw herself into Fanny's capable and equally glad and relieved embrace. But something more crucial is come to an end: Lady Bertram's letters as a felt imagined presence in Fanny's life at Portsmouth: they not only plot important turns in the stories Fanny is an outcast from, and provide suspense to us who are with Fanny and can only see these events from afar. They give us the imagined sense of Mansfield Park as a place ever present in Portsmouth against which we judge Portsmouth as wanting but also not so very different in its moral and emotional life.

It's true the narrator is none too sympathetic towards the literal content and mode of procedure Lady Bertram follows in her continual missives, as when Edmund beats her to the punch and in two brief sentences tells the news of the Grants' removal to Bath, the narrator comments:

"Everybody at all addicted to letter-writing, withouthaving much to say, which will include a large proportionof the female world at least, must feel with Lady Bertramthat she was out of luck in having such a capital piece ofMansfield news as the certainty of the Grants going to Bath,occur at a time when she could make no advantage of it,and will admit that it must have been very mortifyingto her to see it fall to the share of her thankless son,and treated as concisely as possible at the end of along letter, instead of having it to spread over the largestpart of a page of her own. For though Lady Bertram rathershone in the epistolary line, having early in her marriage,from the want of other employment, and the circumstanceof Sir Thomas's being in Parliament, got into the wayof making and keeping correspondents, and formed forherself a very creditable, common-place, amplifying style,so that a very little matter was enough for her; she couldnot do entirely without any; she must have something to write about, even to her niece; and being so soon to lose all the benefit of Dr. Grant's gouty symptomsand Mrs. Grant's morning calls, it was very hard upon herto be deprived of one of the last epistolary uses she could putthem to."

The cogent irony of the above—which I take also to be a comment on most people's letters ("very creditable, commonplace, amplifying" in style—and of course edifying)—leads the reader to forget that a very little matter will do for Lady Bertram, and she is not writing to communicate content but to be present to her niece and to imagine her niece present to her. Let us not knock this aspect of letter-writing—it is after all one of the pleasures of e-mail—the imagined presence, shared interests, and of course kindness of others.

There is in fact a continual stream of letters which keep Fanny and us—for we are in Fanny's epistolary "position"—apprised of what's happening and in suspense. For example, just after Mary's first letter to Fanny telling of her first meeting with Mrs Rushworth and Julia, and a coming party, Fanny receives a letter from Lady Bertram which can be dated as Saturday, Feb 25th, in which Lady Bertram tells Fanny Edmund is headed for London. This news is yet another motive for Fanny's renewed attempts to read with Susan and inspire "a taste for the biography and poetry in which she delighted herself:"

"In this occupation she hoped, moreover, to bury someof the recollections of Mansfield, which were too aptto seize her mind if her fingers only were busy;and, especially at this time, hoped it might be usefulin diverting her thoughts from pursuing Edmund to London,whither, on the authority of her aunt's last letter,she knew he was gone. She had no doubt of what would ensue. The promised notification was hanging over her head. The postman's knock within the neighbourhood was beginningto bring its daily terrors, and if reading could banishthe idea for even half an hour, it was something gained"

The daily terror is that banal letter from Lady Bertram which acutely tells more than Fanny can bear to hear. Fanny's renting and chusing of books like most of our motives satisfies a complicated group of needs.

The next of Lady Bertram's letters which is described and quoted occurs directly after Edmund's first, which we will recall tells the sad story of how he was snubbed by Mary and how he still means to ask her to marry him, but cannot make up his mind whether to do it by letter or in person, and leads to a long powerful stream of consciousness passage coming from Fanny where she longs to see him do something, "Fix, commit, condemn yourself yourself" and at least give Fanny some peace. Or so she thinks: we recall that Elinor did not experience quite that peace of mind she thought she would when she believes she has been told Lucy Steele and Edward Ferrars are now married.

The second of Lady Bertram's letters to be quoted then deepens the mood of the book in a new direction; it is a plot development experienced as an aspect of Fanny's and Lady Bertram's shared consciousness—for a letter is a two-way street. Lady Bertram's "style of writing" is not "warm and genuine," in this one, but when about a week or so later Edmund brings Tom home, we are told the following and then read over Fanny's shoulder this:

"Her aunt did not neglect her: she wrote again and again; they were receiving frequentaccounts from Edmund, and these accounts were as regularlytransmitted to Fanny, in the same diffuse style,and the same medley of trusts, hopes, and fears,all following and producing each other at haphazard. It was a sort of playing at being frightened. The sufferings which Lady Bertram did not see had littlepower over her fancy; and she wrote very comfortablyabout agitation, and anxiety, and poor invalids, till Tomwas actually conveyed to Mansfield, and her own eyes hadbeheld his altered appearance.

Then a letter which shehad been previously preparing for Fanny was finishedin a different style, in the language of real feelingand alarm; then she wrote as she might have spoken. "He is just come, my dear Fanny, and is taken upstairs;and I am so shocked to see him, that I do not knowwhat to do. I am sure he has been very ill. Poor Tom! I am quite grieved for him, and very much frightened,and so is Sir Thomas; and how glad I should be if youwere here to comfort me. But Sir Thomas hopes hewill be better to-morrow, and says we must considerhis journey". Now Fanny does not dread her aunt's letters, she longs for them. (How curious is human psychology; now that it is not Fanny's whose fate is directly threatened and someone is really sick, Fanny is ready to listen patiently, calmly.) Now to talk to Susan is not the same as to read her aunt's letters.

One might remark here that Mrs Price has the same curious gift for the acute if not deeply felt remark when she is told what is in these continual letters: "'My poor sister Bertram must be in a great deal of trouble'". It is true that we are told "A very few lines from Edmund shewed [Fanny] the patient and the sick room in a juster and stronger light than all Lady Bertram's sheets of paper could do," and Lady Bertram is no help at all in the sick room, with her gliding in and out in a state of continual semi- alarmed fret, but they do come and we are entitled to doubt whether Edmund would have written his few lines without his mother's prompting; Lady Bertram's letters also mark time in the narrative and give us a sense of how slow it moves for Fanny as she waits and waits.

The last of Lady Bertram's letters to be quoted and described is placed just before Mary's third letter wherein as we have said Mary reveals to us, if not to Fanny, the dangerous liaison (to coin a phrase) which has been deepening between Henry and Maria; Mary's mysterious worried fourth diverts our and Fanny's minds back to this half-buried love story, a novel within a novel in this phase of *Mansfield Park*. But Lady Bertram's letter is significant; it strikes the central theme of the book: which is Fanny's home? whose daughter is she? whom does she belong to? and by implication her relationship with the man who has become her real father, Sir Thomas.

As I read this letter I in fact find Lady Bertram beginning to rebel against the above husband. Edmund's obtusely-stated reports have continually told Fanny Lady Bertram has reminded (a la Lady Middleton) Sir Thomas some six or seven times a day that Fanny is not here, or where is Fanny, or, why do we not bring Fanny back. The importance of the letter is it clinches Fanny's growing awareness that home is not and cannot be Portsmouth—too many years and roots have been placed in Mansfield Park for that. Why, why are they not sending for her? it is after Easter, more than three months:. Fanny is at first worried lest she hurt her biological parents' feelings. She need not have. They barely listen to her. She is "as welcome to wish herself" at Mansfield as to be at Portsmouth. And then comes the consolation and validationfrom Lady Bertram as she sounds her exasperated note at Sir Thomas's for once powerless dithering about:

"I cannot but say I much regret your being from homeat this distressing time, so very trying to my spirits. I trust and hope, and sincerely wish you may never be absentfrom home so long again" are "most delightful sentences to her," a "private regale".

Since Lady Bertram's letters do not link up to the love story we tend to ignore them, but they are an important part of the texture of the book during Fanny's time at Portsmouth. They underline Fanny's loneliness; they link up to her longing for the beauty of the country, to see spring come again; and, very importantly, they keep before us the overarching structure of the book which is the story of a fringe woman (I refer now to my posting on *The Watsons*) who through a hard struggle and much effort lives on herself, makes herself what she is in despite of the psychological beating she takes from her Aunt Norris and the mortifying careless snubbing and indifference of others, a woman who earns her place, albeitly quietly, at Mansfield Park as the sturdy tree around which all these vines wrap themselves at its close. I always enjoy the joke on Sir Thomas at the book's end: "After settling her at Thornton Lacey with every kind attention to her comfort, the object of almost every day was to see her there, or to get her away from it". It's true his feelings for Fanny were deeper than Lady Bertram's who finds a substitute in Susan, but it was Lady Bertram who wrote to her.

Fanny Delivers the Last Blow to Edmund's Illusions About Mary Crawford

This posting is another written in response to the "Fanny Wars" which have again and again erupted on Austen-L.

I'd like to take up the one scene which most people

mention as Fanny's horribly deplorable sin, revealing how malicious she "really" is, because it is the one place in *Mansfield Park* where Fanny can be found to be doing something which might conceivably promote her self-interest and has on this list been interpreted as mean, cruel, nasty, and superfluously spiteful (just what one might expect from a "passive-aggressive type").

I am, of course, referrring to the passage at the conclusion of Edmund's description of his last interview with Mary Crawford when Fanny at long last informs Edmund that Mary's sudden new-found willingness to listen to Edmund's marriage proposals after months at Mansfield Park where she said she would never become the wife of a rural clergyman (dreadfully dull as "all the world knows" according to Mary), and after giving him an exceedingly icy shoulder in London, is that she believes Tom Bertam may not survive. Fanny tells Edmund of Mary's letter and how Mary made it clear in that letter she was willing to hear of Edmund again and listen to him "affectionately" because now he would have money and sufficient prestige as an heir to offset her intense distaste at the idea of becoming a clergyman's wife which had previously led her to reject him as a husband.

First as Eugene McDonnell's posting alerts us, the scene is 5 pages long. It beings on p 454 of the Oxford. For four long pages Edmund speaks of his pained recognition of Mary's shallowness and indifference not only to sexual mores, but to the deeper emotions such playing with sexual mores elicits and to any permanent pain or injury to the heart or self-respect or reputation with others such playing might cause. Austen has Fanny interrupt once, and it is to the remark Mary made that it is all Fanny's fault: had Fanny married Henry none of this could have occurred; Edmund paraphrases Mary as saying:

"'I shall never forgive [Fanny]. Had she accepted him as she ought, they might now have been on the point of marriage, and Henry would have been too happy and too busy to want any other object. He would have taken no pains to be on terms with Mrs. Rushworth again. It would have all ended in a regular standing flirtation, in yearly meetings at Sotherton and Everingham.' [He continues with his thoughts] Could you have believed it possible?—Buit the charm is broken. My eyes are opened.' *Fanny then bursts out:*

'Cruel!' said Fanny—'quite cruel! At such a moment to give way to gaiety and to speak with lightness, and to you!—Absolute cruelty.'

First, is Edmund hurt by this. No. He dismisses this view.

'Cruelty, do you call it?'—We differ there. No, her's is not a cruel nature. I do not consider her as meaning to sound my feelings. The evil lies yet deeper; in her total ignorance, unsuspiciousness of there being such feelings, in a perversion of mind which made it natural to her to treat the subject as she did...

Edmund goes on to say she talks like other people mostly do. This is how most people feel. To hark back to the play, most people don't pay attention to hurts and slights when they occur to other people, they are so wound up in their own feelings; so you got the part you wanted, and are letting go all you ever wanted to dream of yourself; you don't see the misery of the other; the other doesn't see your misery, when you are sneered at. Here real and not pretend sexuality and appetite is the question, and here Mary dismisses the pain Henry might cause everyone with his "yearly flirtation" with Maria; she also cannot conceive this kind of thing can hurt another who is not involved. Why should they give a damn? she cannot conceive Edmund should be hurt by what occurs to someone else, especially in such an area which no money or real prestige is involved. But he does care; he has been badly hurt by and for his sister, Maria; his whole family is upset.

Edmund does believe sex outside marriage is foul. Fanny says Mary is cruel because she is laughing at this; but Edmund says no, she's not laughing, she just doesn't get it (to use the awful modern phrase). I would add Fanny is utterly human too, and she bursts out with the comment "cruel," because Mary is imagining her Fanny married to Henry. And this touches Fanny to the quick. She didn't want to marry Henry. She doesn't want to be used to keep Henry in line. She wouldn't enjoy that "yearly flirtation" any more than Mr Rushworth. The second real interruption (and both are there in part because our novelist knows long discourses or reports must be broken up or the reader gets restless) is the one referred to above as the one in which everyone accuses Fanny of deliberately maliciously hurting Edmund.

First Edmund has been going on for pages and pages about how his eyes are opened. He's not about to turn back to Mary any more. And then Fanny does not burst out, but thinks a bit and then speaks, and what does the narrator say for her in narrator's discourse turning into indirect:

Fanny, now at liberty to speak openly, felt more than justified in adding to his [Edmund's] knowledge of her [Mary's] real character, by soe hint of what share his brother's state of health might be supposed to have in her wish for a complete reconciliation [it's now okay to marry the dull clergyman, Edmund, no-one will despise me, Mary, for after all, now he's the heir]. This was not an agreeable intimation. Nature [Edmund] resisted it for a while. It would have been a vast deal pleasanter to have had her more disinterested in her attachment; but his vanity was not of a strength to fight long against reason. He submitted to believe, that Tom's illness had influenced her; only reserving for himself this consoling thought, that consdiering the many counteractions of opposing habits, she had certaily been moreattached to him than could have been expected [seeing how she despised country life, clergymen, modest living, &c], and for his sake [that is she really was attracted to him and liked him] been more near doing right. Fanny thought exactly the same; and they were also quite agreed in their opinion of the lasting effect, the indelible impression, which such a disappointment must make on his mind.

First let's note it's thrown into indirect discourse. Austen is uncomfortable with saying this ugly thing. It is true that Fanny stands to gain. But note Fanny says it only *after* she sees Edmund has come to feel horror at Mary, become utterly and permanently alienated from her. Let us think are there other similar situations where other Austen characters suddenly burst out and tell the full ugly truth about someone when they see that the other person knows enough so that telling no longer becomes a matter of personal gain but of solidifying a realization which could be swept away once again. Yes. Colonel Brandon. All along her knew Willoughby was just returned from seducing, impregnating and abandoning Brandon's adopted daughter.

Why does he keep such vicious behavior to himself? Well, because if he told it, the reason would be to alienate Marianne and get Marianne for himself. He waits until after Marianne has the full knowledge of Willoughby for herself, and then he drops the big one [as in Randy Newman's song, "let's drop the big one now"]. Brandon goes on in indirect discourse with all these ugly truths. Now it's true he doesn't tell Marianne; he tells Elinor, but Marianne is ill, weak &c; but he tells Elinor so Marianne shall know.

And it is this final big one that leads Marianne to understand that Willoughby is out. No more turning back. So in part does Fanny tell Edmund. Finis. Yes she wants Edmund for herself, as Brandon wants Marianne. Yet how little is what she tells Edmund in comparison with all he has said. It is a kind of straw on the camel's back. If Brandon's story is the H-bomb, Fanny's is the last lingering shot over the bow. And she's human in being glad to tell to show him fully what Mary is, and human to be so upset to hear Mary speaking so lightly of her as married; but she doesn't think to tell of the connection of Tom's sickness until after Edmund has awakened himself, and there's a sense in which (as with Brandon) as Edmund thinks about it, this last shot (Brandon's bomb) will make Edmund understand he was doing the right thing to walk away from Mary (as Marianne should not walk forward to Willoughby lest he come forward again—as he does, also to Elinor); and it's not done hard or spitefully. First she waited.

And we are told it is "an intimation." She doesn't say it bluntly, the way for example yours truly would have. She hangs in there to insist on it yes, to make him see that Mary's apparent sudden willingness to be willing to marry the solemn clergyman (as all her friends would see it, and Mary sees with "the world's eyes," for these are Mary's eyes too), but she clearly minced words, she said it softly, and then look she then is willing, nay happy to accept the idea and agree with Edmund he will be hurt for a long time because he loved Mary. She is willing to agree Mary is worth it.

How many women could be so self-effacing to sit there and quietly agree that this guy they love so tenderly will be disappointed and hurt for a long time for the love of another woman? Note though that here the narrator's irony is directed at Fanny, but not for malice (the narrator's irony is directed at Fanny in the last phase of the novel throughout Henry's courtship of her because Fanny will not allow herself to see she is flattered by Henry's courtship and could have been led to like him had she not been put off by the early scenes at Rushworth's house where Henry did not bother to hide his cold nature from her). I hear irony in "Fanny thought exactly the same." Fanny is not listening quite; she is so eager to soothe him, so eager to apply balm to his wounds, so eager to remain his confidante, that she barely hears, but it is an act of self-effacement to be able to agree. The narrator's laughing at her kindly-like. Poor Fanny hanging on to this man for dear life. But let's look at Edmund who, like Fanny, takes quite a beating on this list. Look at the deep emotions of this man, how vulnerable he is and caring. It is his mind this indirect discourse is meant to figure forth:

Time would undoubtedly abate somewhat of his sufferings, but still it was a sort of thing which he never could get entirely the better of; and as to his ever meeting with any other woman who could—it was too impossible to be named but with indignation. Fanny's friendship was all he had to cling to. The penultimate sentence ends on an ironic clause; but again the laughter is kindly. He will get over it. But who, I ask, who could want Fanny to marry Henry when she could marry this man, decent, kind, who will never hurt and never forsake her. If he ends up putty in Fanny's hands, it's not her statement about Mary's change of "heart" when Tom gets sick; it's the whole thing, all Edmund has gone through since he fell in love and then the long conversation he held with Mary.

Fanny's little urging to tell a truth which will help her cause is nothing in comparison with how Mary has destroyed herself in front of Edmund; it is Mary who shot herself in the feet with an assault weapon when after Edmund talked and talked "at" her (for she couldn't hear him as he wanted to be heard): 'It was a sort of laugh as she answered, 'A pretty good lecture upon my word. Was it part of your last sermon?'

Fanny never says anything so spiteful as this. I fear on this list spite has been mistaken for wit.

And brava, Tristan! My husband too knows it is hopeless to get me to come away (this time to shovel snow with him) once I get into defending Fanny.

Ellen Moody

In response to yet another browbeating on Fanny Price, I wrote the folowing:

RE: Fanny is to Mary as Catherine is to Isabella

Rereading Fanny's first interruption of Edmund on the day he returns from his last interview with Mary, *viz.*,

'Cruel!' said Fanny—'quite cruel! At such a moment to give way to gaiety and to speak with lightness, and to you!—Absolute cruelty,'

It seemed to me it was also funny, at least when you step back a bit. Fanny is also saying how could she speak to you so cruelly, you Edmund who are so wonderful; oh dear oh dear. In other words Fanny's sense of the "absolute cruelty" of Mary here is a function of her sense of how important and serious a person is Edmund. How could anyone hurt him? Imagine her tone as slightly wide-eyed and horrified and you have the joke, if a joke may be allowed into this scene.

Does it not recall Catherine Morland's worship of Henry Tilney in a way? and the sincerity and naive response is also very much like Catherine's—for which Henry Tilney loves Catherine. But Edmund, who is nowhere as self-conscious as Henry Tilney, is unaware of this really overdone view of him taken by Fanny and consequently that her judgement of Mary's words as "absolute cruelty" as overdone; so he proceeds solemnly to prove Fanny wrong; no, Mary is just shallow; she didn't mean to be so awful to me, Edmund. That is he takes

Fanny's valuation of him as absolutely the right one. So he too is a little bit silly here.

This is sort of comic, even if gently so.

And looking again at Mary's final words to Edmund:

It was a sort of laugh as she answered, 'A pretty good lecture upon my word. Was it part of your last sermon?' What Mary is saying is simply a noise, it's a sneer; the equivalent of "you're another"—she's saying, you are not fooling me, save this hypocritical stuff for fools you must preach to; i.e., you call me a phony, you're another. It's also a rather awkwardly-voiced question, showing how uncomfortable Edmund's presence and point of view makes her.

So too would not James Morland's decency had he really been been able to bring it home to Isabella Tilney (she's far stonier than Mary) have made Isabella Thorpe uncomfortable too? Isabella Thorpe foreshadows Mary Crawford and Catherine Morland Fanny Price.

Jane Austen and Fanny Price as Fringe People

I have still something else I would like to offer up for discussion on this list. In reading Chapters 1-2 and the coming of the child with no money, no status, who is to owe all to Bertrams and yet be kept apart from them, in an attic near the maids (so she will physically from the moment she gets up to the moment she goes to sleep know her place is tenuous, lower, somewhere between "the real family" and the servants), we should remember that Austen herself was not the child of grand people.

The recent biography of Austen by Valerie Grosvenor Myer turned out to be very thin, with little new to say, but it did bring out again and again this aspect of not only Austen but her family. William Price's troubles and profession directly mirror Austen's two sailor brothers. The clergyman profession (which is soon to be so scorned as inadequate in any higher social group by Mary Crawford) was that of Austen's father and two brothers. Two of her brothers were able to go to Oxford because they were founders kin. The move to Bath was as difficult for the Austens as any one of us today might experience in going to buy a new house and finding what we can afford is sadly inadequate to some basic wants. A son was given up by the Austen in order to secure the inheritance that did eventually make some of the family comfortable, and enabled Jane Austen herself to produce her six books in the quiet and solitude of Chawton Cottage—no grand place that either. The Austens were very much fringe types, and when Austen forces us to listen to a speech like that of Sir Thomas on his expectations of what a Fanny Price will probably be (*Mansfield Park*Chapman I:1, 10), and our gorge rises it is because Austen's gorge rises. Sir Thomas is assuming anyone not as high and mighty as the county family in the great house will naturally (it is to be expected) be "vulgar," grossly ignorant, with "mean opinions," and possibly even of a "really bad disposition." Fanny Price here stands in for Austen herself and people of her class as they might be viewed from the viewpoint of the genuinely landed gentry.

And again when Mrs Norris echoes his sentiments, and Lady Bertram worries over the possible harm the little girl might do to Pug (*Mansfield Park*Chapman I:1, 10), and Sir Thomas brings in his plans as to how he will make "distinctions" between his daughters and Fanny, and the worries over what he thinks is the problem of making Fanny remember she is not a "Miss Bertram" while not making her think "too lowly" of herself, not "too far" "depressing her spirits" (*Mansfield Park*Chapman, I:1,10)," Austen is the outsider herself and is using the engendered discomfort and unease this speech engenders to make us sympathize with the child and fear for the child before she even comes, but also to make us look askance at the understanding of this man under whose thumb and moral outlook Fanny will have to live.

The edge we feel, the hardness and distance of the tone is that of the author who is also someone on the fringe. Maybe not in the attic, but in an analogously stigmatized place. Those letters between the time in Bath and the Austen's landing (like cats on their feet, just) in Chawton testify to Austen's sense of how she had come down. How different is the set she moves in now. It is also noticeable (but maybe this is an effect of

Cassandra's having destroyed so many of the letters—the majority it's said) that the invitation to live at Chawton came very quickly after Edward's wife's death. Had she not died.... well, would we have had these books? So Austen identifies closely with Fanny when in these opening chapters Sir Thomas, Mrs Norris, and Lady Bertram, and then the maids, the governess and her cousins (all but Edmund) talk at her in such a way as to mortify her. I should add that Austen does not necessarily think this is a bad thing. The close of the novel tells us that while Maria's devastated future and Julia's diminished one was the result of Mrs Norris's flattery and false emphasis on materialism wholly, Fanny benefited enormously from an education in hardship, struggle, and endurance.

Ordination and Revolution in Mansfield Park.

Now I will try to write of something else:—it shall be a complete Nearly two hundred years after the writing of Mansfield Park , scholars still debate the meaning and degree of emphasis in Austen's famous quotation that the novel was about "ordination." It is suggested here that a too-narrow application of the meaning of ordination solely to Edmund Bertram has stymied fruitful research. The following reading advances an interpretation that explains Austen's comment in new terms and supports Austen's claim that the novel is about ordination. The meaning of ordination was not restricted in 1814 to the meaning of assuming a religious office, nor, indeed, was that its primary definition. A glance at the OED demonstrates that trees, animals, and ideas may all be ordinated. Sub-ordination, as a disposition of ranks or in reference to a hierarchical order, is implicit in the understanding of the term, and only after considering the range of meanings—and especially the primary meaning that Austen would have understood in its fullness—may we arrive at a better understanding of her much-quoted, much-misunderstood, and always-controversial statement that Mansfield Park is about ordination. There are two meanings of the word that are essential to understanding the novel, and while both concern Edmund. the argument here suggests that

Austen applies the concept and mechanism of ordination foremost to the estate of Mansfield Park and to the person of Fanny Price. Ordination, as I believe Austen meant it, is a process of both ordering and ordaining.

What is ordinated in Mansfield Park is not only the estate but also its hierarchy, and the person to be ordained first—in fact as well as in degree of importance—is Fanny Price. Subsidiary to the discussion of ordination is the argument that the concepts of ordination, improvement, and restoration have their antithetical counterparts in subordination, innovation, and revolution. Also, for there to be an ordering, there must first be a disordering and in the universe of Mansfield Park disorders of various kinds "infect" not only Ecclesford (culturally), but the domains of Norfolk and London (morally), Sotherton (spiritually). Portsmouth (familially), and Mansfield Park (socially). While the causes are all local to Mansfield Park, the mode of disseminating infections is the feverish activity whose substance consists of innovative ideas foreign to Mansfield Park. The innovations have their roots in an English Jacobinism, which was inimical to the institutions of church and state and was blamed by many writers of the time for the decadence of the gentry, among other things

[sh Rreview

There's a term for characters like Fanny Price: Mary Sue. And it's not a particularly nice term. Mary Sues are stand-ins for the author, the author idealized, as Fanny surely must be for Jane Austen in *Mansfield Park*. Fanny is beautiful, kind, faultless yet modest, noble of heart and spirit but of humble origins that prevent her from being spoiled. She is, in a word, perfect. Fanny may have pleased Austen herself, but she makes for less than compelling drama for the rest of us, at least in the new adaptation of the novel that just aired on *Masterpiece Theater*, and lands on DVD today.

This is part of the Austen marathon PBS is running this winter, and it's not a total loss — even the worst film version of Austen has its moments. Billie Piper, Rose from *Doctor Who*, seems like a bit of stunt casting as Fanny, but she's probably the best thing about this new made-for-TV movie: she's so genuinely ebullient that you forget that you really should want to hate her for being so impossibly perfect. And weirdly enough, she actually seems less anachronistic here, in the early 19th century, than she did as the Victorian-era girl detective in PBS *Mystery*'s *Ruby in the Smoke* (which is perfectly delightful anyway) — there's something about her bleached blonde hair and contrasting dark eyebrows that simply screams 20th century, at least, if not actually 21st. But she's a good embodiment of the Fanny that director Iain B. MacDonald seems to want to capture: bright and bubbly and not at all the typical demure Austen heroine.

But the rest of the little society at the Bertram manor known as Mansfield Park is pretty dull. Pretty, but dull. Fanny came here as a child to live with her rich relatives — including one played by another girl of geek interest: Michelle Ryan, the new Bionic Woman — and now all manner of typically Austenian matrimonial intrigue threatens to rock the family, and in the process quash her longtime secret in-loved-ness with her cousin Edmund. (Yeah, today we might find it icky to be in love with a cousin, but I guess Austen didn't.) There's a moment when Blake Ritson, as Edmund, finally perks up — it's that a-ha moment when he suddenly realizes he's been in love with Fanny all along, too — but that's a long time coming, and not worth the slog to get to it.

Possessing Jane Austen: Fidelity, authorship, and Patricia Rozema's Mansfield Park

In May 2000, The New Criterion carried an article by Australian writer and historian Keith Windschuttle titled "Rewriting the History of the British Empire," which opened with a discussion of Patricia Rozema's 1999 film Mansfield Park. Windschuttle began by referring to an early scene in the film "that is not in the book", where the ten-year-old Fanny, traveling by coach from Portsmouth to Mansfield, hears someone chanting on a ship that is anchored just off the coast. "Black cargo, miss," says the coachman. Windschuttle's commentary is worth quoting at some length:

Mansfield Park and Film: An Interview with Patricia Rozema

Patricia Rozema is a Canadian film director whose adaptation of Jane Austen's Mansfield Park (Miramax, 1999) produced a torrent of varying receptions, ambivalent at best, denigrating at worst. The novel itself is not highly popular with Austen readers/critics and it was adapted only once for the BBC and broadcast as a miniseries in 1983 before Rozema released her vision of the novel on film in 1999.

This interview is meant to interrogate the choices behind her clearly politicized interpretation of the story. Since she is both the screenwriter and director of the film production, Rozema embodies an interesting case of the reading, envisioning, and rewriting process of literary classics like Austen's and representing them in the twentieth century's most popular medium, the cinema, which has its own methods of communication.

In this interview, I investigate Rozema's reading of the text, the ideological stances that informed, affected, or shaped her reading experience, and her position in relation to the issue of fidelity to the original text, which is still at the core of any critical assessment or indeed general reception of film adaptations of classic/canonic works of literature.

Our dialogue took place through written correspondence and I received the answers to my questions in March 2003, when Rozema was busy working on a film and I was still researching Austen and film adaptations in England. I hope this interview sheds some light on the stages of filming Mansfield Park and highlights some of the central issues regarding film adaptation in general, and that of Austen's novel in particular.* Hiba Moussa: What factors do you think make a book adaptable? Patricia Rozema: The moral core of the piece needs to be built into the turns of events themselves, not just the prose description of those events. Some novels declare themselves in their interpretation of events and some, the ones that are more easily adapted, declare themselves in the very fabric of the causal relations.

HM: How much do socio-historical circumstances, whether those shaping the time you read the, book or the time the book was produced, affect your reading and understanding of a novel?

PR: They affect me very much. In fact, that is what I added to Mansfield Park, the movie. I felt like we couldn't fully understand Austen's subtle statement about captivity if we didn't know that the issue of slavery was raging in every home in Britain at the time. And I felt morally obligated to explain that the extraordinary amount of leisure time these people enjoyed was purchased with the sweat and blood of slaves in the West Indies.

HM: Does English literature have a special significance to you?

PR: Of course it does.

HM: Do you think that studying literature at a university prepared you for the role of adapter and do you think that it is a prerequisite for a successfully well-informed screenplay?

PR: The more you know about different parts of life, the richer your work can be. Acquiring some analytical skills around novels definitely helps.

HM: What is the main purpose behind adapting literary classics in your opinion?

PR: To examine stories that bear re-examination. Tales that are rich in humanity need to be re-interpreted. Re-fashioning them into a different media expands the complexity of our understanding. Collective re-awakening.

HM: How important is fidelity to the original text when you want to adapt it?

PR: Fidelity is critical. The movie should have a different title if it serves an entirely different purpose than the original text. But you cannot underestimate what a radical thing it is to change from one art form to another. An author slaves to start with just the right word, phrase, sentence, and paragraph. The sounds of the words are crucial. But all the demands of words and prose are lifted when you make a movie. The physical presence makes many unnecessary and some necessary ones impossible. So you serve two masters as an adapting filmmaker: the author's intention and the needs of film. Sometimes "fidelity" can mean only focusing on one day of a story told over twenty years in a book. That said, I do sometimes think that if I had changed the title just slightly to say "Letters of Mansfield Park" or "Mansfield Park Revisited," I could have saved myself some grief and managed to get people just to look at it as a movie first and then evaluate its relationship to the original text second.

HM: What kind of changes do you make when rewriting the text?

PR: I make the written word conform to habits of speech. Shorter sentences mostly.

HM: Do you think that reading a novel and re-presenting it from a postmodern point of view and culture entail the risk of imposing meanings and implications that are foreign to the novelist and the novel itself?

PR: Yes. But the whole enterprise is a "risk." But some stories need to be retold, over and over and over again, with this spin and then that. Fairytales are changing all the time. The strongest most important ones will be retold with postmodern and then post-postmodern interpretations. Interpretation is impossible to avoid. It must be openly declared by the filmmakers (writer and director) but "imposing meaning" is impossible to avoid-just selecting the moments we do from a novel is a form of imposed meaning. The effort must be made not to run counter to the novelist's intent, but then the fact of interpretation must be embraced

HM: Mansfield Park as a literary adaptation makes, in my opinion, the least interesting of all Austen's novels a most interesting film version. What made you choose Mansfield Park!

PR: Thank you. I was attracted to the open acknowledgement of slavery in the novel. I felt like I could bring something new to the canon of Austen movies. I liked that it wasn't just another tea party. I felt for Fanny, the injustice with which she is treated right from the start. I liked the implied parallel between the captivity of women and the captivity of slaves.

HM: Some critics think that Mansfield Park is difficult to adapt to film mainly because of the nature of its tone and its main character. What problems did you encounter with the text when writing the screenplay and what risks were you bearing in mind when adapting it?

PR: I did think that the character as written would be too slight and retiring and internal and perhaps judgmental to shoulder a film. So instead of just arbitrarily adding contemporary characteristics to her personality, I became obsessed with Austen herself. I wanted to know everything about her intentions and journey as a writer. It was clear that Mansfield Park was a hugely autobiographical work so I thought I'd add some of the "teller into the tale." I would include Austen, as I understood her, into the character. I tried not to change her behavior in interaction with others. I just allowed the audience into a privileged place inside her mind by making her a writer. Mansfield Park without any alteration would make a lousy film. I knew that. But I thought if I could include just a few things I knew about the period and about the author, it would be fascinating. That was the goal.

HM: Did you read the book as a literary critic, a screenwriter, or a director?

PR: As a human being.

HM: To what extent does your identity (nationality, gender, and class) affect your reading and presentation of this classic text?

PR: I connected to her as a woman. I connected to her experience of starting out life poor and ending up rich (my personal history). I connected to her rage about not being considered central to the real social story. I connected to her insecurity around more educated and elegant individuals. I felt like she was a barely noticed Canadian at a British function.

HM: Why do you think Austen is so popular for contemporary audiences and for screenwriters?

PR: She's one of the best writers in the English language. She understands people. She's extremely funny and her stories are exquisitely structured. Everyone can find themselves in her stories. She tells "romances" but with such an unsentimental voice that we never feel tarnished. We will always be concerned with who sleeps with and marries whom, but without all her economic, psychological, and social layering, it would be mere soap opera.

HM: How did you assimilate your role as a director and screenwriter when you were writing the screenplay, especially in relation to the specific and different natures of film and novel?

PR: I have a short memory. I write it, then as a director I execute the writer's plan. Once in a while I change but I trust what I came up with in the quiet contemplative moments more than the hurly burly of the set. I just try to make it authentic in every way, even the magic.

HM: The film obviously adopts and presents a political voice, specifically feminist and postcolonial, and you mentioned before that you read some criticisms of the novel before re-writing it. Did you read Edward Said's essay, "Jane Austen and Empire," on the novel before writing the script?

PR: Yes, I was very influenced by him. I don't think, however, that Austen was as unaware of her imperialism as he suggests. I do agree with him that Mansfield Park is more about Antigua than it is about England.

HM: Did you think of your audience when writing the screenplay Mansfield Park and visualizing it from a director's point of view?

PR: Yes and no. I just try to please myself and hope that I'm normal enough that it will please others. I knew it could function for some merely on the domestic romantic comedy level and for others more like myself on a political level. I try to make it simple and strong and true for those who don't wish to know that there is really sugar on the pill.

HM: Did you make any changes in the script while the film was being shot? In other words, were there any scenes that looked good on paper but were disappointing in live action and had to be changed?

PR: Not really. I stuck pretty much to the plan. The only big change was going back two months after principal photography had ended and shooting the scene with Sir Thomas Bertram (Harold Pinter) confessing the error of his ways to his dying son, Tom. We felt we needed that resolution otherwise the issue of slavery was never really addressed or completed. What I had originally thought was just a kind of social theme that was always present (the slavery accents) somehow became a subplot and needed resolution. That is what that scene was.

HM: The film has received varied reactions among academic critics. How would you react to some who think this is a completely "unfaithful" version or "against the spirit of Austen" or "not in tune with the novel?"

PR: I would disagree. It is definitely a free and openly interpretive version but I think that if Austen came back as a filmmaker in 1999, she might have adapted her novel into a film in the same way I did. I believe that.

HM: I see the film as an academic rather than mainstream adaptation of Austen's novel (mainly because I could feel a theoretical spirit in it). Do you think that makes it slightly elitist? And how does that reflect on its popularity or status?

PR: I don't think of it as academic. I'm not an academic. It is informed by my research and theory but no, I intended it to be a tale told from one heart to another.

HM: To what extent do you think Harold Pinter's presence in the film added to its critical/ academic tone, if it did at all?

PR: He probably lent it a little credibility with some; his presence might have alerted some to the film's political leanings. But he's not a big draw in suburban mall culture.

HM: The film is being used in seminars on the novel in universities and colleges teaching Austen, especially in relation to postcolonial theory. To what extent do you think your version is also useful for educational purposes and how do you feel about adaptations playing that role?

PR: I feel honored. I think it is quite useful educationally partly because one is forced to read the novel. I don't pretend to have redone the novel (as some filmmakers absurdly claim) in film. I think both the film and the novel are rich territory for postcolonial theory.

HM: Was Mansfield Park's first appearance to Fanny as

"Gothic" meant to contribute to its dark and mysterious side or to the tradition of the novel in Austen's time?

PR: Both.

HM: Why did you put the responsibility on Tom (rather than the more "moral" Edmund) to illuminate the dark side of Mansfield Park and its owner?

PR: It would have been Tom's struggle as the eldest. Would he follow in his father's footsteps?

HM: What future do you envision for Susie as Fanny's successor in the main house?

PR: Questioner of established suppositions.

HM: The film's end, interestingly, is not a closure in the traditional sense. How does that relate to Austen's neat closing of the narrative and what does yours aim to achieve or say about the consequent lives of the characters?

PR: Hmmm. I think it's actually quite a traditional ending. The flying about with the camera was meant to embody that suddenly distant tone Austen takes when she sums everything up. Perhaps I don't understand.

HM: Do you think Sir Thomas repents at the end despite the fact that he is investing in a newer and surely milder form of enslavement, that of tobacco?

PR: It's a partial redemption for jolly old England. Slavery may have been abolished but there were lots of other imperialistic shenanigans after that. That line was me trying to not tie things up quite so sweetly.

HM: If you were to adapt another Austen novel, which one would you choose and why?

PR: I wouldn't. I think I did the most interesting one. And I think that most of the others really should be read and not watched.

HM: Would you consider other literary classics to adapt? If yes, which ones and why?

PR: Yes, The Picture of Dorian Gray. But I haven't figured out how yet.

HM: As a cinematic product, did you ever think of the film as a risk in terms of reception and box office returns?

PR: I try to make a film that engages people I respect-then I let the gods and the distributors have their wicked way with the thing.

HM: Were you involved in the casting and what aspects in terms of actors/actresses did you think were crucial for the success of the film?

PR: I was totally responsible (in consultation with my producers) for the casting.

HM: Did the producers want any changes done to the original draft/script?

PR: It was too long at first and I had to cut a million pounds out of the budget just before shooting so that made me become more and more economical and eliminate any experimental scenes. I was lucky to have extremely smart and literate producers: David Aukin, Allon Riech, Sarah Curtis, and Harvey Weinstein.

PR: Chance. Weather. Actors' moods and love lives. Jonny Lee Miller was divorcing Angelina Jolie and not very happy about it. Frances O'Connor was separated from her long-term boyfriend and open to romantic negotiation, shall we say. Harold raged about all the waiting. The weather rarely cooperated. The size of the cast made quick changes or rethinks very hard, it was like steering a big ocean liner. I wanted to use starlings in Portsmouth but they are of nervous disposition and probably would have died in the boxes, so we used white homing pigeons but the animal wrangler somehow got stuck with nonhoming pigeons and they just stayed there, on our set. Also the language itself had to be checked and double-checked for historical accuracy so there was no ad libbing. I got meningitis during the shoot and everything had to be shut down for a time while I recovered in hospital. Various amusing issues like that.

Patricia Rozema's Mansfield Park

Cinema may not have been Rozema's first career of choice, but it has certainly proven quite the showcase for her talents. The way she tells it, a career in filmmaking was practically a foregone conclusion. "I sometimes look back and I think `My God, it's almost as if I knew I was going to become a filmmaker, so I organized this whole array of experiences that would help me.'"

One of a trio of children born to Dutch immigrants who eventually settled in Sarnia, Ont., Rozema was raised a strict Calvinist who, before the age of 16, had seen only one movie, Snow White and the Seven Dwarfs. Her parents, successful real—estate entrepreneurs, instilled a work ethic and business sense that proved invaluable to her eventual career of choice. "I grew up [learning] how to convince other people that your enterprise is valid and making sure you don't go in the hole doing it; how to save some money and how to plan ahead, basic contracts and even negotiations," she explains.

Acting in plays from the first grade until she finished her B.A., Rozema was busy with a variety of activities in both high school and university. At Lambton Christian High School, Rozema discovered public speaking, and was elected president of her class, an experience that certainly came with an important lesson, and one that reeks of irony. "I remember saying," she recalls, "`never, ever, will I go into politics, ever.' It just drove me mad to be in a situation where I was expected to want to please everyone.

I couldn't do it." Instead, she continued on in a different kind of political arena, the arts. Writing stories in her spare time since she was about eight years old, she coupled this with directing theatre at Calvin College, a small liberal arts university in Grand Rapids, Mich. There, Rozema won awards for her writing and directing in theatre, acted in productions and edited the campus newspaper. On top of that, her approach to her studies, English and Philosophy, proved remarkably astute: "I always tried to arrange my courses so that I would be studying the same period [in] both... so I could be saying `okay, these are the ideas of the 18th century and this is how they worked themselves out in fiction.'" It was also while studying at this Christian college that she discovered her sexuality, one that increasingly involved an attraction to women, and one that inevitably caused a loss of religious faith.

After graduating in 1981, Rozema switched gears and pursued a career in journalism. She had decided to be a novelist but knew that she needed a day job to pay the rent. This new endeavour took her to Chicago (WMAQ-TV) and New York (WNBC-TV) before she finally came back to Canada to work first at Global and then as an associate producer on CBC's The Journal. Here, Rozema learned about constructing stories in a moving-image medium, through writing and editing, and eventually she decided to take a five-week course in 16mm film production.

Before long, she was writing and producing her first film, Passion: A Letter in 16mm , which went on to win the second prize at the Chicago International Film Festival. Coproduced with Alexandra Raffe, shot by Peter Mettler and starring Linda Griffiths, this short is, in retrospect, a veritable who's who of Canadian filmmaking. Essentially a cinematic love letter, Passion introduced audiences to a device that would be a signature of Rozema's style: that of the protagonist breaking the flow of the narrative to address the audience directly. It's usually in these moments that the thoughts, dreams and aspirations of the character are revealed, creating a sense that, structurally speaking, anything can happen. Rozema will be forever remembered as the novice filmmaker who, at the age of 29 took the world by storm with her first feature, I've Heard the Mermaids Singing , winning the Prix de la Jeunesse at the 1987 Cannes Film Festival.

The film charmed critics and audiences alike with its playful style and endearing protagonist. Polly, played to perfection by Sheila McCarthy, is an awkward and surprisingly inept office temp who, despite herself, lands a job working for a successful gallery owner, Gabrielle (Paule Baillargeon). She comes to idolize this woman both personally and professionally, and tries desperately to gain her acceptance on both of these levels. Polly's only refuge comes from her photography and her vivid fantasy life.

These elements, together with her videotaped confession interweave within the basic story line, shaping the film and expanding its form beyond simple storytelling. Instead, Mermaids' form gently actualizes Polly's growing self-awareness to produce a statement that celebrates personal validation over the more tempting public accolades. The stuff that legends are made of, this low-budget film (made for $350,000) has made millions. Besides collecting two Genie Awards for acting (Best Actress, McCarthy, and Best Supporting Actress, Baillargeon), it garnered critical praise internationally and continues to appear on Top Ten lists of the Best Canadian Films of all time.

Persuasion and Cinematic Approaches to Jane Austen

Critics have limited our appreciation and understanding of recent cinematic adaptations of Jane Austen by emphasizing primarily the "literary" aspects of adaptation (e.g., examining what was left in, taken out, and added, the handling of dialogue, drama, and characterization, and so on) and narrowing the genre of these works to the socalled "heritage film," defined largely as a picturesque amalgam of "Grand homes, furnishings, costumes, and hairstyles", productions reducible basically to what Jonathan Miller describes as "our longing for 'a golden age of propriety, decency, courtesy and a highly constituted behaviour which is a sort of sanctuary from the chaos and depression and pessimism of modern life'". This is a premise that when not qualified or carefully applied, echoes a firmly entrenched tradition of oversimplifying, even trivializing, Austen's novels, and may have the same effect on films of those novels.

Surprisingly little attention has been paid to the often remarkably inventive cinematographic styles of these films. I have looked over scores of reviews, particularly of various versions of Emma, Sense and Sensibility, Persuasion, and Pride and Prejudice, and while some are deeply insightful about what Jocelyn Harris rightly calls these "new readings of Jane Austen", only a handful make as much as passing reference to cinematic techniques other than lighting, set design, and casting. Surprisingly, some reviews in film journals seem inattentive to cinematic details.

The reviewer of Emma for Sight and Sound, for example, talks about Austen's worldview without taking the time to discuss the visual details of Douglas McGrath's film-presumably a large part of how such a worldview is conveyed in this medium-and only a complete disregard of the cinematography of the film allows him to claim, even in the midst of a generally positive review, that early on "the movie seems stiff and lifeless". The reviewer claims that, on the whole, it is not "as truly adapted-that is, pared down and reshaped for the camera" as the Ang Lee/ Emma Thompson Sense and Sensibility, and that in general McGrath's "less than adventurous idea is to have the actors recite great wodges of the original dialogue at a succession of dinner tables".

Even detailed academic criticism on Austen adaptations veers from the cinematic. The recent collection of essays, Jane Austen in Hollywood, edited by Linda Troost and Sayre Greenfield, contains much interesting work on the production and reception of some recent adaptations, their ideological inflections, and their reshaping of Austen's texts. But the almost unwavering methodology from beginning to end is what we might call straightforward lit-crit, which works wonderfully with, say, Jane Austen's Persuasion, but less well with Roger Michell's. The title of the introduction announces one of the main intentions of the book, "Watching Ourselves Watching," but what is practiced throughout is a somewhat circumscribed "literary" watching that generates some fine critical commentary but also some remarkable blind spots-including almost no consideration of the films as filmsand an astonishing admission by the editors that "The films are, by necessity, 'E-Z' Austen".

No matter how sophisticated the critic or viewer, a non-cinematic approach to Austen films is, to coin a phrase, clueless-but remediable. We need to supplement and complement the literary approach to Austen films by focusing on how they create powerful visual and emotional effects, establish complex structural and formal patterns, and evoke cinematic codes and contexts that take us far away from the realm of the "authentic literary adaptation." To this end, in what follows I concentrate specifically on a few key cinematic aspects of Roger Michell's Persuasion, I identify a particular repertoire of visual techniques that add up to what might be called the film's spatial strategy,1 a carefully articulated ensemble of repeated devices and effects. Out of many such elements worth discussing, I focus here primarily on various types of camera motion, and also comment briefly on the position of characters in the film frame and a few assorted special effects.

When possible and relevant, I consider ways in which these techniques are visual equivalents or transformations of the novel's themes and style. But if we are to properly understand the film text at hand, I believe that cinematic allusions embedded in the style are equally as important to notice as literary ones. The basic script (plot, dialogue, characters, and so on) may be from Jane Austen but the enunciated and embodied shooting script-the film as we see it-owes much to the traditions and techniques of a host of auteurs and visual contexts that I attempt to identify.

Persuasion, originally made for British television in 1995 but then released theatrically, nicely lends itself to and rewards close cinematic analysis. An experienced play writer and director, Michell relished the opportunity to vary and expand his work beyond the stage. He told an interviewer, "I've got away from doing just theatre, and spent more time behind a camera, which I like-film gives you a huge toyshop of gear with which to tell a story".

That "toyshop" is much in evidence and used to great advantage in Persuasion. Critics have focused on the rumpled realism of the film and its engaging effect: "If you can see a dress is wrinkled at the back," Michell points out, "it makes the shot a Vermeer rather than a Gainsborough. That detail gives you a feeling of being in a room with someone". Michell's penchant for "clothes not costumes", very little prettifying makeup and hair styling, and an abundance of candles, providing light that generates a melancholy warmth, flickering motion, and shadows, all contribute to the "look" and effect of the film, and embody his revisionary aesthetic: one of his most well-known statements is "I'm trying to trash the hotel room of the BBC classic".

But he also uses the "gear" of cinema adventurously in

other ways and for other purposes. As Caryn James notes, in Persuasion "The camera becomes the visual equivalent of Austen's rich, commenting voice, and though it cannot be a complete replacement, it is a more than serviceable one." Part of what makes Persuasion such an intriguing and powerful film is that Michell's remarkably effective and evocative camera work evokes not only Austen's "rich, commenting voice" but rich cinematic traditions as well.

Bibliography

Vows in Mansfield Park: the promises of courtship: Regis, Pamela

Armstrong, Isobel: Jane Austen, Mansfield Park. Penguin, London, 1988.

Austen, Jane. Mansfield Park: Penguin Books, Harmondsworth, England, 1970.

Copeland, Edward: The Cambridge Companion to Jane Austen. Cambridge University Press, Cambridge, 1997.

Looser, Devoney, ed. Jane Austen and Discourses of Feminism. St. Martin's Press, New York, 1995.

Monaghan, David, ed. Jane Austen in a Social Context. Barnes & Noble Books, Totowa, NJ, 1981.

Simons, Judy, ed. Mansfield Park and Persuasion. St. Martin's Press, New York, 1997. (A particularly good collection of essays.)

Steffes, Michael. "Slavery and Mansfield Park: The Historical and Biographical Context." English Language Notes 34(2): 1996.

Tanner, Tony. Jane Austen. Harvard University Press, Cambridge, MA, 1986.

Woolf, Virginia. A Room of One's Own. Harcourt Brace Jovanovich, New York, 1981.